KB039365

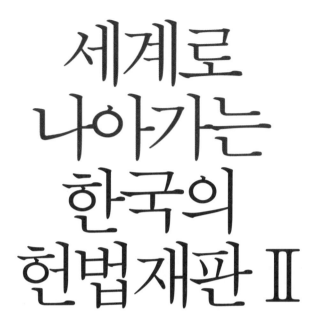

세계로
나아가는
한국의
헌법재판 II

이동흡 편저

박영사

머 리 말

우리나라의 법률문화 발전을 위하여 조금이라도 도움이 될까 하여 「세계로 나아가는 한국의 헌법재판」을 출판하였었다. 그런데 아이러니하게도 위 책자가 저자의 헌법재판소장 인사청문회에서는 헌법재판소장 후보자를 낙마시키기 위한 야당 국회의원들의 주된 공격자료로 사용되었다. 즉 저자의 헌법재판소장 취임을 반대하는 야당 국회의원들은 연구관들이 정리한 부분이 있는데도 저자의 단독저서로 표시한 것은 저작권법 위반이라든지, 헌법재판소 구내식당에서 출판기념회를 연 것이 잘못이라든지, 재판업무가 바쁜데도 너무 자주 외국에 나가 재판업무를 소홀히 하지 않았느냐든지, 외국 출장 시 가족동반을 한 것이 도덕성에 문제가 있지 않느냐 등 갖가지 음해성 공격을 서슴지 않았다.

위 책자는 저자가 헌법재판관 재직 시 외국에서 활동한 내용을 정리한 책자인바, 저자 자신이 저술한 부분 외에도 동행한 헌법재판소 연구관이 있을 경우 동 연구관이 정리한 부분이 있기는 하나 책의 서문뿐만 아니라 해당 내용 중에도 연구관 등이 정리한 것이라고 명시하였을 뿐만 아니라 그 내용조차 저자의 외국에서의 활동상황과 외국 법조인들과의 대담내용 등을 정리한 것으로서 연구관들의 저작물이라고 보기 어려운 면이 있고, 책 출판 시에도 저자명의를 어떻게 하는 것이 좋은지에 대해 관계 당사자들의 상의 하에 결정한 것이므로 저작권법 위반이 될 수 없다고 생각한다고 하였다. 또한 책 출판비용과 헌재 구내식당에서의 출판기념회 비용 등도 저자가 전담하였다고 청문회에서 답변하였으나 야당 국회의원들은 막무가내로 저자의 변소를 받아들이지 않았다.

「세계로 나아가는 한국의 헌법재판」의 초판 발행 이후에도 외국 사

법기관이나 외국대학에서 초청받아 한국의 헌법재판제도나, 판·검사 임
용제도, 국민참여재판 등 기타 사법현황에 대해 발표할 기회가 있어 이
를 정리해 둔 것이 있었는데, 그 자료들을 모아 위 책의 후속판을 발행할
것인지에 대해 고민하였다.

　　그런데 책의 초판을 읽어본 후임 재판관들이나 후배 법조인들로부
터 그 책이 재판관들의 해외출장이나 외국과의 사법교류를 하는 데 있어
큰 도움이 된다는 말씀을 수차 들었다. 위와 같은 말을 듣고 나서는 비
용이 들더라도 책의 후속판을 발행함으로써 저자의 발표자료와 활동내
역을 기록으로 남겨야 한다는 사명감을 느끼게 되어 「세계로 나아가는
한국의 헌법재판 Ⅱ」를 발행하기로 하였다.

　　본서의 내용은 「세계로 나아가는 한국의 헌법재판 Ⅰ」에 이어 제 8
장부터 제12장까지 5부분으로 나누어져 있다.

　　제 8 장은 "타이완 국제회의 참석기 ― 판사, 검사의 임용 및 징계제
도에 관하여―"이다. 이것은 타이완 사법연수소의 초청을 받아 2011.
11. 14. 동 사법연수소에서 주최한 「司法官進用及淘汰制度」 국제 심포지
엄에서 발표한 내용과 같은 달 13일 타이완 司法院에서 대법관, 연구관
들이 참석한 간담회에서 한국의 헌법재판제도를 소개한 내용을 정리한
것이다. 별지로는 「한국의 판사, 검사 임용 및 징계 제도에 관하여」와
논문에 대한 영문본 「Recruitment and Discipline Systems of Judges
and Prosecutors in Korea」 및 중국어본 「韓國法官檢察官的任用與懲戒
制度」를 첨부하였다.

　　제 9 장은 "베트남 국제회의 참석기 ― 헌법상 권력분립에 관하여 ―"
이다. 이것은 아데나워 재단의 초청으로 2012. 2. 28. 하노이 하이야트
호텔에서 개최된 국제회의에서 저자가 발표한 내용과 회의 진행상황들
을 정리한 것이다. 별지로는 「한국 헌법상 권력분립원리의 실현」과 그
영문본인 「Realization of the Principle of Separation of Powers under

the Korean Constitution」과 「Introduction to the Constitutional Court of Korea and its Role in Control of Government Power」를 첨부하였다.

　제10장은 "홍콩 시립대학 법률학원 명사특강 참석기"이다. 2011. 7. 젊은 중국 판사들을 인솔하고 헌법재판소를 방문하였던 王貴國 홍콩 시립대학 법률학원장이 저자가 중국 인민대학에서 헌법재판 강연을 한 사실을 알고 홍콩에 와서도 한국의 헌법재판에 대하여 강연을 해달라고 부탁을 하였는데, 그 뒤 정식 초청이 와서 2012. 3. 1. 홍콩 시립대학에서 '명사특강'의 형식으로 한국의 헌법재판 제도의 발전과 현황을 소개하는 강연회를 개최하였고, 그 강연 내용과 뒷이야기를 정리한 것이다. 말미에는 동 명사특강에서 발표하였던 영문논문 「Development and Current Situation of the Constitutional Adjudication in Korea」와 홍콩 시립대학 홈페이지의 「Justice from Korea Constitutional Court Speaks at Eminent Speaker Lecture Series」를 첨부하였다.

　제11장은 "폴란드 헌법재판소, 루마니아 헌법재판소 및 터어키 이스탄불 지방법원 방문기"이다. 저자는 재판관 임기 중 마지막 해외출장 일정으로 동구권 헌법재판소를 선택하였는데 동 방문기 중 폴란드 헌법재판소장, 루마니아 헌법재판관, 이스탄불 지방법원 법원장과의 대담내용 등을 당시 수행하였던 고일광 연구관(현재 수원지방법원 판사)이 정리한 것이다.

　제12장은 "2012 타이완 사법 민주화 국제회의 참석기"이다. 이것은 저자가 헌법재판관 재임 중 타이완 사법연수소에서 초청을 받아 퇴임 후인 2012. 11. 13. 타이완 사법연수소에서 개최된 "2012 司法民主化及社會化" 국제회의에 참석하여 활동한 내역을 저자가 직접 정리한 것이다. 말미에는 「한국의 국민참여재판」, 그 영문본인 「Citizens Participatory Trials in the Republic of Korea」 및 중국어본인 「大韓民國之國民參與

審判制」를 첨부하였다.

　　끝으로 이 책이 대한민국 사법의 국제화에 조금이라도 보탬이 되었으면 하는 마음이 간절하다. 저자의 은사이시자 초대 헌법재판관과 감사원장을 역임하신 이시윤 박사님께서도 Global化가 우리의 살길이고 발전이라고 늘 강조하셨는데 이 기회를 빌어 은사님의 가르침에 다시 한 번 감사드린다. 이 책의 출간에 온정을 베풀어 주신 박영사 안종만 회장님과 조성호 이사, 이승현 대리에게도 감사드린다. 더불어 인사청문회 이후 온갖 역경 속에서도 꿋꿋하게 이를 인내하고 저자를 격려하고 응원해 준 아내와 가족들에게도 감사를 드린다.

2015. 7.

前 憲法裁判官

李 東 洽

목　차

[별지 1]

Citizens Participatory Trials in the Republic of

타이완 국제회의 참석기

─ 판사, 검사의 임용 및 징계제도에 관하여 ─

제 1. 머 리 말

　　타이완 사법연수소에서 국제회의 참석 여부를 묻는 메일이 온 것은 2011년 7월경이었다. 몇 해 전에 서울에서 열린 세계 여성법관 회의에 참석차 우리나라에 왔던 타이완 여성법관 10여 명이 헌법재판소를 방문했을 때 저자의 방에서 환담을 나눈 적이 있었다. 그런데, 그 때 방문객 중 일행이었던 시옹 성메이(熊 誦梅) 판사가 김복기 헌법재판소 연구관을 통해서 국제회의 참석을 간곡히 부탁하였다. 최근에 타이완에서도 법관징계법을 새로이 제정하고, 미국, 프랑스, 일본과 한국 대표를 초청하여 "판사, 검사의 임용 및 징계제도"를 주제로 5개국이 참여한다는 국제회의를 타이완 사법연수소 주최로 개최한다는 것이었다.

재판업무 때문에 시간을 내는 것이 쉽지 않은 일이었으나 선진국 대표들이 참여하는 국제회의에 일원으로 참가하여 우리나라의 사법제도에 관하여 소개하고 선진 제국의 그것과 비교하는 것이 의미 있는 일이라고 판단되어 초청을 수락하기로 하였다. 11월에 개최되는 국제회의에 발표원고를 9월까지 제출할 것을 요망하였고 논문에 필수적으로 포함되어야 하는 사항을 10개 가량 열거하여 요청하였다.

법원행정처 인사실에 근무하는 배형원 부장판사를 통하여 판사의 임용 및 징계제도에 관한 자료를 모은 다음 헌재 연구관들의 협조를 받아 "한국의 판사, 검사 임용 및 징계 제도에 관하여"라는 제목의 한글 원고를 완성하고 다시 영문으로 번역한 논문까지 2개를 이메일로 보냈다. 논문을 작성하면서 공부해보니 우리나라에서도 2011년 7월 1일자로 법원조직법이 개정되어 법관의 임용자격이 원칙적으로 10년의 변호사 경력이 있어야 하는 것으로 바뀌었고, 로스쿨 제도가 도입되어 앞으로 사법시험 제도가 폐지되는 등 국제회의에서 소개할만한 사항들이 꽤 있었다.

타이완 사법연수소의 국제회의에 참석하는 길에 司法院을 공식방문하는 것도 의미 있는 일이라고 생각되어 타이완 사법원 측에 그 뜻을 전하기로 했다. 지난 번에 내 사무실로 예방했던 쉬 삐후(徐 璧湖)

재판관에게 그 뜻을 메일을 보냈더니 방문을 환영한다고 하면서 사법
원에서 재판관들과 간담회도 가지고 하루 저녁은 지난 번 한국을 방문
했던 여성법관들이 저자를 위해서 만찬도 베풀 것이라고 연락이 왔다.

제 2. 101 빌딩에서의 환영만찬

　　타이완에 도착한 날이 일요일이었음에도 불구하고 타이완 사법
연수소 소장이 저자를 위해서 만찬을 베풀어 주었다. 만찬 장소는 높
이가 101층으로서 아시아에서 현재 가장 높다는 101 빌딩의 80층에
있는 레스토랑이었다. 건물이 너무 높아 구름이 빌딩에 걸쳐 있기도
하고 레스토랑에서 보이는 타이베이 시 야경은 정말 장관이었다. 만찬

〈101 빌딩 레스토랑에서 환영만찬을 마치고 린 후이후앙 사법연수소
소장 등과 기념촬영〉

참석자는 린 후이후앙(林 輝煌) 사법연수소장, 교관인 侯 부장검사, 시옹 성메이 판사, 실무 담당 교관인 Fran(鍾 曉亞) 검사 등이었고 대사관 역할을 하는 무역대표부의 김 영사도 동석하였다. 그런데 타이완에서는 사법연수소가 사법원 소속이 아니라 법무부 소속으로서 사법연수소의 간부들은 모두 판사가 아니고 검사인 것이 특이하였다. 린 소장도 검사장으로서 12년째 소장직을 맡고 있다고 하였다. 린 소장은 미국 유학 경력도 있다고 하였고, 영어도 유창하게 하였다.

제 3. 사법원에서의 간담회와 사법원장과의 오찬

　　2011년 11월 14일(월요일) 9시 50분경 사법원에 도착하였다. 무역대표부의 정 대사가 호텔에까지 마중을 와서 사법원까지 동행하였다. 정 대사는 저자의 사법원장 접견을 준비하기 위해 며칠 전에 사법원장을 예방하고 인사를 드려 놓았다고 하였다. 10시가 되자 라이 하오민(賴 浩珉) 사법원장, 수 잉친(蘇 永欽) 부사법원장, 린(林) 행정처장 외 몇 분 대법관들이 접견실에서 저자를 환영해 주었다. 라이 사법원장은 기념으로 타이완 법관 배지를 저자의 옷깃에 직접 달아 주셨다. 라이 사법원장은 1939년생으로서 평생 변호사 생활을 하시다가 지난 해에 사법원장으로 취임하셨다고 하였고 아주 인자한 인상을 가지신 분이었다. 타이완에서는 대법관의 임기(8년)만 있고 연령제한은 없다고 하였다. 간담회장에는 업무 관계로 사법원장은 직접 참석하지 못하고 부원장이 주재할 것이라고 양해를 구하셨다.
　　접견을 마치고 옆에 있던 대회의실로 자리를 옮겼는데 간담회장에는 수(蘇) 부사법원장을 비롯하여 쉬 삐후(徐 璧湖) 재판관[1] 등 5분의 재판관과 연구관 등 30여 명이 참석하였다. 그런데 특이한 것은 저자가 일본 도쿄대에 가서 "한국의 민주주의 발전에 있어 헌법재판소의 공헌"이라는 제목의 강연을 일본 헌법학회 회원들의 총회 모임에서 하였고, 그 강연 내용이 일본의 유명 법률잡지인 법률시보(法律時報)에 게재된 적이 있었는데, 그 내용을 복사하여 참가자들이 한 부씩 들고 있는 것이었다. 저자가 미리 말하지 않았음에도 불구하고 그러한 정보를 알고 간담회 참석자들에게 미리 자료를 나누어 주어 간담회를 충실하게 하려는 의도를 충분히 알 수 있었다.

간담회는 먼저 수 부사법원장이 인사말을 하고, 저자가 한국의 헌법재판제도 전반에 관하여 한국어로 발표를 하고 우리나라 화교 출신이면서 사법원 직원인 왕정림 씨가 통역을 하는 형식으로 진행하였다. 그런데 질의시간이 되어 참석자들이 질문을 하고 저자가 답변을 하니 통역의 법률 전문지식 부족으로 인하여 의사전달이 잘되지 않는 것 같았다. 그래서 그 이후로는 저자가 영어로 말하면 부사법원장이 중국어로 통역하는 식으로 진행하였다. 수(蘇) 부사법원장은 1951년생으로서 타이완 국립대학 법학교수로 평생 봉직하다가 작년에 재판관으로 임명되어 부사법원장이 되었는데 독일에 유학하여 박사학위도 취득하였다고 하고 영어도 유창하게 구사하였다. 참석자들이 활발하게 여러 가지 질문을 하였는데 그 중에서도 헌법소원에 대하여 많은 질문을 하였다. 처분뿐만 아니라 법률도 헌법소원의 대상이 되는지, 법률에 대하여 헌법소원을 제기할 때 청구기간의 제한이 있

---

[1] 徐 재판관은 그 사이 8년의 임기가 종료되었으나, senior 재판관으로서 여전히 사법원에서 근무하고 있다고 자랑하였다. 우리나라에서도 선진국들의 예와 같이 퇴임 후에도 senior 재판관이나 senior 대법관으로 근무하는 제도의 도입이 필요한 시점이 되었다고 하겠다.

〈사법원에서의 간담회장. 저자의 좌측에 앉아 있는 분이 蘇 부사법
원장〉

는지, 헌법재판소의 한정위헌결정으로 인한 대법원과의 갈등 문제는
어떻게 푸는지 등 수준 높은 질문들이 장시간 이어졌다. 10시 15분경
시작한 간담회가 12시 30분이 되어서도 끝나지 아니하자 부사법원장
이 다음 일정 관계로 마칠 수밖에 없다고 선언하여 겨우 종료하였다.

오찬은 라이 사법원장이 주관하여 호텔 식당에서 베풀어 주었다.
그런데 타이완에서는 손님을 대접하는 법도가 극진함을 알 수 있었는
데, 저자를 주빈석에 앉히고 사법원장은 그 반대편인 입구 쪽 자리에
앉는 것이었다. 오찬에는 사법원장, 부사법원장, 쉬 재판관 등 5분의
대법관, 정 대사, 시옹 판사 등이 자리를 같이 하였는데 1시경에 시작
하여 3시경까지 장시간 식사를 하면서 다양한 화제를 가지고 즐겁고
유익한 시간을 가질 수 있었다. 대화 도중에는 오는 12월에 수 부사
법원장이 타이완의 사절단을 인솔하고 한국을 방문할 예정이라고 하

〈라이 사법원장이 베푼 오찬회장. 저자의 좌측이 정 대사, 우측이 쉬 대법관〉

였다. 한국과 일본이 배심 또는 참심 재판제도를 도입하여 시행하고 있는데 타이완도 곧 시민참여재판을 시행하기 위한 법률을 제정하기 위하여 한국, 일본 등의 제도 시행 상황에 대하여 직접 가서 관찰하고 전문가들과 면담도 가질 예정이라고 하였다. 12월에 한국에 오시면 사절단과 함께 헌법재판소도 꼭 방문하시라고 말하였다.

제 4. 국제회의에서의 발표

사법연수소 대강당에 회의장이 마련되어 있었는데 대형 스크린을 무대의 좌우에 늘어뜨려 한 쪽은 영어로 한 쪽은 중국어로 된 내용을 방청석에서 볼 수 있도록 장치해 놓은 것은 본받을 만한 것이었

〈프랑스, 한국, 중국, 일본, 미국 순의 발표자들이 발표 전에 기념촬영〉

다. 발표자로 일본에서는 전직 검사장 출신의 변호사가 "일본의 검사의 임용 및 징계"에 관하여, 법원장 출신의 로스쿨 교수가 "일본의 판사의 임용 및 징계"에 관하여 발표를 하였다. 발표 내용을 들어보니 실례도 들어가면서 충실하게 발표하였고 파워포인트로도 준비하여 이해가 쉽도록 준비한 것을 알 수 있었다. 두 번째로는 저자가 준비한 원고를 중심으로 주요부분만 발표하는 것으로 진행하였다. 미국 대표로는 시애틀 연방지방법원의 판사가 와서 "미국의 판사, 검사의 임용 및 징계"에 관하여 발표를 하였다. 프랑스 대표로는 프랑스 사법연수원 부원장이 와서 "프랑스의 법관, 검사의 임용 및 징계"에 관하여 프랑스어로 발표를 하고 중국어로 통역이 되었다. 마지막으로는 타이완 대표가 새로이 제정한 법관징계법 등을 중심으로 "타이완의 법관, 검사의 임용 및 징계제도"에 관하여 발표를 하였다.

질의 시간에는 저자에게 5인 가량 청중의 질문이 있었는데 저자가 사례로 소개한 소위 의정부 사건(변호사로부터 판사가 휴가비 등의 명목으로 수백만 원의 금품을 수령한 행위에 대하여 정직 또는 견책의 징계를 내린 사안)의 징계내용이 너무나 경미하지 않느냐는 질문에 대해 답변을 하느라고 진땀을 뺐다.

제 5. 여성법관 회장단과의 만찬

타이완 여성법관들이 우리나라를 방문하는 기회에 저자의 사무실에 들렀을 때 환대해 준 것이 감사하다는 이유로 저자가 타이완을 방문한 기회에 그 답례로서 그 당시 오셨던 여성판사들이 모두 모여 환영만찬을 베풀어 주었다. 전통 중식식당에서 그 동안 맛보지 못했던 여러 가

〈타이완 여성법관 간부들 주최의 환영 만찬을 하기 전에 기념촬영〉

지 중국 음식을 먹으면서 다양한 화제로 즐거운 시간을 보냈다. 그렇
게 많은 수의 여성법관들과 같이 식사를 한 것도 처음이 아닌가 싶었
는데 다행히 시옹 판사의 남편도 동석하였다. 시옹 판사는 타이완에
유학 온 한국 젊은이의 중국어 선생으로 만났는데 결혼에까지 이르렀
고 남편은 현재 타이완 문화대학에서 교수로 근무한다고 하였다. 식
사 분위기가 한창 무르익었을 무렵 저자는 그 동안 공부한 중국어 솜
씨를 뽐낼 겸 唐詩인 張 繼의 7언 절구 楓橋夜泊을 중국어로 암송하
여 참석자들로부터 큰 갈채를 받았다. 린(林) 사법원 행정처장은 저
자에게 중국 술을 선물하였고, 저자는 본인의 저서인 "세계로 나아
가는 한국의 헌법재판"을 선물하였다.

제 6. 결　　어

　　외교관계 문제로 타이완 사법부와는 공식적인 교류관계가 없었
으나 재판소를 방문한 사적인 인간관계가 인연이 되어 현직 재판관
으로는 최초로 타이완에서 주최하는 국제회의에서 발표도 하고, 사
법원 원장 등과 간담회를 하는 등 한국과 타이완과의 사법교류에서
이정표적인 행사를 가졌다고 생각된다. 타이완 사법연수소가 국제회
의를 준비하고 진행하는 것에서 느낄 수 있었지만 국제회의를 진행
하는 수준이 선진국 수준임을 알 수 있었다. 발표 한 달 전에 발표자
로부터 원고를 받아 중국어 번역도 완성하고 회의 전에 핸드북을 마
련하여 회의 시작 전에 나누어 주었을 뿐만 아니라, 회의가 종료된
후에는 회의에서의 질의 응답 내용까지 완벽하게 기재한 회의 결과
물을 우송해 주는 데는 놀라지 않을 수 없었다. 근래에는 중국 본토

와 타이완과의 관계도 긴밀해지고 있고, 타이완의 법률문화 수준이 상대적으로 선진국 수준인 점 등을 참작하면 앞으로는 더욱 개방적인 자세로 타이완 법조사회와 우리나라 법조사회가 긴밀한 협조관계를 맺어나가는 것이 바람직할 것이다.

[별지 1]

Recruitment and Discipline Systems of Judges and Prosecutors in Korea

Dong-Heub LEE*

* Justice, Constitutional Court of Korea.

1. Introduction

For a long time, Korea has been cultivating legal professionals by selecting a limited number of people through a
qualifying examination, or the 'Korean Judicial Examination'
and educating those who passed the Judicial Examination at the
Judicial Research and Training Institute (JRTI), which is
affiliated to the Supreme Court, for two years. Also, under the
Korean legal system, the Chief Justice of the Supreme Court
exerts a strong influence on personnel management of judges
including appointment and reappointment, assignment of
positions, evaluation, etc. Personnel management system of the
Prosecution Service, too, allows the Minister of Justice and the
Prosecutor General to exert a strong influence on that matter.

However, there have been growing voices saying that, the
current Judicial Examination system has limits in training legal professionals who have sound professional ethics based on
considerable sophistication, a deep understanding of people
and society and values oriented to freedom, equality and justice, and who have knowledge and abilities that will allow
professional and efficient resolution of diverse legal disputes,
in order to provide quality legal service responding to the
people's diverse expectations and request. Also, arguments

over the request for judicial reform asking for a new systemic mechanism to improve the personnel management systems for judges and prosecutors for encouraging independence of trial and fairness in investigation have been going on for many years.

As a result of such discussions and debates, the legislature enacted the "Act on the Establishment and Management of Professional Law Schools" in 2008, by which so-called 'law school' system was introduced, and in 2011, a 'Personnel Committee for Judges,' the majority of whose members are composed of non-judges, was established as stipulated in the Court Organization Act. The Prosecution Service also established a 'Recommendation Committee for Candidate to the Prosecutor General' and a 'Personnel Committee for Prosecutor' by stipulating related provisions in the Prosecutors' Office Act.

The year of 2012, when the first law school graduates are to be produced and the Personnel Committees for judges and prosecutors are to be launched, will be evaluated as a critical turning point for the changes in Korea's training system of legal professionals and personnel management of judges and prosecutors.

Meanwhile, as of 2011, the maximum number of judges of all levels of courts is 2,844 as stipulated in the 'Act on the Maximum Number of Judges, etc. of Various Levels of Courts,' and the maximum number of prosecutors is 2,044, as stipulated in the 'Act on the Maximum Number of Prosecutors,' which is a stunning increase compared to the number of judges, 376, in 1963 when the 'Act on the Maximum Number of Judges, etc. of Various Levels of Courts' was first enacted and the number of prosecutors, 190, in 1956 when the 'Act on the Maximum Number of Prosecutors' was first enacted. Even compared to the number of judges and prosecutors in 1990, which is 1,374 and 987 respectively, the number of judges and prosecutors has been increased twice up until now.

Having said that, along with the increase in the number of judges and prosecutors, inappropriate conducts of judges and prosecutors have been singled out as a social problem. To cope with this problem, the Judiciary and the Prosecution Service pronounced the Code of Ethics in 1995 and in 1999, respectively. Nevertheless, the increasing number of cases, in which the application of the Code of Ethics for Judges and the Code of Ethics for Prosecutors becomes controversial, has been reported. At this, more and more attention is paid to the disciplinary system, and further, as a constitutional complaint that requested a review of constitutionality of the statutory provisions providing for causes of disciplinary actions and lawsuit for cancellation of the disciplinary action was filed to the Constitutional Court in 2009, discussions and debates over this issue are getting more heated.

As being in the middle of these various changes and controversies over the training system of legal professionals and the personnel management of the Judiciary and the Prosecution Service, it seems very meaningful to have a bird's eye view of the structure of such systems. Therefore, in this article, overall comparison of appointment, personnel management and disciplinary system between judges whose official status is guaranteed by the Constitution and prosecutors who are the representatives of the public interests as quasi-judicial officers will be discussed, and specifically regarding the disciplinary system, cases in practice will be presented for reviewing the uniqueness and universality of personnel management system of judges and prosecutors.

2. Employment of Judges

(1) Appointment of Judges

The Chief Justice of the Supreme Court shall be appointed by the President of the Republic of Korea with the consent of the National Assembly; Justices of the Supreme Court shall be appointed by the President of the Republic of Korea with the consent of the National Assembly upon recommendation of the Chief Justice of the Supreme Court; and judges shall be appointed by the Chief Justice of the Supreme Court with the consent of the Supreme Court Justices' Council (Article 41 of the Court Organization Act).

Justices of the Constitutional Court shall be appointed by the President of the Republic of Korea and among the nine Justices, three shall be appointed from persons selected by the National Assembly and three appointed from persons nominated by the Chief Justice of the Supreme Court. The President of the Constitutional Court shall be appointed by the President of the Republic of Korea from among the Justices with the consent of the National Assembly (Article 111 Section 2, Section 3 and Section 4 of the Constitution; Article 6 of the Constitutional Court Act).

Meanwhile, in accordance with the observation that it is necessary to reform the personnel management of the Judiciary to answer the social request for judicial reform and thereby the Judiciary can be more respected and trusted by the people, the Court Organization Act was revised on July 18, 2011 and the revised Act is scheduled to be brought into effect on January 1, 2012. The details of the revision to tighten qualifications are as follows: In the case of appointment of Justices of the Supreme Court, there should be a Recommendation Committee for Candidate to Justice, and the Committee shall be composed of members appointed by the Chief Justice of the Supreme Court, including the Senior Justice of the Supreme Court, the Minister of National Court Administration, the Minister of Justice, the President of the

Korean Bar Association, the President of the Korean Law Professors Association, the President of the Korean Association of Law Schools, one judge who is not a Justice and three persons who are not qualified as a lawyer (in this case, at least one of them shall be female) (Article 41-2 of the Court Organization Act). For the appointment of judges, it is newly added that, before going through the aforementioned process, deliberation by a Personnel Committee for Judges is required (Article 41 Section 3, Article 25-2 of the Court Organization Act).

The provision related to the Personnel Committee for Judges was also revised as follows: for the purpose of reviewing important matters on the personnel affairs of judges, members of the Personnel Committee shall be composed of three judges, two prosecutors, two persons who are not qualified as a lawyer (in this case, at least one of them shall be female), appointed by the Chief Justice of the Supreme Court (Article 25-2 of the Court Organization Act).

The Chief Justice and Justices of the Supreme Court shall be appointed from among those who are forty years of age or over, and have been in any of the following offices for not less than 15 years: i) judges, public prosecutor or lawyer; ii) person who is qualified as a lawyer and has been engaged in legal affairs at the government agency, local government, national or public enterprise, government invested institution, or other juristic person; and iii) person who is qualified as a

lawyer, and has been in the office of higher than the assistant professor in jurisprudence at an certified college or university (Article 42 Section 1 of the Court Organization Act). Judges
shall be appointed from among i) those who have passed the
Judicial Examination and completed the required courses of
the Judicial Research and Training Institute and ii) those who
are qualified as a lawyer (Article 42 Section 2 of the Court
Organization Act).

The aforementioned provisions, however, were revised in
July 18, 2011 to fortify the qualification for appointees, so
that the Chief Justice and Justices of the Supreme Court shall
be appointed from among those who are forty five years of
age or over and judges shall be appointed from among those
who have served in the offices specified in Article 42 Section
1 for not less than ten years.[1] This revision will take effect
from January 1, 2013.

Meanwhile, with the launch of the law school system
which replaces the Judicial Examination, 'law clerk' system is
also introduced. The law clerks shall be engaged in investigation and research concerning the deliberation and ad-

---

[1] According to the transitional provision in the Court Organization Act, in
order to be appointed as a judge, a minimum of three years' legal experience is required for those who will be appointed on or after January 1,
2013; a minimum of five years' legal experience for those who will be
appointed on or after January 1, 2020; and a minimum of ten years' legal experience for those who will be appointed on or after January 1,
2022 (Article 2 of the Addenda).

judication of cases and other necessary works, and they shall be hired for a certain period of time not exceeding three years. This system will take effect on January 1, 2012 (Article 53-2 of the Court Organization Act).

Also, with the growing problems of the existing judicial personnel administration system[2] based on 'career judge system'[3] such as judge's lack of social experience (average age of those who are appointed as judge is 28.5), early retirement or retirement in the middle of judge's career,[4] controversies over preferential treatment to the retired judges and bureaucratization of the judicial system, a new movement of 'unitary system of lawyer'[5] has sprouted since 1998. Such changes have been phased over time, and finally the Court Organization

---

2) the Numbers of new judges during the recent three years

	2009	2010	2011
Trainees at the JRTI	92	89	81
Military Judicial Officers	46	52	62
Practicing Attorneys	28	18	-
Total	166	159	143

3) It is also called 'bureaucratic court system,' meaning that a system in which a young lawyer who newly graduated from the Korea Judicial Research and Training Institution is appointed as a judge and builds one's career as a judge within the court system.

4) Number of retired judges and average length of service

Year	Number of retired judges	Average length of service(year)
2009	76	16.3
2010	77	16.8
2011	76	17.2

5) Generally, this term means recruitment of judges from experienced lawyers who possess a certain amount of professional legal career.

Act was revised on July 18, 2011, so that judges shall be recruited from lawyers with a minimum of three to ten years' legal experience from January 1, 2013.

(2) Term of Office of Judges

The Chief Justice of the Supreme Court shall be appointed for a six-year term of office, and may not be reappointed. Justices of the Supreme Court shall be appointed for a six-year term of office and the term may be renewed. Judges shall be appointed for a ten-year term of office, and the term may be renewed. The age limit of the Chief Justice of the Supreme Court shall be seventy years of age; Justices of the Supreme Court, sixty five years of age; and judges, sixty three years of age (Article 45 of the Court Organization Act). But the provisions were revised on July 18, 2011, so that the age limits of the Chief Justice of the Supreme Court and Justice of the Supreme Court shall be seventy years of age, respectively; and judges, sixty five years of age. This revision will take effect on January 1, 2013.

The term of Justices of the Constitutional Court shall be six years and may be renewed. The age limit of Justices of the Constitutional Court shall be sixty five years of age and the age limit of the President of the Constitutional Court shall be seventy years of age. Different from the similar provisions that stipulate the term of office of the Chief Justice and

Justices of the Supreme Court, however, these provisions have yet to be revised.

(3) Guarantee of Judge's Status

Judge's status is guaranteed by the Constitution, stipulating that no judge shall be removed from office except by impeachment or a sentence of imprisonment without prison labor or higher punishment, nor shall he be suspended from office, have his salary reduced or suffer any other unfavorable treatment except by disciplinary action (Article 106 Section 1 of the Constitution). The Court Organization Act also provides for the same provision to guarantee judge's status (Article 46 Section 1 of the Court Organization Act).

3. Employment of Prosecutors

(1) Appointment of Prosecutors

The Prosecutor General shall be appointed from among those who have held a position falling under any of the following subparagraphs for not less than 15 years: i) A judge, prosecutor or lawyer; ii) A person qualified as a lawyer and has been engaged in legal affairs in governmental organizations, local governments, government or public-managed enterprises, public institutions under Article 4 of the Act on the

Management of Public Institutions or other corporations; and iii) A person qualified as a lawyer and has worked as an assistant professor of laws or at a higher position at a college or university (Article 27 of the Prosecutor's Office Act).

Each prosecutor shall be appointed from among those who fall under any of the following: i) A person who has completed courses at the Judicial Research and Training Institute after passing the Judicial Examination; and ii) A person qualified as a lawyer. Appointment of prosecutors and assignment of positions to prosecutors shall be made by the President of the Republic of Korea upon the proposal of the Minister of Justice. The Minister of Justice shall make such a proposal in consideration of the opinion of the Prosecutor General. When the President of the Republic of Korea appoints the Prosecutor General by a proposal of the Minister of Justice, he/she shall undergo personnel hearings held by the National Assembly (Article 34 of the Prosecutor's Office Act).

Also, in order to deliberate on the appointment, change of position of prosecutors and other important matters concerning personnel management, a Personnel Committee for Prosecutor shall be established in the Ministry of Justice. The composition and operation of and matters subject to the deliberation of the Personnel Committee shall be determined by Presidential Decree (Article 35 of the Prosecutor's Office Act).

But, in order to strengthen neutrality and independence of

the Prosecution Service and secure fairness and impartiality in investigation, the Prosecutor's Office Act was revised on July 18, 2011, expecting to be effective from January 1, 2012. According to the revision, when the Minister of Justice makes a proposal for appointment of the Prosecutor General, there should be recommendation of a Recommendation Committee for Candidate to the Prosecutor General. The Recommendation Committee shall be composed of nine members including a former prosecutor, the Deputy Minister for Criminal Affair of the Ministry of Justice, the Vice Minister of the National Court Administration, the President of the Korean Bar Association, the President of the Korean Law Professors Association, the President of the Korean Association of Law Schools and three persons who are not qualified as a lawyer (in this case, at least one of them shall be female) appointed by the Minister of Justice (Article 34-2 of the Prosecutor's Office Act). Also, in cases of prosecutors, the revised Act concretely provides for composition and operation of and matters subject to the deliberation of the Personnel Committee which are currently stipulated in Presidential Decree. The Personnel Committee consists of eleven members, including three prosecutors, two judges, two lawyers, two law professors, two persons who are not qualified as a lawyer, appointed by the Minister of Justice (Article 35 of the Prosecutor's Office Act).

As of February 2011, the maximum number of prosecutors

stipulated in the Prosecutor's Office Act is 2,044, and currently there are 1,846 prosecutors in Korea. The number of newly admitted prosecutors in 2011 is 120, and among them, 65.5% of 90 newly appointed prosecutors who graduated from the Judicial Research and Training Institute (JRTI), excluding 30 people who were military judicial officials, are female.

(2) Employment of Law School Graduates as Prosecutors

From the year 2012, when the law schools will produce their first graduates, to the year 2017, when the Judicial Examination will be completely scrapped, prosecutors will be recruited from both those who pass the Judicial Examination and are trained at the Judicial Research and Training Institute and those who graduate from law school and pass the National Bar Examination.[6]

As of today, regarding law school graduates, concrete plans or substantial standard for their recruitment as prosecutors or fixed ratio for how many law school graduates to be prosecutors have yet to be decided. But, according to the media reports, it has been told that the Ministry of Justice envisions a plan to appoint law school graduates/admittants to the Bar as prosecutors through recommendation from law

---

6) For reference, the passing rate for the National Bar Examination scheduled to be firstly taken by the class of 2012 law school graduates is decided to be 75% of the maximum number of law students (2,000).

schools, interview and internship.

(3) Guarantee of Prosecutor's Status

Different from judges, prosecutor's status, although en-
sured the same level of status guarantee as judges, is guaranteed not by the Constitution, but simply by the Act. According
to the Prosecutor's Office Act, no prosecutor shall be removed
from office, unless he/she is impeached or sentenced to imprisonment without prison labor or heavier punishment, nor
shall he/she be subject to such dispositions as dismissal, removal from office, suspension from office, reduction of salary, reprimand or retirement unless he/she is subject to a
disciplinary disposition or examination of qualifications
(Article 37 of the Prosecutor's Office Act).

Also, with respect to prosecutors (excluding the Prosecutor
General), the evaluation of qualifications shall be conducted every
seven years after they are appointed. And in order to conduct
the aforementioned evaluation, a Prosecutors' Evaluation
Committee composed of nine members shall be established in
the Ministry of Justice and where the Committee deems that a
prosecutor has difficulty in conducting his/her duties normally
as a prosecutor because he/she considerably lacks the ability to
conduct occupational duties, etc., the Committee may propose
to the Minister of Justice the retirement of such a prosecutor
through the resolution of not less than 2/3 of incumbent

members. When the Minister of Justice deems such proposal for retirement reasonable, he/she shall propose that the President of the Republic of Korea issue an order for retirement to the prosecutor concerned (Article 39 of the Prosecutor's Office Act).

4. Discipline of Judges

(1) Judicial Disciplinary Act

Any disciplinary action against a judge shall be taken in any of the following cases: i) where a judge violates obligations or neglects duties; and ii) where a judge commits conduct detrimental to his/her prestige or the dignity of the court (Article 2 of the Judicial Disciplinary Act).[7] When such

---

7) For reference, the Court Organization Act stipulates matters not allowed to be conducted during judge's term of office as follows:
   Article 49 (Prohibited Matters) No judicial officer shall conduct the following acts during his term of office:
   1. To be a member of the National Assembly or a local council;
   2. To be a public official in any administrative agency;
   3. To participate in a political movement;
   4. To be engaged in a paid job without the permission of the Chief Justice of the Supreme Court;
   5. To be engaged in a job for the purpose of any pecuniary profit;
   6. To assume the post, regardless of its reward, as an advisor, officer or employee of a corporation, organization, etc., other than government agencies, without the permission of the Chief Justice of the Supreme Court; and
   7. To perform other matters as prescribed by the Supreme Court Regulations.

causes of disciplinary actions are recognized, disciplinary actions shall be imposed with the following three categories: suspension from office, salary reduction, and reprimand. The period of suspension from office shall be no less than one month but no more than one year, and the judge who is subject to a disposition of suspension shall not be paid during the suspension period. The salary reduction shall be made by reducing no more than one-third of the judge's salary during the period of no less than one month but no more than one year. The reprimand shall require a written warning to a judge about his misconduct (Article 3 of the Judicial Disciplinary Act). And, in order to deliberate on the disciplinary action against a judge, the Judicial Disciplinary Committee[8] shall be established in the Supreme Court and the Committee shall consist of one chairman and six members, with an additional three reserve members (Article 4 of the Judicial Disciplinary Act). The Chief Justice of the Supreme Court disposes and executes a disciplinary action made by the Committee and when a disciplinary action has been taken by the Chief Justice of the Supreme Court, it shall be entered on the Official Gazette

---

8) A justice of the Supreme Court serves as the chairman and the 6 members appointed by the Chief Justice shall include three judges, one lawyer, one professor of law and a person having profound knowledge of and experience with the law (Article 5 Section 1 of the Judicial Disciplinary Act) and reserve members shall be appointed among judges by the Chief Justice (Article 5 Section 2 of the Judicial Disciplinary Act).

(Article 26 of the Judicial Disciplinary Act). If a judge is dissatisfied with a decision of the Committee and wishes to bring a lawsuit for cancellation of the disciplinary action to the Supreme Court, he/she must do so within fourteen days of being notified of the decision to bring the lawsuit without going through an administrative appeal process. The Supreme Court will review the lawsuit for cancellation of the disciplinary action by a single-trial system (Article 27 of the Judicial Disciplinary Act).

(2) Code of Ethics for Judges

Judges, by guaranteeing the fundamental human rights of citizens and the legitimate exercise of the rights, should protect freedom, equality and justice. Judges should conduct their judicial authority in compliance with the law and according to conscience to establish democracy and the rule of law. In order to implement the stated missions, judges should uphold the independence and honor of the Judiciary and obtain public confidence and respect. Therefore, judges should perform the judicial duties based on impartiality and integrity, and must observe high standards of professional responsibilities deemed as indispensable to judges. For this, the Judiciary has pronounced the Code of Ethics for Judges by which all judges should abide based on self-responsibility and regulations to exert their best efforts to fulfill their missions and duties (please refer to Appendix 1 for the complete text).

(3) Cases

Cases of disciplinary action against inappropriate conducts of judges are followed as below:

① A judge campaigned for her husband. Her salary had been reduced for 6 months for damaging the dignity of judge and integrity of the court.

② A summary order was issued to a judge for his committing an obstruction of the performance of official duties. The judge was reprimanded for damaging the dignity of judge.

③ A judge was reprimanded by his drunk driving because the dignity of judge and the integrity of the court were damaged.

④ The dignity of judge and the integrity of the court were impaired for the absence without permission. The judge was reprimanded.

⑤ A judge conveyed a request of a litigant. The judge had been suspended from office for 10 months for damaging the dignity of judge.

⑥ A judge had repeated a groundless allegation that a presiding judge of the High Court was wrongfully assigned to a position through the internal communication network of the court, group electronic emails, and the contribution and interview to the press despite the repeating abstention instruction of the chief judge of the competent court. The judge had been suspended from his office for 2 months because the dignity of judge and the integrity of the court were damaged.

⑦ Some judges of a branch court located in the suburbs of Seoul accepted several millions KRW from a lawyer. The judges had been suspended from office for 10 months to 6 months and reprimanded for impairing the dignity of judge and the integrity of the court.

⑧ A judge proceeded with a case, not recusing himself from the case, despite the judge had been told about the dispute from the stockholders and reviewed related documents. Besides, the judge contacted the stock-holder litigant for several times near trials and con-veyed the opinion of the stockholder litigant to a pre-siding judge of another judge panel. The judge had been suspended from office for 10 months by impairing the dignity of judge and the integrity of the court.

⑨ A judge had been suspended from office for 5 months for impairing the dignity of judges and the integrity of court as he conducted inappropriate act which cast doubts on his impartiality and integrity, such as appointing his brother and friend as auditors for the company under his legal management.

(4) Constitutional Complaint Case on the Judicial Disciplinary Act

1) Overview of the Case

The complainant, who is a judge at the court, had spread the groundless allegation for more than 20 times that a presiding judge of the High Court was wrongfully assigned to a position, through the internal communication network of the court, group emails and the contribution and interview to the press for 6 months since February 20, 2007, despite the repeating abstention instruction of the chief judge of the competent court. He had also repeatedly insisted on the disciplinary or impeachment against the Chief Justice of the Supreme Court and mislead that the specific case management unfairly affected the personnel management of his colleague judges, seriously impairing the confidence of the people in the independence and fairness of trial as well as the fame of the colleague judges. With these reasons that he had repeated the allegations beyond the limit of the reasonable expression as a judge, he had been suspended from office for 2 months due to the caused damages on the dignity of judge and the integrity of the court.

The complainant appealed the above disciplinary action, filing a lawsuit for confirmation of nullity or claim for cancellation of the above disciplinary action in the Supreme Court, and filed a motion to request for the constitutional review on Article 2 Item 2 of the Judicial Disciplinary Act providing the ground for disciplinary action that applied to the complainant and Article 27 of the Judicial Disciplinary Act stipulating the disciplinary procedure is under the mandatory jurisdiction of the Supreme Court. The Supreme Court rejected both the lawsuit for confirmation of nullity or claim for cancellation of the disciplinary action and motion to request for the constitutional review on the above provisions; nevertheless, the complainant filed a constitutional complaint to dispute the unconstitutionality of the provisions (2009 Hun-Ba 34) in the Constitutional Court.

2) Issues of the Case

① Whether the "degradation of dignity of judges or impairment of the integrity of the court" as prescribed in Article 2 Section 2 of the Judicial Disciplinary Act violates the principle of clarity that should be observed by the legislation restricting the basic rights as a way of the rule of law.

② Whether it is appropriate to be resolved from the perspective of the freedom of expression of judges and from the perspective of the rule against excessive restriction; whereas the basic rights restricted by Article 2 Section 2 of the Judicial Disciplinary Act may include the freedom of expression, the general freedom of action and the freedom of occupation.

③ Whether Article 27 of the Judicial Disciplinary Act that stipulates the appeal against disciplinary actions of judges as the single trial system under the jurisdiction of the Supreme Court infringes on the right to trial by judges.

④ Whether the single trial system prescribed by Article 27 of the Judicial Disciplinary Act violates the right to equality, unreasonably discriminating against judges, compared to a person engaged in public affairs, such as a prosecutor or public officer, who can go through an administrative appeal process.

5. Discipline of Prosecutors

(1) Discipline of Prosecutors Act

A public prosecutor falling under any of the following shall be subject to disciplinary action: i) where he/she violates Article 43 of the Public Prosecutor's Office Act[9]; ii) where

---

9) Public Prosecutor's Office Act
   Article 43 (Prohibition of Political Activities, etc.)
       No prosecutor shall perform any act falling under any of following subparagraphs while in office:
       1. Become a member of the National Assembly or a local council;
       2. Get involved in any political activity;

he/she violates any of his/her official duties, or neglects any of his/her duties; and iii) where he/she commits any conduct detrimental to his/her prestige or dignity as a public prosecutor, regardless of whether it is related to his/her official duties (Article 2 of the Discipline of Prosecutors Act).

Disciplinary action against prosecutors shall be classified into dismissal, removal, suspension from office, salary reduction, and reprimand. Suspension from office means suspending a public prosecutor from performing his/her official duties for a period of between not less than one month and not more than six months without salary. Salary reduction means reducing a salary by not more than 1/3 for a period of between not less than one month and not more than one year. Reprimand means having a public prosecutor reflect on the misconduct he/she has committed while engaging in his/her official duties (Article 3 of the Discipline of Prosecutors Act). And, in order to deliberate on disciplinary action against public prosecutors, a Public Prosecutor Disciplinary Committee shall be established in the Ministry of Justice, and the Committee shall be comprised of seven members including a chairperson with three reserve members (Article 4 of the Discipline of

---

3. Engage in business, the purpose of which is to obtain monetary profits;
4. Engage in other remunerative duties without the permission of the Minister of Justice.

Prosecutors Act). When taking disciplinary action against any public prosecutor, it shall be published in the Official Gazette (Article 23 of the Discipline of Prosecutors Act).

If a prosecutor is dissatisfied with a decision of the Committee and wishes to bring a lawsuit for cancellation of the disciplinary action, he/she can do so by going through an administrative appeal process since there is no specific provision, different from the case of lawsuit for cancellation by judge, stipulating that the Supreme Court will review the lawsuit for cancellation of the disciplinary action by a single-trial system.

(2) Code of Ethics for Prosecutors

As prosecutors have duties to protect citizens from crimes and realize a free and stabilized society based on democracy by protecting human dignity and rights of citizens through the 'rule of law,' they should carry out such missions on the basis of responsibility and sense of duty with the highest level of morality and professional ethics. In order to make prosecutors deeply recognize the dignity of their missions and thereby be wholeheartedly trusted by the people, ethical standards and rules of action are established. Prosecutors are required to keep the standards and rules and be responsible for the results of their conducts (for detail, please see Appendix 2).

(3) Cases

① A prosecutor accepted $5,000 given by a company president at the overseas airport. The prosecutor's salary had been reduced for 3 months for damaging the dignity of prosecutor.

② A prosecutor played golf with a company president who was introduced at the private club whose members are from the same county. The prosecutor had accepted $5,000 twice and had been asked for favorable arrangements with related to the case subject to the investigation by the company president by telephone. The prosecutor had been suspended from office for 6 months for damaging the dignity of prosecutor.

③ A prosecutor played golf with an acquaintance of the accuser of a case being investigated by another prosecutor who belongs to the same team with him; and the prosecutor borrowed money, totaled 230 million KRW, to invest in stocks from a junior prosecutor who is advised by him but defaulted on a part of the debts due to the drop in stock prices. The prosecutor had been suspended from office for 3 months for damaging the dignity of prosecutor.

④ A prosecutor impaired his dignity as a prosecutor by accepting treats that amount 2,150,000 KRW in total, extending over 5 times, from a person who has a fraud record and was committing fraud at that time. He was also negligent in performances of his duties because he wrongfully directed the effect of the suspension of sentence to be lost, which resulted in 13 days of illegal detention. The prosecutor's salary had been reduced for 3 months.

⑤ A prosecutor wrongfully directed the lapse of suspension of sentence, resulting 48 days of illegal detention, because of his miscalculation of the point of consummation of the crime. The prosecutor was reprimanded due to his negligence in performing his duties.

⑥ A prosecutor had an acquaintance with a president of a construction company and received a company card by the representative, spending 97,660,000 KRW in total during 38 months. The prosecutor had been dismissed from his office.

⑦ A prosecutor had been paid 2,500,000 KRW per month as dividends, totaled 80 million KRW, from his investment of 100 million KRW despite his assumption that the place of his investment is related to usury. His salary had been reduced for 2 months.

⑧ A prosecutor assaulted his wife twice, injuring chin sprain that required 3 weeks treatment. His salary had been reduced for 1 month.

⑨ A prosecutor impaired the dignity of prosecutors by inappropriate word and behavior during the investigation. He also infringed the Rule for the Protection of Human Rights during Investigation, violating his professional obligation. The prosecutor had been suspended from office for 2 months.

⑩ A prosecutor refused to follow the Prosecutor General's direction to attend at the Supreme Prosecutor's Office for cross-examination with an attorney with related to the inspection of the case of bribery from an attorney. Despite the prosecutor was advised his resignation due to the above bribery suspicion, he left his office without permission of the Prosecutor General in order to issue a statement that blamed the Prosecutor General in Seoul. He held a press conference at the pressroom of the Supreme Prosecutor's Office, causing social chaos and impairing the chain of command. The prosecutor had been removed from office due to the damages in honor and dignity of prosecutors.[10]

⑪ A prosecutor was treated dinner, was entertained at hostess bar and accepted cash from a constructor under his jurisdiction. The prosecutor had been removed

---

10) Nevertheless, in the following administrative lawsuit, the above removal action has been revoked due to its illegality that violates the principle of proportionality and abuses the discretion.

from office.[11]

⑫ A prosecutor had been removed from office for damaging dignity and honor of prosecutors and violating the duty to remain politically neutral as he was indicted for maintaining his status as a member of the Democratic Labor Party and Open Uri(Our) Party even after being appointed as a prosecutor.

⑬ A prosecutor had been removed from office for impairing dignity and honor of prosecutor as he forcefully kissed a female trainee of the Judicial Research and Training Institute who served a practical apprenticeship at the Prosecution Office while drunken at a social gathering.

⑭ At a social gathering, a prosecutor impaired dignity and honor of prosecutor by inappropriate words and behavior, including forcing a female trainee of the Judicial Research and Training Institute who served a practical apprenticeship at the Prosecution Office to dance with him. His salary had been reduced for 2 months.

---

11) With regard to this disciplinary action, the lawsuit of claim for cancellation has been filed, leading the favorable judgment for the complainant at the first trial but pending in the appellate trial, appealed by the defendant.

6. Conclusion

Although there are some disciplinary cases against judges or prosecutors in Korea, in general, it can be said that they have maintained fairly high level of moral integrity and professional competency. This is so because their morality and professional competency are tested throughout the extremely rigorous passage of passing the Korean Judicial Examination. Moreover, the social status of judges or prosecutors, as the ones who are respected and admired by the people in Korea, attracts many young and talented individuals with a sense of duty and commitment to the social justice.

From the systemic perspectives regarding the employment and discipline of judges and prosecutors, although there are some parts to be improved, the system has been managed gearing toward assuring fair and independent trial, and the Judiciary itself has been making its utmost effort to reinforce fairness and transparency in the process of the employment or discipline of judges in order to achieve continuous respect and trust from the people.

Meanwhile, it is expected that there will be fundamental changes in the employment of judges and prosecutors in the near future. The basic idea of Korea's judge employment system, since Korea's liberalization from Japanese colonial rule, has been the 'career judge system,' which is prevalent in civil law countries and the system also correspondingly applies to the prosecutor's employment. This personnel management system itself, in which those who passed the Judicial Examination and were educated at the Judicial Research and Training Institute are appointed as judges or prosecutors, trained by their seniors and accumulate their own career within the hierarchical system, has both weakness and strength as any other system does. And its success or failure depends on how well the system is operated corresponding to the realities of our situation, and it is true that the operation has been proven to be satisfactory in its own way so far.

The recent introduction of the law school system and the revision to the related Acts aiming to realize the 'unitary system of lawyer,' however, rekindled debates and controversies over the personnel management system of judges and prosecutors in Korea, thereby providing a critical juncture for the systemic change in the legal profession where more and more lawyers with various legal specialty go into society and judges are employed among those who have sufficient experiences in both legal profession and life. This systemic change is achieved as a result of exchanging and collecting opinions and ideas from various corners of society to make trials be more trusted by the people, and I strongly believe that, if this new climate in the legal profession is successfully established as initially planned, far better personnel system of the Judiciary will also take root. For the successful introduction of the system, not only the endeavor of the Judiciary but also the support and understanding of the people is required.

Also, I sincerely hope that I can have another chance to share the experiences of the advanced personnel management system of Korean judges and prosecutors, expected to be achieved by the aforementioned changes currently undergoing, with you in the near future.

Appendix 1

Code of Ethics for Judges

Canon 1. (Protection of Judicial Independence)

A judge should uphold the independence of the Judiciary against all extraneous influences.

Canon 2. (Preserving Dignity)

A judge should have respect for honor and preserve dignity.

Canon 3. (Impartiality and Integrity)

① A judge should be impartial and uphold integrity, should not act in a manner that their impartiality or integrity might reasonably be questioned.

② A judge should discharge the judicial duties without prejudice or discrimination on the basis of blood relationship, regional or alma mater connections, sex, religion, financial abilities as well as social status.

Canon 4. (Performance of Judicial Duties)

① A judge should conduct faithfully all judicial duties as-signed, and exert constant efforts to maintain and enhance professional competence in the law.

② A judge should administer proceedings promptly and efficiently, hear cases carefully and prudently to guarantee a fair trial.

③ A judge should be kind and courteous to litigants, law-yers and others with whom the judge deals in an official capacity.

④ A judge, except for the occasions necessary to dis-charge the judicial duties, should avoid contacting with or meeting litigants, lawyers and others with whom the judge deals in an official capacity.

⑤ A judge, except for the purpose of education, scholarly research and accurate media reports, should avoid public comment or opinion on the merits of a pending or impending action.

Canon 5. (Extrajudicial Activities of Judge)

① A judge may participate in the extrajudicial activities such as participation in academic societies or membership of religious, cultural entities so far as the judge does not have difficulty in preserving dignity and discharging the judicial duties.

② A judge should not be involved in other's legal disputes, or act to influence on the cases of judicial colleagues.

③ A judge should not provide legal advice or information on the Judiciary personnel including lawyers on the occasions where the proceedings would be influenced or judge's impartiality might reasonably be questioned.

Canon 6. (Limits on the Financial Activities)

A judge should not be engaged in financial transactions such as lending or borrowing money, and should not receive economic benefits including donation on the occasions where the judge's impartiality might reasonably be questioned or the discharge of the judicial duties would be disturbed.

Canon 7. (Political Neutrality)

① A judge should preserve political neutrality in performing the judicial duties.

② A judge should not serve as a member or a board member of an organization involved with political activities, and avoid activities undermining the political neutrality of the judge including political campaign activity.

Appendix 2

Code of Ethics for Prosecutors

Article 1 (Vision)

A prosecutor shall establish the order of law, protect the human rights, and apply justice as a representative of the public interests.

Article 2 (Service for Citizens)

A prosecutor shall serve citizens with faith and modesty, remembering that the prosecuting authority is delegated by citizens.

Article 3 (Political Neutrality and Fairness)

① A prosecutor shall preserve political neutrality in performing the duties, being irrelevant to political campaigns.

② A prosecutor shall not discriminate a suspect, a victim or any other person related to the case without reasonable grounds and shall not be affected by any pressure, temptation and interests; but a prosecutor shall perform impartially and fairly the duties according to the law and conscience.

Article 4 (Dignity and Honor)

A prosecutor shall preserve strict dignity and morality, and respect for honor in the public and personal life.

Article 5 (Self-Improvement)

A prosecutor shall continue to improve the competences in order to understand the changing social phenomenon and cultivate insight and intelligence that are required by society.

Article 6 (Respect for the Human Rights and Due Process)

A prosecutor shall respect the human rights of a suspect, the accused, a victim and any other person related to the case and observe the procedure of the Constitution and law.

Article 7 (Appropriateness in the Exercise of Prosecution)

A prosecutor shall not abuse the prosecuting authority by collecting evidence according to the legal proceedings and applying appropriately the law.

Article 8 (Promptness in the Exercise of Prosecution)

A prosecutor shall perform faithfully and diligently the

duties, thereby realizing promptly the national right to punishment.

Article 9 (Self Recusal)

① In cases where a prosecutor is a relative of a suspect, a victim or any other person related to the case (in cases where the person involved in the relevant case is a corporate person, chief executive officer or controlling shareholder) under Article 777 of the Civil Act, has previously served as a lawyer for them or has a personal interest in the outcome of the proceeding, he/she shall recuse himself/herself from participating in the proceeding.

② A prosecutor may recuse himself/herself in the event of any special relationship other than the personal relationship stated in ① that could be adversely affect the required appearance of impartiality.

Article 10 (Attitude to Related Parties of the Case at issue)

A prosecutor shall abide by the Rule for the Protection of Human Rights during Investigation, carefully listen to the arguments of the related parties of the case at issue including a suspect and a victim and do his/her best to treat the related parties with neutrality and impartiality.

Article 11 (Attitude to Lawyers)

A prosecutor, while recognizing and guaranteeing the legal representative's right to defense, shall not personally communicate with all legal representatives of the related parties of the case involved or their staffs without due cause.

Article 12 (Attitude to Seniors)

A prosecutor shall respect his/her seniors with decorum and politeness and obey seniors' order and supervision in relation to performing the duties: Provided that in cases of objection to the legality or legitimacy of the order and supervision by his/her seniors, a prosecutor can raise objection by going through proper proceeding.

Article 13 (Attitude to Management of Judicial Police)

A prosecutor, as a leader who presides over investigation process, shall control and supervise management of judicial police.

Article 14 (Relationship with People outside the Prosecution Office)

A prosecutor shall not have relationship with people whose contact with him/her may cause the prosecutor's impartiality in conducting the duties to be questioned and be careful in his/her behavior.

Article 15 (Restriction on Personal Contact with Related Parties)

Prosecutors shall not personally contact with the parties related to the case at hand such as a suspect and a victim, etc. and other interested parties (hereinafter, 'related parties, etc.') without legitimate reasons.

Article 16 (Misuse of Position of Power etc. Forbidden)

① A prosecutor shall draw a clear line between official and private matters and shall not misuse his office or position of power for the benefit of his or others' interest.

② A prosecutor shall not utilize the facts or information which are disclosed to him while on his duty.

Article 17 (Engagement in Financial Activities etc. Forbidden)

A prosecutor shall not be engaged in the business seeking monetary profit and, without permission of the Minister of Justice, in the office with salary. Neither shall a prosecutor hold an additional position except in the case permitted by law.

Article 18 (Interceding and Soliciting etc. Forbidden)

① A prosecutor shall not intercede with or solicit or unduly influence other prosecutors or agencies about the cases of which they are in charge.

② A prosecutor shall not be involved in others' legal disputes to gain an unfair profit.

Article 19 (Accepting Money Forbidden)

A prosecutor shall not accept money, monetary profit, treatment or financial benefit without good reason from the person who could disturb the impartiality of his duty under Article 14 or from the relevant person under Article 15.

Article 20 (Introducing or Suggesting a Lawyer Forbidden)

A prosecutor shall not introduce or suggest a lawyer to the suspect, indicted, or other relevant person about the case of which he or his colleague prosecutors in the same district office are in charge.

Article 21 (Rule on Contributing or Presenting Opinion to the Public)

A prosecutor should obtain permission of the head of public prosecutor's office he belongs to, when to contribute or present the content or his opinion about the case under his duty or investigation to the public using his office title.

Article 22 (Maintaining the Official Secrecy)

A prosecutor should maintain the secrecy on the items

under investigation, personal information of the relevant person, facts disclosed to him while on his duty. In addition, he should pay attention when using telephone, facsimile, e-mail or other communication devices, not to let those secrets disclosed.

Article 23 (Guiding and Supervising Office Staff)

A prosecutor should respect office staff, a judicial apprentice, other public servicemen relating to his duty. He should guide and supervise them not to be engaged in the illegal or unjust act or not to disclose or misuse the official secret.

韓國法官檢察官的任用與懲戒制度

李　東　洽[*]

黃　慧　儀　翻譯[**]

---

* 韓國憲法法院大法官
** 國立台灣大學法律學系碩士

1. 前 言

韓國長久以來透過檢覈或韓國司法特考，遴選少部分人以培養司法專業人才，而通過司法特考的人員，於隸屬最高法院的司法研究與訓練所(Judicial Research and Training Institute，簡稱 JRTI)中，接受爲期二年的培訓教育。此外，依據韓國的司法制度，韓國最高法院院長(Chief Justice of the Supreme Court)對法官之任用、再任、職務分派、評鑑等人事管理事項，均有重大的影響力。而檢察署的人事管理制度，也讓法務部長與檢察總長對司法人事有重大的影響力。

不過，越來越多的輿論議論現行司法特考制度對於訓練司法人才的缺失，司法人才的職業倫理應立於對人民和社會有相當經驗和深切體察的基礎之上，並重視自由、平等和公平，且須具有知識和能力，可專業並有效率地解決不同法律紛爭，以改善人民對於司法品質的期待和需求。而國內關於要求司法改革、改進法官及檢察官人事管理制度之新機制，以促進司法審判獨立和偵查公平之爭議，已存在多年。

由於這些討論與爭辯，韓國於2008年立法制定法學院設立與管理法(Act on the Establishment and Management of Professional Law Schools)並引進所謂法學院系統；接著在2011年依法院組織法(Court Organization Act)設立法官人事委員會(Personnel Committee for Judges)，其委員主要非法官所組成。檢察署亦於檢察署法(Prosecutors' Office Act)訂定相關條文，設立檢察總長人選建議委員會(Recommendation Committee for Candidate to the Prosecutor General)和檢察官人事委員會(Personnel Committee for Prosecutor)。

　　於2012年，法學院第一批畢業生將產出，且法官檢察官的人事委員會將啓動，此將成爲韓國法律專業人才的訓練制度和法官檢察官人事管理的重大轉振點。

　　同時，依「各級法院法官人數上限法」(Act on the Maximum Number of Judges, etc. of Various Levels of Courts)規定，從2011年起各級法院中所有法官的人數最多爲2844位；檢察官人數依「檢察官人數上限法」(Act on the Maximum Number of Prosecutors)，人數最多爲2044位。此與1963年「各級法院法官人數上限法」(Act on the Maximum Number of Judges, etc. of Various Levels of Courts)初立法時的367位法官，和1956年「檢察官人數上限法」(Act on the Maximum Number of Prosecutors)初立法時的190位檢察官人數相比，有非常驚人的增加。即使與1990年的1374位法官與987位檢察官的人數相比，現今的法官和檢察官人數已增加超過二倍強之多。

　　隨著法官和檢察官人數增加，法官及檢察官的不當行爲已被獨立出來爲社會問題，爲解決此問題，最高法院與檢察署在1995和1999分別公布了倫理規範(Code of Ethics)。然而，隨著適用法官倫理規範(the Code of Ethics for Judges)和檢察官倫理規範(Code of Ethics for Prosecutors)之爭議實例越來越多，時有不當行爲案件數量增加之報導。因此，懲戒制度越來越受關注；另外加上2009年發生了向憲法法院起訴請求對規定懲戒處分理由之條文爲違憲審查，以及請求撤銷懲戒處分的訴訟，使得此議題的爭論更加劇烈。

　　由於我們處於這些關於司法專業人員訓練及司法與檢察部門人事管理的轉變之中，鳥瞰這些制度的結構是相當重要的。因此，本篇文章將討論並整體比較受憲法保障公職身分的法官，和代表公共利益具準司法官地位之檢察官的任用、人事管理和懲戒制度，並且特別介紹懲戒制度和實際案例，以檢視法官和檢察官人事管理制度的特殊性和共通性。

2. 法官之任用

(1) 法官之任命

最高法院院長須經國會同意，由大韓民國國總統任命。最高法院的大法官由最高法院院長提名，經國會同意，由大韓民國總統任命。法官則須經最高法院法官會議同意，由最高法院院長任命(法院組織法第41條)。

憲法法院的大法官由大韓民國總統任命，九位大法官中，三位爲經國會所選之人任命，三位爲經最高法院院長指名之人任命。憲法法院之主席應自大法官中選出，經國會同意，由大韓民國總統任命(憲法第111條第2項、第3項、第4項、憲法法院法Constitutional Court Act第6條)。

同時，基於認爲司法院人事管理有必要回應社會對司法改革之要求，使司法院更受人民尊敬與信任，法院組織法於2011年7月18日修法，新修正的法律將於2012年1月1日生效。修正後，更嚴格限定資格如下：就最高法院大法官的任命，應設立法官人選建議委員會(Recommendation Committee for Candidate of Justice)，委員會由最高法院院長任命的委員組成，其包括最高法院的先任大法官、國家法院行政部長(Minister of National Court Administration)、法務部長、韓國律師協會會長(President of the Korean Bar Association)、韓國法律教授協會會長(President of the Korean Law Professors Association)、韓國法學院協會會長(President of the Korean Association of Law Schools)、一位非最高法院大法官之法官、三位非律師之人士(至少一位必須是女性，法院組織法第41之2條)。就法官之任命，新增規定除了上述程序外，要求必須經過法官人事委員會審查(法院組織法第41條第3項、第25之2條)。

　　關於法官人事委員會的規定也修正如下：爲審查法官之重要人事事項，人事委員會的委員應由三位法官、二位檢察官、二位非律師之人士(至少一位須爲女性)組成，經最高法院院長任命(法院組織法第25之2條)。

　　最高法院的院長和大法官應就40歲以上、曾任下列職位15年以上之人中任用之：ⅰ)法官、檢察官或律師，ⅱ)具律師資格，曾任公務機關、地方政府、國公營企業體、政府投資機關中辦理法律業務者，或其他法務人員，ⅲ)具律師資格，曾任獨立學院或大學法律領域高於助理教授以上職位者(法院組織法第42條第1項)。法官應就符合下列資格者任用之：ⅰ)經司法特考及格，並完成司法研究與訓練所必修課程者，與ⅱ)具律師資格者(法院組織法第42條第2項)。

　　上述規定在2011年7月18日經修正，增加受任用者的資格要求，規定最高法院院長和最高法院大法官必須就45歲以上者任用之，而法官必須就曾任第42條第1項所定之職務10年以上者任用之[1]。修正條文將於2013年1月1日生效。

　　同時，隨著取代司法特考的法學院系統之啓動，也開始採用「法官助理」(law clerk)制度。法官助理須從事與案件之審議與判決有關的調查和研究、以及其他相關必要的工作，且僱用的期間不超過3年。此制度將於2012年1月1日生效(法院組織法第53之2條)。

　　再者，由於在職業法官體系[2]下現存法官人事管理制度[3]日益嚴重，

---

1) 依此一變更的法院組織法條文，爲了要被任用爲法官，在2013年1月之後被任用者，必須有至少3年的法律實務經驗；在2020年1月1日之後任用者，必須有至少5年的法律實務經驗；在2022年1月1日後任用者，必須有至少10年的法律實務經驗(附錄第2條)。

2) 近三年的新任用法官人數

	2009	2010	2011
司法研究與訓練所學員	92	89	81
軍 法 官	46	52	62

如法官缺乏社會經驗(任用年齡平均爲28.5歲)、提早退休或在法官生涯中途退休[4]、法官優退待遇的爭議、以及司法制度官僚化等問題，促使「律師一元體系」(unitary system of lawyer)[5]的新運動於1998年萌生。這些轉變已同步前進多時，最後法院組織法終於在2011年7月18日修正，因此自2013年起，法官應自具備至少3至10年法律實務經驗之律師中進用。

(2) 法官之任期

最高法院院長任期爲6年，不得連任。最高法院大法官任期爲6年，可連任。一般法官的任期爲10年，可連任。年齡限制(退休年齡)爲：最高法院院長是70歲；最高局院的大法官是65歲；其他法官是63歲(法院組織法第45條)。但在2011年7月18日條文修正後，最高法院院長和大法官是70歲、一般法官爲65歲。此修正規定將於2013年生效。

憲法法院大法官的任期是6年，可連任。退休年齡的規定不同於最高法院的規定，憲法法院大法官是65歲，擔任憲法法院院長之大法官則是70歲，這些規定並未修正。

(3) 法官身分保障

法官身分受憲法保障，除非被彈劾、受不得易服勞役之有期徒刑裁

執業律師	28	18	－
總　數	166	159	143

3) 此亦稱爲「官僚法院體系」(bureaucratic court system)，指自韓國司法研究與訓練所甫畢業的年輕律師被任用爲法官，然後在法院體系中發展法官職業。

4) 退休法官人數和平均服務年限

年份	退休法官人數	服務平均期間(年)
2009	76	16.3
2010	77	16.8
2011	76	17.2

5) 大致上來說，此名詞意指從有經驗、已從事相當多法律專業職務之律師中招募法官。

判、或更重之刑罰處分，法官不得被免職。除非經懲戒程序，不得被停職、減薪或受到其他不利處分(憲法第106條第1項)。法院組織法也有同樣的規定保障法官身分(法院組織法第46條第1項)。

3. 檢察官之任用

(1) 檢察官之任用

檢察總長應就曾任下列各款職務15年以上者，任用之：ⅰ)法官、檢察官或律師；ⅱ)具律師資格，於公務機關、地方政府、國公營企業體、公法人管理法第4條之公法人或其他組織從事法律業務；ⅲ)具律師資格，曾任學院或大學法律領域助理之教授或高於助理教授之職位者(檢察署法第27條)。

檢察官應就符合下列資格者任用之：ⅰ)經司法考試及格並完成司法研究與訓練所課程者。ⅱ)具律師資格。檢察官任用和職位分派，應經法務部長提名，由大韓民國總統任命之。法務部長之提名應參考檢察總長之意見。大韓民國國總統依法務部長提名任命檢察總長時，應接受國會質詢(檢察署法第34條)。

再者，爲了審慎考慮任用事項、檢察官職位改變、或其他人事重要事項，法務部必須設立檢察官人事委員會(Personnel Committee for Prosecutor)。人事委員會審議之組成和運作應依總統命令(Presidential Decree)定之(檢察署法第35條)。

但是爲了強化檢察官的中立與獨立性，確保調查的公平與公正，檢察署法於2011年7月18日修正，並將於2012年1月1日生效。依據修正規定，法務部長決定檢察總長之提名時，必須有檢察總長候選人推薦委員會(Recommendation Committee for Candidate to the Prosecutor General)的推薦。推薦委員會應由九位委員組成，九位委員中應包括一位前檢察官、法務部刑事處副處長(Deputy Minister for Criminal Affair of the Ministry of Justice)、國家法院行政部副部長(Vice Minister of the National Court Administration)、韓國律師協會會長、韓國法律教授協會會長、韓國法學院協會會長、以及三位不具律師資格者(至少一人須爲女性)。委員由法務部長任命(檢察署法第34之2條)。

再者，就檢察官而言，修正的法律具體規範了現行由總統命令規定的人事委員審議之組成與運作事項。人事委員會由十一位委員組成，包括三位檢察官、二位法官、二位律師、二位法律教授、二位不具律師資格者，由法務部長任命之(檢察署法第35條)。

從2011年2月開始，檢察署法規定的檢察官人數上限爲2044人，而目前在韓國有1846位檢察官。2011年的新任檢察官人數爲120位，除了30位爲軍事司法官外，90位新任用檢察官爲自司法研究與訓練所畢業，其中有65.5%爲女性。

(2) 任用法學院畢業生爲檢察官

自2012年起，法學院將出產第一批的畢業生，而至2017年司法特考完全被瓦解之前，檢察官將由通過司法特考並經司法研究和訓練所訓練者，以及通過國家律師考試的法學院畢業生中進用[6]。

到目前爲止，就法學院畢業生任用爲檢察官的具體計畫和實質標準、或是任用多少比例的法學院畢業生，都尚未決定。然而，根據媒體報導，法務部預計透過法學院推薦、面試和實習，來任用法學院畢業生/

---

6) 2012年首批法學院畢業生參加國家律師考試的及格率，定爲全部法學院學生(2000人)的百分之75。

通過律師考試者爲檢察官。

⑶ 檢察官身分保障

檢察官身分雖然受到與法官同樣等級的身分保障，但不同於法官，其並非受憲法保障，而僅受法律保障。依檢察署法，檢察官除非被彈劾、或受不得易服勞役之有期徒刑裁判或更重之刑罰處分，不得被免職。除非經懲戒處分或資格評鑑，不得被撤職、免職、停職、減薪、申誡、命令退休(檢察署法第37條)。

此外，檢察官(檢察總長除外)任用後每七年進行一次資格評鑑。爲了進行上述評鑑，法務部須設立由九位委員組成的檢察官評鑑委員會(Prosecutors' Evaluation Committee)而且當委員會認爲受評鑑檢察官因欠缺能力執行工作，而認定該檢察官執行檢察官職務有困難時，經三分之二以上委員同意，委員會得向法務部提議該檢察官退休。若法務部長認爲提議合理，法務部長應向韓國共和國總理申請核發命令該檢察官退休(檢察署法第39條)。

4. 法官之懲戒

⑴ 法官懲戒法(Judicial Disciplinary Act)

下列情形法官應受懲戒：ⅰ)違背職務上義務或怠於職行職務；ⅱ)行爲有損法官形象或法院尊嚴(法官懲戒法第2條[7])。確定懲戒處分的原因

---

7) 法院組織法第49條(禁止事項) 法官在任職期間不得爲下列行爲：
　　1. 爲國會或地方議會之議員。
　　2. 爲行政府署之公務員。
　　3. 參與任何政治活動。
　　4. 未經最高法院長同意從事有報酬的職務。

時，應爲下列三種懲戒處分：停職、減俸、和申誡。停止職務期間爲1個月以上，1年以下。受停職處分的法官於停職期間不得支薪。減俸不得大於三分之一的薪水，期間爲1個月以上，1年以下。申誡應通知其不當行爲(法官懲戒法第3條)。再者，爲了審議法官懲戒處分，最高法院應設立法官懲戒委員會(Judicial Disciplinary Committee)[8]，委員會應包括1位主席和6位委員，另外還有三位預備委員(法官懲戒法第4條)。由最高法院院長裁定並執行委員會所作之懲戒處分，最高法院院長作出懲戒處分時，應公布於政府公報(法官懲戒法第26條)。若法官對委員會的決定不服，欲提起訴訟主張撤銷懲戒處分，必須於收到處分通知後14天內向最高法院提起訴訟，不必經過行政救濟程序。最高法院將以單一審級(Single-Trial System)進行審查撤銷懲戒處分的訴訟(法官懲戒法第27條)。

(2) 法官倫理規範

法官，爲保障人民基本人權和權利之合法實行，應確保自由、平等和正義。法官應依據法律執行司法權力，並本於良心建立民主法治。爲履行上述任務，法官應維護司法獨立與尊嚴，並得到大眾信任與尊敬。因此，法官應秉持公平正直，執行司法職務，並須遵守法官必需之高尚專業責任標準。質是之故，法官倫理規範宣示所有法官必須基於自我負責遵守法官倫理規範與規定，以盡最大努力完成使命與職務(完整內容請參照附件1)。

---

5. 從事以取得金錢利益爲目的之業務。
6. 未經最高法院同意，報酬有無不問國家機關外法人、團體等之顧問、任員、職員等職位就任。
7. 其他最高法院規則規定之工作。
8) 由最高法院的大法官擔任主席，最高法院院長任命的6位委員應包括三名法官、一名律師、與一名具豐富法律知識與經驗者(法官懲戒法第5條第1項)。以及預備委員應就法官中選出由最高法院院長任命(法官懲戒法第5條第2項)。

⑶ **案　例**

對法官不當行為的懲戒處分案例如下：

1）法官為丈夫競選，被減俸6個月，以賠償其損害法官尊嚴和法院公信。

2）法官被裁定妨礙公務員執行公務，該法官因損害法官尊嚴被申誡。

3）法官因酒駕，損害法官尊嚴和法院公信，被申誡。

4）法官無故缺席，損害法官尊嚴和法院公信，因此被申誡。

5）法官傳達訴訟當事人的要求，該法官因損害法官尊嚴被停職10個月。

6）法官不顧有管轄權法院審判長重複地指示應放棄主張，仍透過法院內部通訊網路、群組電子郵件、媒體投稿和訪談，重複提出無理由的上訴，指摘某高等法院審判長不應被分派該職務。該法官因損害法官尊嚴與法院公信被停職2個月。

7）數名在韓國首爾郊區地方法院的法官，收受律師交付數百萬韓元，法官們因損害法官尊嚴和法院公信被停職10至6個月，並被申誡。

8）法官曾被股東告知紛爭且看過相關文件，卻未迴避審判。此外，該法官於接近審判時與股東當事人聯繫數次，並向另一審判庭的法官傳達股東當事人的意見，該法官損害法官尊嚴和法院公信，被停職10個月。

9）法官之不當行為，如指定兄弟和朋友擔任受其司法管理之公司的監督人，使公正和公信受到質疑，因損害法官尊嚴和法院公信，被停職5個月。

⑷ **法官懲戒法的憲法訴願案件**

1）**案件簡介**

請求人為地方法院法官，自2007年2月2日起，在6個月內，不顧有管轄權法院重複指示應放棄主張，仍透過法院內部通訊網路、群組電子郵件和媒體投稿和採訪，散佈超過20次的無理由之上訴，使得高等法院審判長誤被分派職務。該法官不斷堅持最高法院院長應接受懲戒或彈劾，並錯誤地指摘該特定案件管理不公正、影響其法官同仁的人事，該法官嚴重損害人民對審判公平獨立的信任和其法官同仁的名聲。基於其重複的主張，已超出法官合理言論表達的限度，該法官因損害法官尊嚴和法院公信，被停職2個月。

請求人對上述懲戒處分提起上訴，向最高法院起訴請求確認處分無效或撤銷處分，並請求對法官懲戒法第2條第2款此一懲戒請求人的法律依據規定進行違憲審查，以及對法官懲戒法第27條關於懲戒程序繫屬最高法院強制管轄之規定進行違憲審查。最高法院駁回請求確認處分無效或請求撤銷懲戒處分的主張，亦駁回對上述規定進行違憲審查的請求；然而，請求人向憲法法院提起2009Hun-Ba34條文是否違憲之憲法訴願。

2) 案件爭點：

① 法官懲戒法第2條第2款「損害法官尊嚴與損害法院公信」之規定，是否違反法治國限制基本權利應有法律保留之明確性原則。

② 法官懲戒法第2條第2款限制的權利，可能包括言論自由、一般的行動自由和職業自由，以法官言論表達自由和過度限制權利來解決是否妥適。

③ 法官懲戒法第27條規定對懲戒處分異議，為最高法院單一審級管轄，是否侵害裁判請求權。

④ 法官懲戒法第27條規定單一審級，使法官不能與其他公務員或檢察官一樣，能透過行政救濟程序異議，是否為對法官不合理的差別待

遇，違反平等權。

5. 檢察官懲戒

(1) 檢察官懲戒法

　　符合下列各款情形，檢察官應受懲戒：i)違反檢察廳法第43條[9]；ii)違反法定職務，或怠於執行職務；iii)爲損害身爲檢察官之形象與尊嚴之行爲，不論該行爲是否與職務相關(檢察官懲戒法第2條)。

　　對檢察官的懲戒處分應分爲撤職、免職、停職、減俸、及申誡。停職指檢察官暫時停止職行職務，期間爲1個月以上，6個月以下，不支薪。減俸指減少三分之一以下比例的薪水，期間爲1個月以上，1年以下。申誡指於在職時令檢察官反省所爲之不當行爲(檢察官懲戒法第3條)。再者，爲了審議檢察官懲戒處分，法務部須設立檢察官懲戒委員會，委員會應由七位委員組成，其中包括一位主席與三位預備委員(檢察官懲戒法第4條)。對任何檢察官爲懲戒處分時，應公布於公報上(檢察官懲戒法第23條)。

　　若檢察官對委員會決定不服，欲提起訴訟請求撤銷懲戒處分，與法官起訴請求撤銷的情形不同，法官的情形有特別規定由最高法院單一審級審理請求撤銷懲滅處分的訴訟，檢察官因爲沒有特別規定，故可經由行政上訴程序。

---

9) 檢察廳法第43條(禁止政治活動)
　檢察官在任職期間不得爲下列行爲：
　　1. 爲國會或地方議會之議員。
　　2. 參與任何政治活動。
　　3. 從事以取得金錢利益爲目的之商業活動。
　　4. 未經法務部長同意從事其他有報酬的職務。

(2) 檢察官倫理規範

鑑於檢察官有職責保護人民免於犯罪，並透過法治保護人民之人性尊嚴和權利，以實現立基於民主的自由穩定社會，檢察官應秉持最高倫理和專業道德的責任感，履行上述任務。爲使檢察官深切體認其受任務的尊嚴，並因此受人民全心地信賴，須建立倫理準則與行爲規範。檢察官須遵守準則和規範並對其行爲之結果負責任(詳細請見附件2)。

(3) 案　例

1) 檢察官於國外機場接受公司董事長給予的5,000元美金，該檢察官因損害檢察官尊嚴被減俸3個月。

2) 檢察官與在私人俱樂部認識的公司董事長一起打高爾夫球，該俱樂部會員皆來自同一縣。檢察官接受5,000元美金兩次，並曾打電話向該公司董事要求與公司董事長的投資案有關之優惠待遇。該檢察官因損害檢察官尊嚴被停職6個月。

3) 檢察官與案件告訴人的朋友一起打高爾夫球，而該案件告訴人的案件正由同屬一組的其他檢察官調查中。另外，該檢察官向一名其指導的檢察官借了總共2億3千萬韓元去投資股票，但因股價下跌而拖欠部分債務。該檢察官因損害檢察官尊嚴被停職3個月。

4) 檢察官接受有詐欺前科且當時正在從事詐欺犯罪之人所給予總共價值215萬韓元的招待，且次數超過5次，損害身爲檢察官的尊嚴。此外，該檢察官於執行職務有過失，錯誤執行緩刑，造成13天的非法拘禁，被減俸3個月。

5) 檢察官因爲計算犯罪行爲完成時點錯誤，使緩刑時效經過，造成48天不合法的拘禁，該檢察官因執行職務的過失被申誡。

6）檢察官與建設公司董事長熟識，透過代表人收到公司的信用卡，在共38個月的期間內，花費9,766萬韓元。檢察官被撤職。

7）檢察官雖然預見投資的對象與高利貸有關，仍投資1億韓元，每月收到分期支付250萬韓元，總共8千萬韓元，該檢察官被減俸2個月。

8）檢察官傷害其妻子兩次，造成須3週治療的下巴挫傷，被減俸1個月。

9）檢察官因調查中的不當言詞和行為損害檢察官尊嚴。並在調查中違反人權保障規則(Rule for the Protection of Human Rights)，違背職務上義務，該檢察官被停職2個月。

10）檢察官就最高檢察署有關律師賄賂他的案件調查，拒絕依檢察總長之指揮，出席與該律師對質之調查。雖然該檢察官因賄賂嫌疑被建議辭職，但其為了在首爾發表譴責檢察總長的聲明，未經檢察總長即許可擅離崗位。他在最高檢察署的記者室舉行記者會，造成社會混亂傷害檢察一體。該檢察官因損害檢官名譽和尊嚴被免職[10]。

11）檢察官接受晚餐招待和接受酒吧小姐娛樂，並自其轄區內的建商收受現金，該檢察官被免職[11]。

12）檢察官因損害檢察官之尊嚴與聲譽，以及因在被任命為檢察官後，仍維持民主勞動黨(Democratic Labor Party)和開放的我們黨[12](Open Uri Party)黨員的身分而被起訴，違反保持政治中立之義務，故被免職。

13）檢察官於聚會中喝醉，強吻一位在檢察署實習的司法研究與訓

10）不過，在接下來的行政訴訟，前述免職處分被撤銷，理由為處分違反比例原則與濫用裁量權。

11）就此懲戒處分，已提起撤銷訴訟，第一審判決原告勝訴，被告上訴，上訴審仍在審理中。

12）譯按：譯名請參考蕭新煌、李明峻，亞太論壇第28期，2005. 6，註1。

練所女學員，因損害檢察官之尊嚴與名譽被免職。

　　14)　檢察官於聚會時爲不當言詞與行爲，包括強迫在檢察署實習的司法研究與訓練所女學員與其共舞，因損害檢察官之尊嚴與名譽被減俸2個月。

6. 結　論

　　雖然韓國有發生法官和檢察官的懲戒案例，但大體上來說，法官和檢察官仍可說是保持相當高的道德標準和專業能力。因爲他們的道德和專業能力乃經過非常嚴格的韓國司法考試的測試。甚且，法官或檢察官的社會地位，在韓國是受人民所尊崇的，吸引許多抱有爲社會正義貢獻和責任感的青年才俊。

　　由制度面的觀點看法官和檢察官任用和懲戒制度，雖然有些部分需要改進，此制度已開始朝向確保審判公平與獨立，且司法院已盡最大努力加強法官任用和懲戒的程序公平性和透明度，以獲得人民持續的尊敬和信任。

　　同時，未來將可期待法官和檢察官的任用制度出現根本性的轉變。韓國法官任用制度的基礎理念，自從韓國自日本殖民統治解放後，已是「職業法官制度」，此在民主法治國家相當普遍，且此制度亦同樣適用於檢察官的任用。此人事管理制度，爲通過司法特考者於司法研究與訓練所接受訓練後被任命爲法官或檢察官，接著由前輩訓練，在官僚制度中累積職業經驗；此制度與其他制度一樣，兼有缺點與優點。制度的成敗端視能否與我們的現今情況相符，且運作得當；而此制度運作，至今仍應令人滿意。

　　最近採用法學院制度和相關法律修正主要目的是爲實現「律師一元體系」，不過也燃起了韓國法官和檢察官人事管理制度的爭議和討論，因此帶來法律職業在制度上改變的重大契機，越來越多不同法律專長的律師走入社會，法官則就同時具備法律專業和人生經驗者任用之。此制度性的改變是因爲有來自社會不同角落的聲音，爲了使審判更受人民信賴，彼此互相交換意見和想法所造就，我深信若此番法律職業新氣象能依最初計畫成功地建立，更好的司法人事制度將會生根發展。欲能成功地適用此制度，不僅需要司法院的努力，也需要人民的支持與理解。

　　上述正在進行中的改變，被期望能成就更進步的韓國法官與檢察官人事管理制度，我誠摯地希望將來還有機會與各位分享更進一步的經驗。

[附件 1]

法官倫理規範

第 1 條(保護司法獨立)

法官應捍衛司法獨立，不受任何外來影響。

第 2 條(維護尊嚴)

法官應重視名譽並維護尊嚴。

第 3 條(公正與正直)

法官應公正並保持正直，不得從事使公正或正直被質疑之行為。

法官執行職務時，不得因血統、地域或教育背景、性別、宗教、社會經濟地位，表現偏見或歧視。

第 4 條(執行司法職務)

法官應忠誠執行受分派之司法職務，並隨時注意保持和充實執行職務所需之法律專業能力。

法官應妥速並有效率地指揮程序，仔細並謹慎聽審以保障公平審判。

法官應對當事人、律師或其他法官執行職務相關之人溫和有禮。

法官除執行職務有必要外，應避免與當事人、法官執行職務相關之人聯繫或會面。

　　法官除爲教育、學術研究和端正媒體報導外，應避免對進行中之訴訟公開發表評論或意見。

第 5 條(法官職務外活動)

　　只要不與司法職責和維護尊嚴之義務相衝突，法官得參與職務外活動，如參與學術團體、宗教會員、或文化組織。

　　法官不得涉入他人之司法紛爭，不得爲影響法官同仁案件之行爲。

　　於程序會被影響或法官公正可能受質疑之情形，法官不得向司法相關人士，包括律師，提供法律意見或資訊。

第 6 條(財務活動之限制)

　　於法官公正可能受質疑、或司法職責會被擾亂之情形，法官不得參與財務交易，如金錢借貸；亦不得接受經濟利益，包括捐款在內。

第 7 條(政治中立)

　　法官執行職務時，應保持政治中立。

　　法官不得擔任政治活動組織之會員或委員。應避免損害法官政治中立的活動，包括政治選舉活動。

[附件 2]

檢察官倫理規範

第 1 條(期望)

檢察官應確立法治、保障人權，並爲實現正義之公共利益代表人。

第 2 條(服務人民)

檢察官應忠誠並謙遜服務人民，謹記檢察職權來自人民授權。

第 3 條(政治中立與公正)

檢察官執行職務應保持政治中立，遠離政治選舉活動。

檢察官不得歧視犯罪嫌疑人、被害人、或其他案件關係人。並不得因任何壓力、誘惑和利益受影響；檢察官應依據法律，本於良心正直，公正地執行職務。

第 4 條(尊嚴與名譽)

檢察官應保有高尚尊嚴與道德，並重視公共生活和私人生活之名譽。

第 5 條(自我充實)

檢察官應隨時充實能力,以通達社會現象和培養社會要求之洞察力與智。

第 6 條(重視人權和正當法律程序)

檢察官應重視犯罪嫌疑人、被告和其他案件關係人之人權,並注意憲法和法律之程序。

第 7 條(適當執行檢察事務)

檢察官應依法律程序蒐集證據,適當適用法律,不得濫用檢察職權。

第 8 條(妥速執行檢察事務)

檢察官應忠誠謹勉執行職務,妥速實現國家刑罰權。

第 9 條(自行迴避)

檢察官爲犯罪嫌疑人、被害人或其他案件關係人(若涉及案件之人爲法人的情形,指總裁,或控制股東)、民法第777條之親屬或律師、或就訴訟結果有個人利益,應自行迴避,不得參與程序。

檢察官有前項規定以外之特殊關係,可能影響公正性之情形,得自行迴避。

第10條(對案件關係人之態度)

檢察官調查時應遵守人權保障規則,仔細聆聽案件關係人,包括犯罪嫌疑人和被害人,並應盡力中立公正地對待關係人。

第11條(對律師之態度)

檢察官，於肯認並保障訴訟代理人的防禦權，不得無正當理由而私自與案件相關者之訴訟代理人或其員工溝通。

第12條(對前輩之態度)

檢察官應尊重前輩、恪守禮節、態度有禮，並遵守前輩於職行職務有關之命令與監督：對於前輩命令與監督的合法性有異議之情形，檢察官得循適當程序提起異議。

第13條(管理司法警察之態度)

檢察官，身爲指揮調查程序之領導者，應掌控並監督司法警察。

第14條(檢察職務外之人際關係)

檢察官不得接觸可能對檢察官執行職務之公正有影響之人，檢察官應對自己行爲謹慎爲之。

第15條(與當事人聯繫之限制)

檢察官無正當理由不得與處理中案件之關係人，如犯罪嫌疑人、被害人，或其他關係人(下稱「關係人等」)私下聯繫。

第16條(禁止濫用職權)

檢察官應嚴分公務與私人事務，並不得濫用公務或職權圖利自己或他人。

檢察官不得利用於職務上所知之事實和資訊。

第17條(禁止參與財務活動)

檢察官不得參與商業活動謀取金錢利益；未得法務部長同意，不得從事其他有薪之職務。除非法律允許，檢察官亦不得兼任其他職務。

第18條(禁止關說與行賄)

檢察官不得對其他檢察官或機關所主管之案件為關說或行賄。

檢察官不得參與他人的法律紛爭謀取不正利益。

第19條(禁止收受金錢)

檢察官不得無理由接受第14條規定會擾亂職務之人，或第15條規定之關係人所給予之金錢、金錢利益、招待、或經濟利益。

第20條(禁止介紹或推薦律師)

檢察官不得對自己主管案件，或其他同區辦公室之檢察官同仁主管案件之犯罪嫌疑人、被訴人、或其他關係人介紹或推薦律師。

第21條(公開發表言論或投稿之規範)

檢察官欲以職稱投稿或公開發表關於其職務或調查之意見或內容，應取得所屬檢察署首長之許可。

第22條(保守公務秘密)

檢察官就調查事項、相關人士個人資料、職務上得知之事實，應保守秘密。此外，檢察官使用電話、傳真、電子郵件或其他通訊裝置，應注意不使秘密外洩。

第23條(指導與監督公務人員)

檢察官應尊重公務人員、學習司法官、其他與檢察官職務相關之公務員。檢察官應指導與監督公務人員不得從事不法或不正行為，並不得揭露或濫用公務秘密。

한국의 판사, 검사 임용 및 징계 제도에 관하여

이　동　흡*

---

* 대한민국 헌법재판소 재판관.

1. 서　론

한국은 오랜 기간 '사법시험'이라는 자격시험을 통하여 일정한 인원을 선발하고, '사법연수원'이라는 대법원에 속한 조직에서 사법시험 합격자들을 2년 동안 교육하는 과정을 거쳐 법조인력을 양성하여 왔고, 법관의 임용, 보직, 근무평정, 연임 등에 있어 대법원장이 실질적으로 강한 영향력을 끼칠 수밖에 없는 인사제도가 실시되어 왔으며, 검찰 역시 인사에 있어 법무부장관과 검찰총장의 영향력이 크게 미치도록 제도가 설계되어 있었다.

그러나 국민의 다양한 기대와 요청에 부응하는 양질의 법률서비스를 제공하기 위하여 풍부한 교양, 인간 및 사회에 대한 깊은 이해와 자유·평등·정의를 지향하는 가치관을 바탕으로 한 건전한 직업윤리관과 복잡다기한 법적 분쟁을 전문적·효율적으로 해결할 수 있는 지식 및 능력을 갖춘 법조인을 양성하기 위하여는 사법시험 제도로는 한계가 있다는 견해가 대두되었고, 재판의 독립과 수사의 공정을 위하여 법관·검찰 인사의 공정성을 제고하기 위한 제도적 장치가 요청된다는 등의 사법 개혁 요구에 따른 논의가 수년간 계속되었다.

이러한 논의의 결과 입법자는 2008년 '법학전문대학원 설치·운영에 관한 법률'을 제정하여, 소위 '로스쿨'제도를 도입하였고, 2011년 '법원조직법'상 과반수 이상이 법관이 아닌 자로 구성되는 인사관련 심의기관인 인사위원회 제도를 도입하였으며, 같은 해 '검찰청법'상 검찰총장후보추천위원회 제도와 검찰인사위원회 제도를 도입하였다.

법학전문대학원의 첫 졸업생이 배출되고, 법관과 검찰의 인사위원회 제도가 처음 시행되는 2012년은 한국의 법조인력 양성시스템과 법관·검찰 인사제도의 중대한 전환점으로 평가될 수 있을 것이다.

한편 현행 '각급 법원 판사 정원법'상 각급 법원 판사의 수는 2,844명이고, 현행 '검사정원법'상 검사의 정원은 2,044명인데, 이는 1963년 '각급 법원 판사 정원법' 제정 당시의 판사 정원 376인, 1956년 검사정원법 제정 당시 검사 정원 190명과 비교하여서는 물론이고, 1990년 당시 정원인 판사 1,374인, 검사 987인과 비교하여도 2배로 늘어난 상태이다. 이와 같은 법관과 검사의 수의 증가와 함께 종래 드물었던 법관·검사의 부적절한 처신이 사회적으로 문제되는 경우가 발생하였고, 이에 법원은 1995년, 검찰은 1999년 각각 윤리강령을 제정하여 행위지침을 마련하였으나, 법관징계법과 검사징계법의 적용이 문제되는 사례가 증가하고 있는 추세이다. 이에 징계제도에 대한 관심이 높아지고 있고, 나아가 법관의 징계제도와 관련하여 징계사유 및 불복절차를 규정한 법률의 위헌 여부를 다투는 헌법소원심판이 2009년 청구됨에 따라 논의가 계속되고 있는 상황이다.

이렇듯 법조인력 양성시스템 및 법관·검찰 인사제도의 여러 변화와 논란의 가운데, 위와 같은 제도의 구성을 전체적으로 살펴보는 것은 매우 의미있는 작업이 되리라 생각하며, 본고에서는 헌법상 신분이 보장되는 법관과 준사법기관으로서 공익의 대표자인 검사의 임용, 인사, 징계제도를 전체적으로 비교하고, 징계제도의 경우 실제 사례를 고찰함으로써 법관과 검사의 인사제도의 특수성과 보편성을 살펴보기로 한다.

2. 판사의 임용제도

가. 판사의 임명

대법원장은 국회의 동의를 얻어 대통령이 임명하고, 대관관은 대법원장의 제청으로 국회의 동의를 얻어 대통령이 임명하며, 판사는 대법관회의의 동의를 얻어 대법원장이 임명한다(법원조직법 제41조). 헌법재판관은 법관의 자격을 가진 자 중에서 대통령이 임명하는데, 9명의 재판관 중 3인은 국회에서 선출하는 자를, 3인은 대법원장이 지명하는 자를 임명하고, 헌법재판소의 장은 국회의 동의를 얻어 재판관 중에서 대통령이 임명한다(헌법 제111조 제2항, 제3항, 제4항, 헌법재판소법 제6조).

다만, 법원이 국민으로부터 신뢰와 존경을 받을 수 있도록 사법제도의 개혁이 필요하다는 사회적 요청에 부응하여 사법부의 인사제도를 개선할 필요가 있다는 지적에 따라 2011. 7. 18. 법이 개정되었고, 2012. 1. 1. 시행예정이다. 법관의 임용자격을 강화하고자 법관의 임명 부분에 관하여 개정된 내용은 다음과 같다. 대법관의 경우, 대법원장이 제청할 대법관 후보자의 추천을 위하여 대법관후보추천위원회를 두고, 그 위원은 선임대법관, 법원행정처장, 법무부장관, 대한변호사협회장, 한국법학교수회 회장, 법학전문대학원협의회 이사장, 대법관이 아닌 법관 1명, 변호사의 자격을 가지지 아니한 사람 3명(1명 이상은 여성이어야 함)에 해당하는 사람을 대법원장이 임명하거나 위촉하도록 하였고(법원조직법 제41조의2), 판사의 경우, 현행법과 같은 위 절차 이전에 인사위원회의 심의를 거치는 것을 추가하도록 하였다(법원조직법 제41조 제3항, 제25조의2).

법관의 인사에 관한 중요 사항을 심의하기 위한 법관인사위원회
는 그 위원으로 법관 3명, 검사 2명, 변호사 2명, 법학교수 2명, 변
호사의 자격이 없는 사람 2명(이 경우 1명 이상은 여성이어야 함)에 해
당하는 사람을 대법원장이 임명하거나 위촉하여야 하는 것으로 개정
되었다(법원조직법 제25조의2).

대법원장과 대법관은 15년 이상 ⅰ) 판사·검사·변호사, ⅱ) 변
호사의 자격이 있는 자로서 국가기관, 지방자치단체, 국·공영기업
체, 정부투자기관 기타 법인에서 법률에 관한 사무에 종사한 자, ⅲ)
변호사의 자격이 있는 자로서 공인된 대학의 법률학 조교수 이상의
직에 있던 40세 이상의 자 중에서 임용하고(법원조직법 제42조 제 1
항), 판사는 ⅰ) 사법시험에 합격하여 사법연수원의 소정 과정을 마
친 자, ⅱ) 변호사의 자격이 있는 자 중에서 임용한다(법원조직법 제
42조 제 2 항). 다만, 개정법은 그 임용자격을 강화하였는바, 대법원장
과 대법관은 45세 이상의 사람 중에서, 판사는 10년 이상 법원조직
법 제42조 제 1 항 각 호의 직에 있던 사람[1] 중에서 임용하는 것으로
2011. 7. 18. 개정되었고, 이는 2013. 1. 1. 시행예정이다.

한편, 사법시험을 대체하는 로스쿨제도가 도입되면서 '재판연구
원' 제도를 도입하였는바, 각급 법원은 재판연구원을 두어 사건의 심
리 및 재판의 조사·연구, 그 밖에 필요한 업무를 수행하게 하고, 총
3년의 범위에서 기간을 정하여 채용하도록 하고 있으며, 이는 2012.
1. 1. 시행예정이다(법원조직법 제53조의2).

---

1) 법원조직법은 경과규정을 마련하여 2013. 1. 1.부터 임용하는 사람은 3년 이상,
   2018. 1. 1.부터 임용하는 사람은 5년 이상, 2020. 1. 1.부터 임용하는 사람은
   7년 이상, 2022. 1. 1.부터 임용하는 사람은 10년 이상의 경력을 요구하도록 하
   였다(부칙 제 2 조).

또한, 종래 '경력법관제[2]'로 구성[3]되던 사법부의 인사제도가 법관의 일천한 사회경험(신규법관 임용 평균 연령 28.5세), 조기·중도 퇴직현상,[4] 전관예우 시비, 사법관료화 현상 등의 문제점을 지적받고, 1998년부터 일정 경력 이상의 법조 경력자 중에서 법관을 선발하여 '법조일원화[5]'의 움직임을 보이기 시작하였다. 앞으로도 점차 그 비중을 늘려 2013. 1. 1.부터는 경력 3년 내지 10년 이상의 법조 경력자 중에 한하여 법관을 선발하는 것으로 2011. 7. 18. 법원조직법이 개정되었다.

나. 판사의 임기

대법원장의 임기는 6년으로 하며, 중임할 수 없고, 대법관의 임기는 6년으로 하며, 연임할 수 있으며, 판사의 임기는 10년으로 하며, 연임할 수 있다. 대법원장의 정년은 70세, 대법관의 정년은 65세, 판사의 정년은 63세이다(법원조직법 제45조). 그러나 이 또한 대법원장과 대법관의 정년은 각각 70세, 판사의 정년은 65세로 하는

2) 자격시험을 통과한 젊은 법조인을 법관으로 임명하여 법원 내에서 경력을 쌓아가게 하는 제도를 말하는데, '관료형 법관제'라고 하기도 한다.

3) 신규법관 분포

	2009	2010	2011
사법연수생	92	89	81
군법무관	46	52	62
재야임용	28	18	-
합 계	166	159	143

4) 퇴직자 수, 퇴직자 평균 근무기간

구 분	퇴직자수	평균 근무기간
2009	76	16.3
2010	77	16.8
2011	76	17.2

5) 통상적으로 일정 경력 이상의 법조 경력자 중에서 법관을 선발한다는 의미로 사용되고 있다.

것으로 2011. 7. 18. 개정되어, 2013. 1. 1. 시행예정이다.

헌법재판관의 임기는 6년이며, 연임할 수 있다. 헌법재판관의 정년은 65세이며 헌법재판소장인 재판관의 정년은 70세이다. 그러나 대법원장과 대법관의 정년을 규정한 법원조직법이 개정되어 시행예정인 것과는 달리, 헌법재판소장과 헌법재판관의 정년을 규정한 헌법재판소법은 아직 개정 전이다.

다. 판사의 신분보장

법관의 신분은 헌법에 의하여 보장되고 있는바, 법관은 탄핵 또는 금고 이상의 형의 선고에 의하지 아니하고는 파면되지 아니하며, 징계처분에 의하지 아니하고는 정직·감봉 기타 불리한 처분을 받지 아니한다(헌법 제106조 제1항). 이러한 내용은 법원조직법에서도 동일하게 규정되어 법관의 신분을 보장하고 있다(법원조직법 제46조 제1항).

3. 검사의 임용제도

가. 검사의 임명

검찰총장은 15년 이상 ⅰ) 판사, 검사 또는 변호사, ⅱ) 변호사 자격이 있는 사람으로 국가기관 등에 종사한 사람, ⅲ) 변호사의 자격이 있는 사람으로 대학의 법률학 조교수 이상으로 재직하였던 사람 중에서 임명하고(검찰청법 제27조), 검사는 ⅰ) 사법시험에 합격하여 사법연수원 과정을 마친 사람, ⅱ) 변호사 자격이 있는 사람 중에서 임명한다(검찰청법 제29조). 검찰총장을 임명할 때에는 대통령이 법무부장관의 제청으로 하되, 국회의 인사청문을 거쳐야 한다. 검사의 임명과 보직은 법무부장관의 제청으로 대통령이 하며, 이 경우 법무부장관은 검찰총장의 의견을 들어 검사의 보직을 제청한다(검찰청법 제34조). 또한, 검사의 임용, 전보, 그 밖의 인사에 관한 중요 사항을 심의하기 위하여 법무부에 검찰인사위원회를 두는데, 검찰인사위원회의 구성·운영 및 심의사항은 대통령령으로 정하도록 하고 있다(검찰청법 제35조).

　다만, 검찰의 정치적 중립성과 독립성을 강화하고, 수사의 공정성을 확보하기 위한 필요성에 따라 2011. 7. 18. 법이 개정되었고, 2012. 1. 1. 시행예정이다. 검사의 임명에 관하여 개정된 내용은 다음과 같다. 검찰총장의 경우, 법무부장관이 검찰총장을 제청할 때에는 검찰총장후보추천위원회의 추천을 받도록 하는데, 그 위원은 검사로 재직하였던 사람, 법무부 검찰국장, 법원행정처 차장, 대한변호사협회장, 한국법학교수회 회장, 법학전문대학원협의회 이사장, 변호사 자격을 가지지 아니한 사람 3명(1명 이상은 여성이어야 함)에 해당하는 사람을 법무부장관이 임명하거나 위촉하도록 하였고(검찰청법 제34조의2), 검사의 경우, 그 임용, 전보, 그 밖의 인사에 관한 중요사항을 심의하는 검찰인사위원회는 현재 대통령령으로 규정되어 있는 구성과 운영 및 심의사항에 관한 내용을 법률에 구체적으로 정하였고, 그 위원은 검사 3명, 판사 2명, 변호사 2명, 법학교수 2명, 변호사 자격을 가지지 아니한 사람 2명에 해당하는 사람을 법무부장관이 임명하거나 위촉하도록 하는 것으로 개정되었다(검찰청법 제35조).

　2011. 2. 기준으로 검사 정원은 2,044명, 현원은 1,846명이다. 2011년에 120명이 검사로 신규 임용되었으며, 그 중 군법무관 전역자 30명을 제외한 사법연수원 출신 90명 중 65.6%가 여성으로 구성

되어 있다.

나. 향후 로스쿨 졸업자의 검사 임용

로스쿨제도 시행 이후 로스쿨 졸업자가 처음 배출되는 2012년부터 사법시험이 유지되는 2017년 사이에는 사법시험 합격자와 로스쿨을 졸업하고 변호사시험에 합격한 자 중에서 검사를 임용하게 된다.[6]

현재까지 로스쿨 졸업자에 대한 구체적인 검사 임용방안, 검사 임용비율, 검사 임용기준이 확정되지 않은 상태이다. 다만, 언론보도 내용에 의하면, 법무부에서는 로스쿨을 졸업하고 변호사시험에 합격한 자 중에서 로스쿨의 추천, 면접, 실무 수습을 거쳐 검사로 임용하는 방안을 검토하고 있다고 한다.

다. 검사의 신분보장

검사 역시 법관과 동일한 신분상의 보장을 받으나, 법관과 달리 헌법이 아닌 법률에 의한 신분보장을 받음에 그친다. 이에 따라 검사는 탄핵이나 금고 이상의 형을 선고받은 경우를 제외하고는 파면되지 아니하며, 징계처분이나 적격심사에 의하지 아니하고는 해임·면직·정직·감봉·견책 또는 퇴직의 처분을 받지 아니한다(검찰청법 제37조).

그리고 검사(검찰총장은 제외한다)에 대하여는 임명 후 7년마다 적격심사를 하고, 위 심사를 위하여 법무부에 9명의 위원으로 구성하는 검사적격심사위원회를 두어 검사가 직무수행 능력이 현저히 떨어지는 등 검사로서 정상적인 직무수행이 어렵다고 인정하는 경우에

---

6) 참고로 2012년 로스쿨 졸업생에 대한 변호사시험 합격률을 입학정원(2,000명)의 75%로 결정하였다.

는 재적위원 3분의 2 이상의 의결을 거쳐 법무부장관에게 그 검사의
퇴직을 건의하고, 위 퇴직 건의가 타당하다고 인정되면 대통령에게
그 검사에 대한 퇴직명령을 제청한다(검찰청법 제39조).

4. 판사의 징계제도

가. 법관징계법

법관에 대한 징계 사유는 ⅰ) 법관이 직무상 의무를 위반하거나
직무를 게을리한 경우, ⅱ) 법관이 그 품위를 손상하거나 법원의 위
신을 떨어뜨린 경우이다(법관징계법 제2조).[7] 이러한 징계사유가 인정
될 경우 법관에 대한 징계처분은 정직·감봉·견책의 세 종류로 하는
데, 정직은 1개월 이상 1년 이하의 기간 동안 직무집행을 정지하고,
그 기간 동안 보수를 지급하지 아니하고, 감봉은 1개월 이상 1년 이하
의 기간 동안 보수의 3분의 1 이하를 줄이며, 견책은 징계 사유에 관
하여 서면으로 훈계한다(법관징계법 제3조). 그리고 법관에 대한 징계
사건을 심의·결정하기 위하여 대법원에 법관징계위원회[8]를 두며, 위

---

7) 참고로 법원조직법에서는 법관의 직무상 금지사항을 다음과 같이 규정하고 있다.
　　법원조직법 제49조(금지사항) 법관은 재직 중 다음의 행위를 할 수 없다.
　　　1. 국회 또는 지방의회의 의원이 되는 일
　　　2. 행정부서의 공무원이 되는 일
　　　3. 정치운동에 관여하는 일
　　　4. 대법원장의 허가 없이 보수 있는 직무에 종사하는 일
　　　5. 금전상의 이익을 목적으로 하는 업무에 종사하는 일
　　　6. 대법원장의 허가 없이 보수의 유무를 불문하고 국가기관 외의 법인·단체
　　　　　등의 고문·임원·직원 등의 직위에 취임하는 일
　　　7. 기타 대법원규칙으로 정하는 일
8) 법관징계위원회의 위원장은 대법관 중에서 대법원장이 임명하고, 위원은 법관

원회는 위원장 1인과 위원 6명으로 구성하고, 예비위원 3명을 둔다
(법관징계법 제 4 조). 대법원장이 법관징계위원회의 결정에 따라 징계
처분을 하고, 이를 집행하게 되며, 이 때 이를 관보에 게재한다(법관
징계법 제26조). 피청구인이 징계처분에 대하여 불복하려는 경우에는
징계처분이 있음을 안 날부터 14일 이내에 전심(前審) 절차를 거치지
아니하고 대법원이 징계처분의 취소를 청구하여야 하며, 대법원은 위
취소청구사건을 단심(單審)으로 재판한다(법관징계법 제27조).

나. 법관윤리강령

법관은 국민의 기본적 인권과 정당한 권리행사를 보장함으로써,
국민으로부터 부여받은 사법권을 법과 양심에 따라 엄정하게 행사하
여 민주적 기본질서와 법치주의를 확립하여야 하는바, 이 같은 사명
을 다하기 위하여 사법관의 독립과 법관의 명예를 굳게 지켜야 하고,
국민으로부터 신뢰와 존경을 받아야 한다. 그러므로 법관은 공정하
고 청렴하게 직무를 수행하며, 법관에게 요구되는 높은 수준의 직업
윤리를 갖추어야 하는데, 이를 위하여 법관이 지녀야 할 윤리기준과
행위전범을 마련하여 법관으로서의 자세와 마음가짐을 바로 하고,
법관의 사명과 책무를 다하기 위하여 「법관윤리강령」을 마련하여 이
를 스스로의 책임과 규율 아래 지키도록 하고 있다(자세한 내용은 [부
록 1] 참조).

3명과 변호사, 법학교수, 그 밖에 학식과 경험이 풍부한 사람에 해당하는 사람
중 각 1명을 대법원장이 각각 임명하도록 규정되어 있으며(법관징계법 제 5 조
제 1 항), 예비위원은 법관 중에서 대법원장이 임명하도록 규정되어 있다(법관
징계법 제 5 조 제 2 항).

다. 구체적 사례

판사의 비위 사실로 인하여 징계처분이 내려진 구체적 사례는 다음과 같다.

① 남편을 위한 선거운동을 함으로써 법관으로서의 품위를 손상하고 법원의 위신을 실추시켰다는 이유로 감봉 6월

② 공무집행방해죄로 약식명령을 받음으로써 법관으로서의 품위를 손상하고 법원의 위신을 실추시켰다는 이유로 견책

③ 음주운전을 함으로써 법관으로서의 품위를 손상하고 법원의 위신을 실추시켰다는 이유로 견책

④ 무단결근을 함으로써 법관으로서의 품위를 손상하고 법원위 위신을 실추시켰다는 이유로 견책

⑤ 사건당사자로부터 부탁을 전달하였다는 등 법관으로서의 품위를 손상하고 법원의 위신을 실추시켰다는 이유로 정직 10월

⑥ 소속 법원장의 거듭된 자제 지시에도 불구하고, 사법부 내부 통신망에 게시하거나 집단 전자우편으로 보낸 글 및 외부 언론기관에 기고한 글과 인터뷰를 통하여, 근거 없이 고등법원 부장판사 보임 인사가 위법하다 등의 주장을 반복함으로써 법관으로서의 품위를 손상하고 법원의 위신을 실추시켰다는 이유로 정직 2월

⑦ 서울 근교의 지방법원 소속 법관이 변호사로부터 수백만 원의 금품을 수수함으로써 법관으로서의 품위를 손상하고 법원의 위신을 실추시켰다는 이유로 정직 10월 내지 6월 및 견책

⑧ 모 회사의 주요 주주로부터 분쟁에 관한 설명을 듣고, 관련 서류를 검토한 사실이 있음에도 불구하고, 그 후 위 주주의 재판을 회피하지 아니한 채 진행하고, 각 재판을 전후하여 재판 당사자인 위

주주와 수 회 접촉하고, 다른 재판부에서 진행 중이던 사건에 관하여 담당 재판관에게 위 주주의 의견을 전달함으로써 법관으로서의 품위를 손상하고 법원의 위신을 실추시켰다는 이유로 정직 10월

⑨ 자신이 법정관리하는 기업의 감사에 친형과 친구를 자신이 임명하는 등 공정성과 청렴성을 의심받을 행동을 함으로써 법관으로서의 품위를 손상하고 법원의 위신을 실추시켰다는 이유로 정직 5월

라. 법관징계법에 대한 헌법소원 사건

(1) 사건의 개요

청구인은 현직 판사로서, 소속 법원장의 거듭된 자제 지시에도 불구하고, 2007. 2. 20.부터 6개월간 20여 차례에 걸쳐, 사법부 내부통신망에 게시하거나 집단 전자우편으로 보낸 글 및 외부 언론기관에 기고한 글과 인터뷰를 통해, 근거 없이 고등법원 부장판사 보임 인사가 위법하다고 주장하면서 이를 이유로 대법원장에 대한 징계 또는 탄핵 소추를 반복적으로 요구하거나, 동료 법관들이 구체적 사건의 처리 결과에 따라 인사상 이익 또는 불이익을 받았다고 오인토록 하여 재판의 독립 및 공정성에 대한 국민의 신뢰를 심각하게 손상함과 동시에 동료 법관들의 명예를 훼손하는 등 법관으로서의 정당한 의견표명의 한계를 벗어난 주장을 반복함으로써, 법관으로서의 품위를 손상하고 법원의 위신을 실추시켰다는 이유로 정직 2개월의 징계처분을 받았다.

청구인은 위와 같은 징계처분에 불복하여 대법원에 징계처분 무효확인 및 취소소송을 제기하고, 청구인에게 적용된 징계사유를 정한 법관징계법 제2조 제2호 및 대법원의 전속관할을 정한 법관징

계법 제27조에 대한 위헌법률심판 제청신청을 하였다. 그러나 법원
이 위 징계처분 무효확인 및 취소청구 및 위헌법률심판 제청신청을
모두 기각하자, 위 각 법률조항의 위헌확인을 구하는 헌법소원심판
을 청구(2009헌바34)하였다.

(2) 위 헌법소원 사건의 쟁점

① 법관징계법 제2조 제2호가 징계사유로 규정한 "법관이 그
품위를 손상하거나 법원의 위신을 실추시킨 경우"가 법치국가원리의
한 표현으로서 모든 기본권 제한 입법에 대하여 요구되는 명확성 원
칙에 위반되는지 여부

② 법관징계법 제2조 제2호에 의하여 제한되는 기본권은, 구
체적인 사정에 따라 표현의 자유, 일반적 행동의 자유, 직업의 자유
등 매우 다양한데, 이 사건에서 법관의 표현의 자유의 침해 여부의
문제로서 접근하는 것이 상당한지 여부 및 과잉금지원칙에 위반되는
지 여부

③ 법관에 대한 징계처분에 관한 불복소송을 대법원 단심제로
규정한 법관징계법 제27조가 법관에 의한 재판을 받을 권리를 침해
하는지 여부

④ 법관징계법 제27조가 검사나 다른 공무원 등 공익적 업무에
종사하는 자에 대한 징계처분 불복소송과 달리 단심제를 규정한 것
이 합리적 이유 없는 차별취급으로서 평등권을 침해하는지 여부

5. 검사의 징계제도

가. 검사징계법

검사가 ⅰ)「검찰청법」제43조[9]를 위반하였을 때, ⅱ) 직무상의 의무를 위반하거나 직무를 게을리하였을 때, ⅲ) 직무 관련 여부에 상관없이 검사로서의 체면이나 위신을 손상하는 행위를 하였을 때의 어느 하나에 해당하면 그 검사를 징계한다(검사징계법 제 2 조). 이때 징계는 해임, 면직, 정직, 감봉 및 견책으로 구분되는데, 정직은 1개월 이상 6개월 이하의 기간 동안 검사의 직무 집행을 정지시키고 보수를 지급하지 아니하는 것을 말하고, 감봉은 1개월 이상 1년 이하의 기간 동안 보수의 3분의 1 이하를 감액하는 것을 말하며, 견책은 검사로 하여금 직무에 종사하면서 그가 저지른 잘못을 반성하게 하는 것을 말한다(검사징계법 제 3 조). 위와 같은 징계 사건을 심의하기 위하여 법무부에 검사 징계위원회를 두는데, 위원회는 위원장 1명을 포함한 7명의 위원으로 구성하고, 예비위원 3명을 둔다(검사징계법 제 4 조). 검사에 대한 징계처분을 한 때에는 그 사실을 관보에 게재하여야 한다(검사징계법 제23조 제 2 항). 검사의 징계처분에 불복하고자 하는 경우, 판사에 대한 징계처분에 불복하는 경우와 같이 대법원의 단심으로 한다는 특별 규정이 없으므로 행정소송으로 다툴 수 있다.

---

9) 검찰청법 제43조(정치운동 등의 금지) 검사는 재직 중 다음 각 호의 행위를 할 수 없다.
　1. 국회 또는 지방의회의 의원이 되는 일
　2. 정치운동에 관여하는 일
　3. 금전상의 이익을 목적으로 하는 업무에 종사하는 일
　4. 법무부장관의 허가 없이 보수를 받는 직무에 종사하는 일

나. 검사윤리강령

검사는 범죄로부터 국민을 보호하고, '법의 지배'를 통하여 인간의 존엄과 권리를 보장함으로써 자유롭고 안정된 민주사회를 구현하여야 할 책임이 있는바, 검사는 이 책임을 완수하기 위하여 스스로 높은 도덕성과 윤리 의식을 갖추고 투철한 사명감과 책임감을 바탕으로 이 직무를 수행하여야 한다. 검사는 주어진 사명의 숭고함을 깊이 인식하고 국민으로부터 진정으로 신뢰받을 수 있도록 일정한 윤리기준과 행동 준칙을 마련하고, 이에 따라 실천하고 스스로 그 결과에 대하여 책임을 지도록 하고 있다(자세한 내용은 [부록 2] 참조).

다. 구체적 사례

① 모 그룹 회장의 지시에 의하여 교부된 5,000불을 해외 공항에서 수수하여 검사로서의 위신을 손상하였다는 이유로 감봉 3월

② 동향출신 모임에서 모 그룹 회장을 만나 알게 된 후, 위 회장이 운영하는 골프장에서 위 회장과 함께 골프를 치고, 위 회장으로부터 5,000불을 교부받았으며, 위 회장으로부터 수사중인 사건과 관련하여 선처 받을 수 있게 해달라는 취지의 청탁전화를 받은 후, 5,000불을 수수하여 검사로서의 위신을 손상하였다는 이유로 정직 6월

③ 같은 부 소속 검사가 수사중인 사건의 고소인측 지인과 골프 회동을 한 후, 그 비용을 위 지인으로 하여금 대납토록 하였고, 자신의 지도를 받고 있던 초임검사로부터 주식투자금 등 명목으로 합계 2억 3,000만원을 빌렸다가 주가의 하락으로 일부 금원을 변제하지 아니하는 등 검사로서의 위신을 손상하였다는 이유로 정직 3월

④ 사기죄 등 처벌받은 전력이 있고, 계속 사기범행을 저지르고

있는 사람과 5회에 걸쳐 215만원 상당의 향응을 수수하여 검사로서
의 위신을 손상하고, 만연히 집행유예 실효지휘를 하여 13일간 불법
구금되게 하여 검사로서의 직무를 태만히 하였다는 이유로 감봉 3월

⑤ 범죄의 기수시기를 잘못 인식한 나머지 집행유예 실효지휘를
하여 48일간 불법 구금되게 하여 검사로서의 직무를 태만히 하였다
는 이유로 견책

⑥ 모 건설 대표를 만나 교류하면서 위 대표로부터 법인카드를
교부받아 38개월간 총 9,766만원 상당을 사용하여 검사로서의 위신
을 손상하였다는 이유로 해임

⑦ 모 씨가 고리사채업을 하는 것으로 추측하면서도 1억원의 투
자금을 맡기고, 매월 금 250만원씩 합계 8,000만원을 이익배당금으
로 교부받아 검사로서의 품위를 손상하였다는 이유로 감봉 2월

⑧ 두 차례에 걸쳐 처를 폭행하여 약 3주간의 치료를 요하는 턱
관절염좌상을 가하는 등 검사로서의 품위를 손상하였다는 이유로 감
봉 1월

⑨ 피의사건 수사중 부적절한 언행을 하여 검사로서의 품위를
손상하고, 인권보호수사원칙에 위배되는 행위를 하여 직무상 의무를
위반하였다는 이유로 정직 2월

⑩ 변호사로부터 금품과 향응을 수수한 혐의로 감찰조사를 받던
중 위 변호사와의 대질신문을 위하여 대검찰청에 출석하라는 검찰총
장의 명령을 전달받고도 정당한 이유 없이 출석을 거부하고, 위와 같
은 비리혐의로 인하여 사표제출을 권유받자 서울에서 검찰총장 등을
비난하는 성명을 발표할 목적으로 검찰총장의 승인을 받지 않은 채
근무지를 무단으로 이탈하는 등 직무상 의무를 위반하였으며, 대검
찰청 기자실에서 기자회견을 하면서 사회적 물의를 야기하고, 검찰

의 지휘체계를 훼손하는 등 검사로서의 체면과 위신을 손상케 하였다는 사유로 면직[10]

⑪ 관할지역 건설업자로부터 식사대접을 받고, 룸살롱에서 향응과 현금을 수수하였다는 등의 사유로 면직[11]

⑫ 검사로 임용된 뒤에도 민주노동당과 열린우리당 당원신분을 유지하고 있다가 기소되어 정치적 중립에 관한 직무상 의무를 위반하고 검사로서의 위신을 손상하였다는 이유로 면직

⑬ 검사 실습을 나온 여성 사법연수원생과 노래방에서 술을 마시다 강제로 입을 맞추어 검사로서의 위신을 손상하였다는 이유로 면직

⑭ 회식 자리에서 검사 직무대리 여성 사법연수원생에게 춤을 추자며 강제로 손을 잡아 끄는 등 부적절한 언동을 하여 검사로서의 위신을 손상하였다는 이유로 감봉 2월

6. 결 론

약간의 징계사례가 있긴 하지만, 대체적으로 한국 판·검사들의 윤리의식과 직무충실도는 높은 편에 속한다고 할 수 있다. 판·검사로 임용되기 위해 사법시험을 통과하는 과정에서 고도의 전문지식과 윤리의식을 검증받는데다가, 판·검사라는 직위가 사회적인 존경과

---

10) 그러나 이후 이어진 행정소송에서 위 면직처분은 비례원칙에 위반된 재량권 남용으로서 위법하다고 보아 취소되었다(대법원 2001. 8. 24. 선고 2000두 7704 판결).

11) 이에 대하여는 위 면직처분 취소청구 소송을 제기하여, 1심에서 승소판결을 선고받았고, 이에 피고가 항소하여 현재 재판 계속 중이다.

선망의 대상으로서 젊은 인재들로부터 선호되어 왔기 때문이다.

임용 및 징계관련 제도적인 면에서 보더라도, 세부적인 면에서 개선되어야 할 부분들도 있으나, 공정하고 독립된 재판을 보장하는 방향으로 관련 제도를 운영해 왔으며, 사법부 스스로 판사 임용절차나 징계제도의 운영 과정에서 국민으로부터 꾸준한 신뢰와 존경을 얻기 위해 공정성과 투명성을 강화하고 있다.

다만, 판·검사의 임용과 관련하여서는 향후 근본적인 변화가 있을 것으로 예상된다. 우리나라가 해방 이후부터 현재까지 기본적으로 취해 온 판사 임용제도는 대륙법계 국가들의 그것인 직업법관제였고, 검사 임용방식 역시 이에 준하여 운영되어 왔다. 즉, 사법시험에 합격하고 사법연수원을 졸업한 후 판·검사로 임용돼 선배 판·검사로부터 교육을 받으며 경력을 쌓아가는 방식의 인사시스템이었는데, 모든 제도가 그렇듯이, 나름의 장단점이 있고, 그 성공 여부는 얼마나 우리 현실에 맞게 제도를 잘 운영하느냐에 달려 있으며, 현재까지 나름대로 성공적으로 운영되어 온 것도 사실이다. 하지만, 최근 로스쿨제도가 도입되고 법조일원화를 목표로 한 법률이 개정되면서 한국의 판·검사 인사시스템은 다시 한 번 중요한 고비를 맞이하게 되었다. 다양한 분야의 전문지식을 갖춘 법률가들이 사회로 진출하고, 수년간의 법조경력과 인생경험을 갖춘 사람 중에서 판사가 배출될 수 있는 제도적 기반이 마련된 것이다. 보다 국민이 신뢰할 수 있는 재판을 해야 겠다는 각계의 의견이 모아져 이루어진 제도적 변화인데, 위 제도들이 도입취지대로 성공적으로 정착된다면 보다 훌륭한 사법부 인사시스템이 구축될 것으로 확신한다. 사법부를 비롯한 법조계의 제도적 노력뿐만 아니라 재판을 받는 국민들의 이해와 성원이 더욱 필요한 시점이다.

아울러, 언젠가는 다시 한 번 이 자리에 계신 여러분들에게, 위 변화된 제도들로 말미암아 더욱 향상된 한국 판·검사 인사시스템에 관해서 경험을 나눠 드릴 수 있는 기회가 오길 개인적으로 희망해 본다.

[부록 1]

법관윤리강령

제1조(사법권 독립의 수호) 법관은 모든 외부의 영향으로부터 사법권의 독립을 지켜 나간다.

제2조(품위 유지) 법관은 명예를 존중하고 품위를 유지한다.

제3조(공정성 및 청렴성) ① 법관은 공평무사하고 청렴하여야 하며, 공정성과 청렴성을 의심받을 행동을 하지 아니한다.

② 법관은 혈연·지연·학연·성별·종교·경제적 능력 또는 사회적 지위 등을 이유로 편견을 가지거나 차별을 하지 아니한다.

제4조(직무의 성실한 수행) ① 법관은 맡은 바 직무를 성실하게 수행하며, 직무수행 능력을 향상시키기 위하여 꾸준히 노력한다.

② 법관은 신속하고 능률적으로 재판을 진행하며, 신중하고 충실하게 심리하여 재판의 적정성이 보장되도록 한다.

③ 법관은 당사자와 대리인 등 소송 관계인을 친절하고 정중하게 대한다.

④ 법관은 재판업무상 필요한 경우를 제외하고는 당사자와 대리인 등 소송 관계인을 법정 이외의 장소에서 면담하거나 접촉하지 아니한다.

⑤ 법관은 교육이나 학술 또는 정확한 보도를 위한 경우를 제외하고는 구체적 사건에 관하여 공개적으로 논평하거나 의견을 표명하지 아니한다.

제 5 조(법관의 직무 외 활동) ① 법관은 품위 유지와 직무 수행에 지장이 없는 경우에 한하여, 학술 활동에 참여하거나 종교·문화 단체에 가입하는 등 직무 외 활동을 할 수 있다.

② 법관은 타인의 법적 분쟁에 관여하지 아니하며, 다른 법관의 재판에 영향을 미치는 행동을 하지 아니한다.

③ 법관은 재판에 영향을 미치거나 공정성을 의심받을 염려가 있는 경우에는 법률적 조언을 하거나 변호사 등 법조인에 대한 정보를 제공하지 아니한다.

제 6 조(경제적 행위의 제한) 법관은 재판의 공정성에 관한 의심을 초래하거나 직무수행에 지장을 줄 염려가 있는 경우에는, 금전대차 등 경제적 거래행위를 하지 아니하며 증여 기타 경제적 이익을 받지 아니한다.

제 7 조(정치적 중립) ① 법관은 직무를 수행함에 있어 정치적 중립을 지킨다.

② 법관은 정치활동을 목적으로 하는 단체의 임원이나 구성원이 되지 아니하며, 선거운동 등 정치적 중립성을 해치는 활동을 하지 아니한다.

[부록 2]

검사윤리강령

제 1 조(사명) 검사는 공익의 대표자로서 국법질서를 확립하고 국민의 인권을 보호하며 정의를 실현함을 그 사명으로 한다.

제 2 조(국민에 대한 봉사) 검사는 직무상의 권한이 국민으로부터 위임된 것임을 명심하여 성실하고 겸손한 자세로 국민에게 봉사한다.

제 3 조(정치적 중립과 공정) ① 검사는 정치운동에 관여하지 아니하며, 직무수행을 할 때 정치적 중립을 지킨다.

② 검사는 피의자나 피해자, 기타 사건 관계인에 대하여 정당한 이유 없이 차별 대우를 하지 아니하며 어떠한 압력이나 유혹, 정실에도 영향을 받지 아니하고 오로지 법과 양심에 따라 엄정하고 공평하게 직무를 수행한다.

제 4 조(청렴과 명예) 검사는 공·사생활에서 높은 도덕성과 청렴성을 유지하고, 명예롭고 품위 있게 행동한다.

제 5 조(자기계발) 검사는 변화하는 사회현상을 직시하고 높은 식견과 시대가 요구하는 새로운 지식을 쌓아 직무를 수행함에 부족함이 없도록 하기 위하여 끊임없이 자기계발에 노력한다.

제 6 조(인권보장과 적법절차의 준수) 검사는 피의자·피고인,

피해자 기타 사건 관계인의 인권을 보장하고, 헌법과 법령에 규정된 절차를 준수한다.

제 7 조(검찰권의 적정한 행사) 검사는 적법한 절차에 의하여 증거를 수집하고 법령의 정당한 적용을 통하여 공소권이 남용되지 않도록 한다.

제 8 조(검찰권의 신속한 행사) 검사는 직무를 성실하고 신속하게 수행함으로써 국가형벌권의 실현이 부당하게 지연되지 않도록 한다.

제 9 조(사건의 회피) ① 검사는 취급 중인 사건의 피의자, 피해자 기타 사건 관계인(당사자가 법인인 경우 대표이사 또는 지배주주)과 민법 제777조의 친족관계에 있거나 그들의 변호인으로 활동한 전력이 있을 때 또는 당해 사건과 자신의 이해가 관련되었을 때에는 그 사건을 회피한다.

② 검사는 취급 중인 사건의 사건 관계인과 제 1 항 이외의 친분관계 기타 특별한 관계가 있는 경우에도 수사의 공정성을 의심받을 우려가 있다고 판단했을 때에는 그 사건을 회피할 수 있다.

제10조(사건 관계인에 대한 자세) 검사는 인권보호수사준칙을 준수하고, 피의자, 피해자 등 사건 관계인의 주장을 진지하게 경청하며 객관적이고 중립적인 입장에서 사건 관계인을 친절하게 대하도록 노력한다.

제11조(변호인에 대한 자세) 검사는 변호인의 변호권행사를 보장하되 취급 중인 사건의 변호인 또는 그 직원과 정당한 이유 없이 사적으로 접촉하지 아니한다.

제12조(상급자에 대한 자세) 검사는 상급자에게 예의를 갖추어 정중하게 대하며, 직무에 관한 상급자의 지휘·감독에 따라야 한다.

다만, 구체적 사건과 관련된 상급자의 지휘·감독의 적법성이나 정당성에 이견이 있을 때에는 절차에 따라서 이의를 제기할 수 있다.

제13조(사법경찰관리에 대한 자세) 검사는 수사의 주재자로서 엄정하고 합리적으로 사법경찰관리를 지휘하고 감독한다.

제14조(외부 인사와의 교류) 검사는 직무 수행의 공정성을 의심받을 우려가 있는 자와 교류하지 아니하며 그 처신에 유의한다.

제15조(사건 관계인 등과의 사적 접촉 제한) 검사는 자신이 취급하는 사건의 피의자, 피해자 등 사건 관계인 기타 직무와 이해관계가 있는 자(이하 '사건 관계인 등'이라 한다)와 정당한 이유 없이 사적으로 접촉하지 아니한다.

제16조(직무 등의 부당 이용 금지) ① 검사는 항상 공·사를 분명히 하고 자기 또는 타인의 부당한 이익을 위하여 그 직무나 직위를 이용하지 아니한다.

② 검사는 직무와 관련하여 알게 된 사실이나 취득한 자료를 부당한 목적으로 이용하지 아니한다.

제17조(영리행위 등 금지) 검사는 금전상의 이익을 목적으로 하는 업무에 종사하거나 법무부장관의 허가 없이 보수 있는 직무에 종사하는 일을 하지 못하며, 법령에 의하여 허용된 경우를 제외하고는 다른 직무를 겸하지 아니한다.

제18조(알선·청탁 등 금지) ① 검사는 다른 검사나 다른 기관에서 취급하는 사건 또는 사무에 관하여 공정한 직무를 저해할 수 있는 알선·청탁이나 부당한 영향력을 미치는 행동을 하지 아니한다.

② 검사는 부당한 이익을 목적으로 타인의 법적 분쟁에 관여하지 아니한다.

제19조(금품수수금지) 검사는 제14조에서 규정한 직무 수행의

공정성을 의심받을 우려가 있는 자나 제15조에서 규정한 사건관계인 등으로부터 정당한 이유 없이 금품, 금전상 이익, 향응이나 기타 경제적 편의를 제공받지 아니한다.

제20조(특정 변호사 선임 알선 금지) 검사는 직무상 관련이 있는 사건이나 자신이 근무하는 기관에서 취급 중인 사건에 관하여, 피의자, 피고인 기타 사건 관계인에게 특정 변호사의 선임을 알선하거나 권유하지 아니한다.

제21조(외부 기고 및 발표에 관한 원칙) 검사는 수사 등 직무와 관련된 사항에 관하여 검사의 직함을 사용하여 대외적으로 그 내용이나 의견을 기고·발표하는 등 공표할 때에는 소속 기관장의 승인을 받는다.

제22조(직무상 비밀유지) 검사는 수사사항, 사건 관계인의 개인정보 기타 직무상 파악한 사실에 대하여 비밀을 유지하여야 하며, 전화, 팩스 또는 전자우편 그리고 기타 통신수단을 이용할 때에는 직무상 비밀이 누설되지 않도록 유의한다.

제23조(검사실 직원 등의 지도·감독) 검사는 그 사무실의 검찰공무원, 사법연수생, 기타 자신의 직무에 관여된 공무원을 인격적으로 존중하며, 그들이 직무에 관하여 위법 또는 부당한 행위를 하거나 업무상 지득한 비밀을 누설하거나 부당하게 이용하지 못하도록 지도·감독한다.

베트남 국제회의 참석기

― 헌법상 권력분립에 관하여 ―

제 1. 머 리 말

아데나워 재단 베트남 지부에서 국제회의 참석을 바라는 메일이 왔다. 회의 주제는 헌법상 권력분립과 권력분립에 있어서 헌법재판소의 역할이었다. 베트남 국회에서 앞으로 헌법 개정을 염두에 두고 아데나워 재단과 공동으로 헌법상 권력분립을 주제로 세계적인 전문가들을 초청하여 세미나를 개최하려는데 저자가 다른 국제회의에서 성공적으로 발표한 것을 알고 저자를 한국의 대표로 초청한다는 것이었다. 처음에는 바쁜 재판 일정 때문에 망설이기도 하였으나 국제적으로 한국의 헌법재판소를 알리는 데는 좋은 기회라고 생각되어 초청을 승낙하였다. 그 후 연구관들의 도움을 받아 바쁜 시간을 쪼개어 "한국 헌법상 권력분립원리의 실현" 및 "권력분립에 있어 한국 헌법재판소의 역할"이라는 제목의 두 가지 논문을 영문으로 작성하여 이메일로 미리 보냈다.

제 2. 회의에서의 발표

회의 참석자는 유럽 각국 및 미국 헌법상 권력분립에 관하여 발표하는 독일 본 대학 교수, 아시아 각국의 헌법상 권력분립에 관하여 비교하여 발표하는 싱가폴 대학 교수, 필리핀 헌법상 권력분립에 대하여 발표하는 전 필리핀 대법원장, 공산주의 체제 하의 권력분립에 관하여 발표하는 헌법위원회 위원 그리고 한국을 대표한 저자였다. 회의는 2012년 2월 28일부터 29일에 걸쳐 하노이 하이야트 호텔에서 열렸는데 참석자들이 200명 가까이 되었으며 특히 베트남 학자들이 많이 참석하여 발표자들의 발표 후에 활발히 질문을 하였다. 특히 저자에 대한 질문이 다른 발표자에 비해 많았는데 참석자들이 다른 어느 나라보다도 한국의 권력분립제도 및 헌법재판제도에 대하여 관심이 많은 것을 알 수 있었다. 발표원고인 "한국 헌법상 권력분립원리의 실현"의 한글판은 [별지 1]로, 영문판은 [별지 2]로 첨부하였고, "권력분립에 있어 한국 헌법재판소의 역할"의 영문판은 [별지 3]으로 말미에 첨부하였다.

〈하노이 하이야트 호텔에서 주제발표를 하고 있는 저자〉

　　하루 종일 회의에 참석했던 한국 대사관의 서기관 등도 저자가 성공적으로 발표한 것 같다면서 한국에서 고위관리가 베트남에 와서 이렇게 성공적으로 발표하는 것을 본 것이 처음이라고 하였다. 발표와 질의 응답을 마치고 내려오니 아데나워 재단 베트남 지부 대표의 첫 마디가 "다음에 초청해도 오시겠습니까?"였다.

　　베트남은 근래에 경제적으로 발전하고 있으며 정치적으로도 민주화를 위한 국가적 움직임을 보이고 있고, 독일 아데나워 재단이 그러한 움직임을 후원하는 것을 알 수 있었다. 게다가 베트남인들은 문화적이나 민족적인 면에서 한국과 밀접한 감정을 가지고 있어 앞으로 우리나라가 베트남과 긴밀한 관계를 유지하는 것이 바람직할 것이라는 생각이 들었다.

〈주제 발표자들 및 아데나워 재단 베트남 지부장과 기념촬영〉

[별지 1]

한국 헌법상 권력분립원리의 실현

이 동 흡*

I. 서 론

　권력분립원리란 국가권력을 그 성질과 기능에 따라 여러 기관으로 분산시켜 기관이 서로 견제와 균형을 하도록 함으로써, 국민의 자유와 권리를 보호하고자 하는 국가기관의 구성원리를 의미한다. 이것은 과거 절대왕권이 입법, 행정, 사법권 모두를 행사하였던 역사를 거울삼아 국가권력으로부터 시민의 자유를 수호하기 위하여 고안된 원리로서, 국가권력의 비대화를 방지하고 국가권력 상호간의 견제와

---

* 대한민국 헌법재판소 재판관.

균형을 통하여 국민의 기본권을 보장하기 위하여 필요한 제도이다.

현행 한국 헌법에서는 권력분립을 개별 조항에서 명시하고 있지 않지만, 국가권력을 국회의 입법권, 정부의 행정권, 법원의 사법권, 헌법재판소의 헌법재판권으로 분할하고 있다. 이들 통치기구는 각기 자기에게 배분된 권능에 따라 그 기능을 수행하는 한편, 필요에 따라 상호 협동과 견제를 하고 있다.

II. 국가권력의 분할

한국 헌법은 국가권력을 입법권, 집행권(통치권 및 협의의 행정권), 사법권, 헌법재판권으로 나누어 분할하고, 입법권은 국회에(헌법 제40조), 집행권은 국가원수인 대통령을 행정수반으로 하는 정부에 (헌법 제66조 제 4 항), 사법권은 법원에(헌법 제101조 제 1 항), 헌법재판권은 헌법재판소에(헌법 제111조) 각각 귀속시키고 있다.

이러한 권력의 분할을 뒷받침하기 위하여 국회의원은 대통령의 직무를 겸할 수 없고(헌법 제43조, 국회법 제29조 제 1 항 제 2 호), 대통령은 국무총리·국무위원·행정각부의 장이 될 수 없다(헌법 제83조). 또한 국회의원과 일반 공무원의 겸직이 금지되고(국회법 제29조 제 1 항), 법관의 독립(헌법 제103조) 및 헌법재판소 재판관의 정치관여금지(헌법 제112조 제 2 항) 규정을 두고 있다.

그리고 한국 헌법은 지방자치단체 제도를 규정하고 있다(헌법 제117조, 제118조). 지방자치단체와 중앙정부는 수직적 권력분립관계이고, 지방자치단체 내에서는 다시 지방자치단체장과 지방의회로 수평적 권력분립을 하여 각 관할권을 배분함으로써 권력분립과 기능 배분이 이루어져 있다.

한편, 헌법은 국가권력을 담당하는 헌법기관이 서로 지배력을 행사할 수 없도록 하기 위하여 임기제를 두고 있다. 국회의원의 임기는 4년(헌법 제42조), 대통령의 임기는 5년(헌법 제70조), 대법원장·대법관·헌법재판소장·헌법재판소재판관·선거관리위원회위원의 임기를 6년으로 하고 있다(헌법 제105조 제1항·제2항, 제112조 제1항, 제114조 제3항).

공직의 겸직금지(헌재 1993. 7. 29. 91헌마69, 판례집 5-2, 145)

교육위원의 교원 겸직금지를 규정한 지방교육자치에관한법률 제9조 제1항에 대한 위헌확인

"일반적으로 입법상의 공직 겸직금지제도가 마련되는 이유로는 첫째, 직무전념 내지 직무수행의 이념상 일반직의 국가공무원 또는 지방공무원이 다른 직종을 겸직하는 것을 원칙적으로 금지하고 있는 경우와 둘째, 제도상 직무상호간에 권력분립의 필요성이 있는 경우로서 국회의원과 일반직 공무원간의 겸직금지, 지방자치단체의 장과 지방의회 의원간의 겸직금지 등이 그 예이며 셋째, 직무의 공정성과 전념성 및 정치적 중립성의 확보를 위한 목적으로 겸직금지의 규정을 두고 있는 경우가 있다."

공직의 겸직금지(헌재 2004. 12. 16. 2002헌마333·451(병합), 판례집 16-2 하, 535)

지방공사 직원의 지방의회의원 겸직금지규정에 대한 위헌확인

"원래 공직자에 대한 입후보제한 및 겸직금지는 "입법과 행정간의 권력분립"이라는 헌법상의 원칙을 유지하고 실현시키는 데 그 입법취지가 있다. 구체적으로 말하면 법률의 집행이나 적용을 맡고 있는 공직자가 동시에 법률의 제정에 관여하는 현상, 즉 집행공직자가 의원겸직을 통하여 행정의 통제자가 되어 자신을 스스로 통제하는 것을 허용하지 않고 이로써 이해충돌의 위험성을 방지하자는 것이다."

Ⅲ. 한국의 현행 헌법상 정부형태(government regime)와 권력분립

1. 서 론

정부형태란 국가에 있어 입법부와 집행부의 관계를 설정하는 구조와 그 작동형태를 의미하는 권력분립원리의 조직적 실현형태를 의미한다. 각 나라마다 권력분립을 어떻게 구체화할 것인가를 정하기 위해서는 다양한 요소를 고려하여야 할 것인데, 권력을 분할하여 남용을 방지하고, 국가권력으로부터 국민의 자유와 권리를 보장하여야 하며, 국가운영의 효율성을 확보하여야 한다. 한편, 이러한 보편적인 요소 외에도 각 국가가 처한 정치·사회·경제적 여건도 아울러 고려하여야 할 것이다.

한국 헌법이 규정하는 정부형태는 기본적으로 대통령제의 범주에 속하는 것이라고 할 수 있으나, 의원내각제의 요소를 가미하고 있다.

2. 한국의 정부형태

(1) 대통령제의 요소

① 대통령은 국가원수인 동시에 집행부 수반의 지위와 권한을 보유하고 있으므로(헌법 제66조 제1항·제4항), 집행에 관한 최고의 권한과 최종적인 책임은 대통령에게 귀속되어 있다.

② 대통령은 국민에 의하여 직접 선출되므로(헌법 제67조 제1항), 국민으로부터 직접 그 대표성을 부여받고 있다.

③ 대통령은 5년의 임기 동안(헌법 제70조) 탄핵소추의 경우를 제외하고는 국회에 대하여 정치적 책임을 지지 아니하며, 국회도 대통령에 대하여 불신임결의를 할 수 없다.

④ 대통령이 국회해산권을 가지고 있지 아니하므로 권력분립의 원리가 충실히 반영되어 있다.

⑤ 대통령은 법률안 거부권을 행사함으로써(헌법 제53조 제2항) 국회의 경솔과 전제를 방지할 수 있다.

(2) 의원내각제의 요소

① 외형상 의원내각제의 내각과 유사한 국무회의를 설치하여 집행부의 권한에 속하는 중요정책을 심의하도록 하고 있고(헌법 제88조 제1항), 대통령을 그 국무회의의 의장으로 하고 있다.

② 국무총리를 임명함에 있어 국회의 동의를 얻도록 하고 있다(헌법 제86조 제1항).

③ 국무총리는 대통령의 명을 받아 행정각부를 통할하고(헌법 제86조 제2항), 국무위원의 임명을 대통령에게 제청하며, 국무위원의 해임을 건의할 수 있다(헌법 제87조 제1항·제3항).

④ 국회는 국무총리와 국무위원에 대한 해임을 대통령에게 건의할 수 있다(헌법 제63조 제1항).

⑤ 대통령의 국법상 행위에는 국무총리와 관계 국무위원의 부서가 있어야 한다(헌법 제82조).

⑥ 정부도 법률안을 제출할 수 있다(헌법 제52조).

⑦ 국무총리·국무위원·정부위원은 국회나 그 위원회에 출석하여 발언할 수 있고, 국회와 그 위원회도 이들을 출석시켜 답변을 요구할 수 있다(헌법 제62조 제1항·제2항).

3. 현행 한국 헌법상 통치제도의 특색

한국의 현행 헌법은 첫째, 대통령의 국회해산권을 폐지하고 비상조치권을 폐지하여 대통령의 국회에 대한 견제권을 대폭 축소시켰다. 둘째, 국회의 연간 개회일수제한규정을 폐지하고, 대통령이 소집을 요구한 임시회에서의 처리안건제한규정을 없앰으로써 국회의 독립성을 강화하였다. 셋째, 헌법재판소를 두어 국가기관간의 권한쟁의를 심판하도록 함으로써 권력분립제도를 유지하도록 하고 있다. 넷째, 국회는 국정감사권을 가지고, 헌법재판소는 국회입법에 대한 구체적 규범통제권을 가지며, 법원은 행정입법과 행정처분에 대한 통제권을 가짐으로써 통치기구간의 견제권을 강화하였다.

[표 1] 역대 한국 헌법의 정부형태 및 정부와 국회의 관계

	정부형태	정부와 국회의 관계
건국헌법 (1948)	· 대통령제 : 간선제(국회), 임기 4년, 1차 중임 허용 · 부통령제	· 대통령의 법률안 거부권, 임시 국회소집요구권 · 정부의 법률안제출권 및 출석 · 발언권
제 1 차 헌법개정	· 대통령제 : 직선제 개헌	· 국회의 국무원불신임권 · 국무총리 · 국무위원의 연대책임
제 2 차 헌법개정	· 대통령제 : 초대 대통령에 한하여 중임제한 철폐	· 국무총리제 폐지 · 국무위원의 개별적 책임
제 2 공화국 헌법 (1960)	· 의원내각제 · 행정권은 국무원 · 상징적 국가원수로서 대통령 존속 : 임기 5년, 2선 허용, 양원합동회의에서 간선	· 국무원의 민의원해산권 · 국무총리와 국무위원의 과반수는 국회의원으로 구성 · 민의원의 국무원불신임권 및 국무원의 연대책임
제 3 공화국 헌법 (1962)	· 대통령제 : 직선제, 임기 4년	· 대통령의 법률안 거부권, 임시 국회소집요구권 · 정부의 법률안제출권 · 국회의 국무총리 · 국무위원 해임건의권
제 4 공화국 헌법 (1972)	· 대통령제 : 간선제(통일주체 국민회의), 임기 6년	· 통일주체국민회의에서 선출하는 국회의원에 대한 대통령의 추천권 · 대통령의 긴급조치 · 국회의 국무총리임명동의권
제 5 공화국 헌법 (1980)	· 대통령제 : 간선제(선거인단), 단임제, 임기 7년	· 대통령의 국회해산권, 법률안 제출권, 비상조치권 · 국회의 국무총리 · 국무위원 출석요구권, 국무총리 · 국무위원 해임의결권
제 6 공화국 헌법 (1987~현재)	· 대통령제 : 직선제, 임기 5년, 단임제	· 대통령의 법률안제출권 및 법률안 거부권 · 국회의 국무총리 임명동의권 · 국회의 국무총리 · 국무위원 출석요구권, 국무총리 · 국무위원 해임건의권

4. 권력의 분산

현행 헌법은 권력분립적인 정부형태를 채택하고 있다. 입법권은 국회에, 집행권은 대통령과 행정부에, 사법권은 법원에 부여하고 있다. 특히 헌법보장기관으로서 헌법재판소를 두어 권력 상호간의 견제와 균형을 유지하고 있다.

(1) 국 회

국회는 입법권을 행사할 뿐만 아니라(헌법 제40조), 국가의 예산안을 심의·확정하고(헌법 제54조), 조약의 체결·비준에 대하여 동의권을 가지며(헌법 제60조 제1항), 선전포고, 국군의 해외파견, 외국군대의 국내주류 등에 대하여 동의권을 갖는다(헌법 제60조 제2항). 그리고 국회는 국무총리·국무위원 또는 정부위원에 대하여 출석·답변을 요구할 수 있고(헌법 제62조), 국무총리 또는 국무위원에 대하여 해임건의권을 갖는다(헌법 제63조). 또한 대통령·국무총리·국무위원·행정각부의 장·헌법재판소 재판관·법관·중앙선거관리위원회 위원·감사원장·감사위원 기타 법률이 정하는 공무원에 대한 탄핵소추권을 갖는다(헌법 제65조).

(2) 대 통 령

대통령은 국가의 원수로서 국가의 독립, 영토의 보전, 국가의 계속성과 헌법수호의 책임을 지며, 조국의 평화적 통일을 실현할 의무를 진다(헌법 제66조). 대통령은 외국과의 관계에서 국가를 대표하고(헌법 제66조), 조약을 체결·비준하며(헌법 제73조), 국군통수권(헌법

제74조), 국가긴급시의 긴급명령권 및 긴급재정·경제처분 및 명령권
(헌법 제76조), 계엄선포권(헌법 제77조)을 갖는다.

이외에도 국민투표 회부권(헌법 제72조), 국무총리·국무위원 임
명권(헌법 제86조, 제87조), 감사원장과 감사위원의 임명권(헌법 제98
조), 대법원장과 대법관 임명권(헌법 제104조), 헌법재판소 소장 및 재
판관 임명권(헌법 제111조 제 2 항·제 4 항), 중앙선거관리위원회 위원
임명권(헌법 제114조) 등의 공무원 임면권(헌법 제78조)과, 사면·감
형·복권권을 가지고(헌법 제79조), 훈장과 영전수여권(헌법 제80조)을
가지며, 국회출석발언권(헌법 제81조), 위임명령과 집행명령을 제정할
수 있고(헌법 제75조), 헌법개정발의권(헌법 제128조), 법률안거부권(헌
법 제53조), 국회임시회 소집요구권(헌법 제47조) 등을 가져 국권행사
의 최고기관으로서의 지위를 가진다.

(3) 행 정 부

행정권은 대통령을 수반으로 하는 정부에 속한다. 정부는 대통
령과 국무총리 그리고 국무위원으로 구성되는데(헌법 제88조), 국무
총리는 대통령을 보좌하고 행정에 관하여 대통령의 명을 받아 행정
각부를 통할한다(헌법 제86조 제 2 항). 국무위원은 국정에 관하여 대
통령을 보좌하며 국무회의의 구성원으로서 국정을 심의한다(헌법 제
87조 제 2 항). 행정각부의 장은 소관사무에 관하여 행정을 집행하고
부령을 발할 수 있다(헌법 제95조). 감사원은 국가의 세입·세출의 결
산과 회계감사 및 공무원의 직무감사를 한다(헌법 제97조).

(4) 법　　원

사법권은 법관으로 구성된 법원에 속한다(헌법 제101조). 법원은 명령·규칙·처분이 헌법이나 법률에 위반되는지 여부가 구체적 소송 사건에서 재판의 전제가 된 경우에 대법원은 이에 대해 최종적으로 심사할 권한을 갖는다(헌법 제107조).

(5) 헌법재판소

헌법재판소는 위헌법률심사권, 탄핵심판권, 정당해산심판권, 권한쟁의심판권, 헌법소원심판권을 갖는다(헌법 제111조 제 1 항).

5. 권력의 견제와 균형

(1) 국회와 정부 상호간

국회는 정부에 대하여 국무총리 임명동의권(헌법 제86조 제 1 항), 국무총리·국무위원의 해임건의권(헌법 제63조), 대통령 기타 고위직 공무원에 대한 탄핵소추권(헌법 제65조), 예산안의결권(헌법 제54조), 중요조약의 체결·비준 동의권(헌법 제60조 제 1 항), 국정감사·조사권(헌법 제61조), 선전포고 등 외교행위에 대한 동의권(헌법 제60조 제 2 항), 긴급명령 및 긴급재정·경제처분명령에 대한 승인권(헌법 제76조), 계엄해제요구권(헌법 제77조 제 5 항), 대통령이 제안하는 헌법개정안의 의결권(헌법 제130조 제 1 항), 대통령의 일반사면에 대한 동의권(헌법 제79조 제 2 항), 국무총리·국무위원·정부위원에 대한 출석답변요구권(헌법 제62조) 등의 권한을 가지고 대통령과 행정부를 통제할 수 있다.

이에 대하여 정부는 국회에 대하여 임시국회소집요구권(헌법 제
47조), 법률안거부권(헌법 제53조), 계엄선포권(헌법 제77조), 국회출석
발언권(헌법 제62조, 헌법 제81조), 국가간위에 관한 중요정책의 국민
투표회부권(헌법 제72조), 헌법개정안발의권(헌법 제128조) 등을 가지
고 있어 이에 대항하여 견제할 수 있다.

한나라당 대통령후보 이명박의 주가조작 등 범죄혐의의 진상규명을 위한
특별검사의 임명 등에 관한 법률 제 3 조에 대한 위헌확인(헌재 2008. 1.
10. 2007헌마1468, 판례집 20-1 상, 1)

대법원장으로 하여금 특별검사 후보자 2인을 추천하도록 한 특검법 제 3 조가
권력분립원칙에 위배되는지 여부

"헌법상 권력분립의 원칙이란 국가권력의 기계적 분립과 엄격한 절연
을 의미하는 것이 아니라, 권력 상호간의 견제와 균형을 통한 국가권력
의 통제를 의미하는 것이다. 따라서 특정한 국가기관을 구성함에 있어
입법부, 행정부, 사법부가 그 권한을 나누어 가지거나 기능적인 분담을
하는 것은 권력분립의 원칙에 반하는 것이 아니라 권력분립의 원칙을
실현하는 것으로 볼 수 있다.

특별검사제도는 검찰의 기소독점주의 및 기소편의주의에 대한 제도
적 견제장치로서 권력형 부정사건 및 정치적 성격이 강한 사건에서 대
통령이나 정치권력으로부터 독립된 특별검사에 의하여 수사 및 공소제
기·공소유지가 되게 함으로써 법의 공정성 및 사법적 정의를 확보하기
위한 것이다. 이처럼 본질적으로 권력통제의 기능을 가진 특별검사제도
의 취지와 기능에 비추어 볼 때, 특별검사제도의 도입 여부를 입법부가
독자적으로 결정하고, 특별검사 임명에 관한 권한을 헌법기관 간에 분

산시키는 것이 권력분립의 원칙에 반한다고 볼 수 없다."

(2) 정부와 법원, 헌법재판소 상호간

대통령은 법원과 헌법재판소에 대하여 예산편성권(헌법 제54조)을 가지고, 사면·감형·복권권(헌법 제79조), 긴급명령권(헌법 제76조), 계엄선포권(헌법 제77조)을 가지고 있어 어느 정도의 견제를 할 수 있다. 또한 대통령은 대법원장, 대법관의 임명권(헌법 제104조 제1항·제2항)을 가지고, 헌법재판소 재판관 중 3인의 지명권 및 헌법재판소 소장과 재판관의 임명권을 가져(헌법 제111조) 법원과 헌법재판소를 견제할 수 있다.

반면, 법원은 명령이나 규칙·처분이 헌법과 법률에 위반되는지 여부가 구체적 소송 사건에서 재판의 전제가 된 경우에는 이에 대한 심사권을 가지고(헌법 제107조), 헌법재판소는 국민의 기본권을 직접 침해하는 행정입법(명령이나 규칙)이 있는 경우, 그것이 헌법에 위반되는지 여부에 대한 심사권을 가지며(헌재 1990. 10. 15. 89헌마178, 판례집 2, 365), 또한 헌법재판소는 국회가 체결·비준한 조약과 대통령의 긴급명령, 긴급재정·경제명령·처분에 대한 위헌여부를 판단할 수 있고, 일정 고위공무원에 대한 탄핵심판권 및 정당해산심판권을 가지기 때문에 정부를 어느 정도 견제할 수 있다.

(3) 국회와 법원, 헌법재판소 상호간

국회는 법원과 헌법재판소에 대하여 대법원장·헌법재판소장 임명동의권(헌법 제104조 제1항, 제111조 제4항), 대법관 임명동의권(헌

법 제104조 제 2 항), 헌법재판소 재판관 3인의 선출권(헌법 제111조 제 3
항) 등을 통하여 어느 정도의 견제를 할 수 있다. 또한 법원과 헌법재
판소에 관한 법률제정권(헌법 제102조 제 3 항, 제113조 제 3 항) 및 예산
심사의결권(헌법 제54조), 헌법재판소 재판관과 법관에 대한 탄핵소추
권(헌법 제65조 제 1 항), 일반사면동의권(헌법 제79조 제 2 항), 국정감
사·조사권(헌법 제61조) 등의 견제권을 가지고 있다.

　　이에 대하여 법원은 국회의 입법에 대하여 위헌심사제청권을 가
지고(헌법 제107조 제 1 항), 헌법재판소는 위헌결정으로 법률의 효력
을 상실시킬 수 있어(헌법 제111조 제 1 항) 국회를 견제할 수 있다.

(4) 법원과 헌법재판소 상호간

　　대법원장은 헌법재판소 재판관 중 3인에 대한 지명권을 갖는다
(헌법 제111조 제 3 항). 반면, 헌법재판소는 법원의 구성에 대한 통제
권을 가지지 않고, 법원의 재판은 원칙적으로 헌법소원심판의 대상
이 아니다(헌법재판소법 제68조 제 1 항). 그러나 예외적으로 법원의 재
판이 헌법소원심판의 대상이 되는 경우에는 헌법재판소가 법원을 통
제할 수 있다(헌재 1997. 12. 24. 96헌마172·173(병합), 판례집 9-2,
842). 또한 헌법재판소는 법관에 대하여 탄핵심판권을 가진다(헌법
제111조 제 1 항 제 3 호).

Ⅳ. 결　　론

　　이상으로 한국의 정부형태와 권력분립원리를 실현하기 위한 국
가권력의 견제와 균형에 관하여 살펴보았다. 한국의 정부형태는 의

원내각제의 요소를 일부 포함하고 있지만, 기본적으로 대통령제를 취하고 있다. 대통령의 비상대권을 포함한 강력한 권한을 가졌던 과거의 헌법과 비교하면, 현행 헌법은 입법부의 권한을 강화하고 통치권 행사의 절차적 정당성을 강조하는 내용을 보완함으로써 입법부와 행정부의 견제와 균형을 도모하였다고 평가할 수 있다.

그러나 여전히 대통령선거에서 상대다수 득표에 의한 당선을 인정하고 있으므로(plurality system) 유효투표의 반수 미만 득표로 대통령 당선이 가능하다는 점, 민주적 정당성이 없는 국무총리가 대통령의 권한대행권을 가진다는 점, 집행부와 입법부가 대립하고 갈등하여 정국의 불안정이 초래되는 경우(분점정부, divided government)에 이를 조정할 수 있는 제도적 장치가 마련되어 있지 않은 점 등은 앞으로 한국이 해결해 나아가야 할 과제라고 하는 헌법학자들의 의견이 있다.

[별지 2]

Realization of the principle of separation of powers under the Korean Constitution

Dong-Heub LEE*

---

* Justice, Constitutional Court of Korea.

I. Introduction

The doctrine of separation of powers means the principle of state institution formation that divides the state powers into several branches based on their nature and function and makes it possible for the different branches to check and balance each other, so that the rights and freedoms of all people can be protected. This principle was the vehicle designed to protect freedom of people against encroachment by the state power, considering the history in which an absolute monarch exercised all the legislative, executive and judicial powers. The separation of powers is necessary to protect people's fundamental rights by preventing excessive expansion of state powers and maintaining checks and balances among state powers.

The current Korean Constitution does not stipulate the principle of separation of powers in a separate provision. But it divides state power into the following four: legislative power vested in the National Assembly, executive power vested in the Executive Branches, judicial power vested in courts and constitutional adjudication power vested in the Constitutional Court. Each governing power conducts its own functions with separate and independent powers and responsibility while also cooperating and checking each other, if necessary.

II. Division of State Powers

The Korean Constitution divides state powers into legislative power, executive power (power of sovereignty and administrative power in a narrow sense), judicial power and constitutional adjudication power. The legislative power is vested in the National Assembly (Article 40 of the Constitution), the executive power is vested in the Executive Branch headed by the President (Article 66 Section of the Constitution), the judicial power is vested in courts (Article 101 Section 1 of the Constitution) and the constitutional adjudication power is vested in the Constitutional Court (Article 111 of the Constitution).

In order to support such separation of powers, members of the National Assembly shall not concurrently hold any other office including public official in general service prescribed by Act (Article 43 the Constitution and Article 29 of the National Assembly Act), the President shall not concurrently hold the office of Prime Minister, a member of the State Council, the head of any Executive Ministry, nor other public or private posts as prescribed by Act (Article 83 of the Constitution), judges shall rule independently (Article 103 of the Constitution) and the

Justices of the Constitutional Court shall not join any political party nor shall participate in political activities (Article 112 Section 2 of the Constitution).

Also, the Constitution stipulates the local government system (Article 117 and Article 118 of the Constitution). The vertical separation of powers is maintained between the local governments and the national government, and within the local governments, the powers are horizontally divided between the head of local government and the council of local government, thereby each conducts its own function based on independent and separate powers and responsibilities.

Meanwhile, the Constitution provides the terms of office in order to prevent the constitutional institutions from exercising its control over each other. The term of office of members of the National Assembly is four years (Article 42 of the Constitution), the term of office of the President is five years (Article 70 of the Constitution) and the terms of office of the Chief Justice and Justices of the Supreme Court; the President and Justices of the Constitutional Court; and the members of the Election Commission are six years (Article 105 Section 1 and Section 2; Article 112 Section 1; and Article 114 Section 3 of the Constitution).

Prohibition of Concurrent Service Case (5-2 KCCR 145, 91Hun-Ma69, July 29, 1993)

Constitutional complaint against Article 9 Section 1 of the Act on Autonomy of Local Education which prohibits members of the board of education from concurrently serving as teacher

- "In general, the reasons for legally prohibiting concurrent service of public offices are as follows: first, due to the public officials' duty to devote themselves to conduct their duties, public officials in general service and local public officials are prohibited to be concurrently engaged in any other duties; second, due to systemic necessity for the separation of powers between duties, for example, members of the National Assembly cannot concurrently take the position of public officials in general service and vice versa, and a head of local government cannot concurrently work as a member of the local council; and third, in order to guarantee fairness and commitment to duties and political neutrality, a statutory provision that prohibits concurrent service exists."

Prohibition of Concurrent Service Case (16-2(B) KCCR 535, 2002Hun-Ma333 · 451 (consolidated), December 16, 2004)

Constitutional complaint against a statutory provision that prevents employees of local public cooperation from concurrently being member of the local council

- "Originally, the legislative purpose of statutory provisions that restrict public officials' candidacy or prohibit concurrent service of public officials is to maintain and realize the constitutional principle of 'separation of powers between the Legislature and Executive.' Concretely speaking, such restriction is imposed to prevent such a case where a public official, in charge of execution or application of law, is concurrently engaged in the process of legislation, or in other words, to prevent a public official who executes law from checking himself/herself by becoming a controller of the executive as a member of the local council, so that the risk of conflict in interests can be precluded."

III. Current Government Regime in Korea and Separation of Powers

1. Introduction

Government regime is a systemic realization of the principle of separation of powers which means the structure establishing relation between the Legislature and the Executive and its working mechanism in a country. In order to decide how to concretize the separation of powers, each country may consider various factors, including prevention of abuse of state powers by dividing them, protection of people's rights and freedoms and guarantee of efficiency in managing national affairs. Meanwhile, other than the general factors mentioned before, specific political, social and economic situations in which each country is located should also be taken into consideration.

It can be said that the government regime defined by the Korean Constitution basically comes under the category of the Presidential System, but it also contains the elements of the Parliamentary Cabinet System.

2. The Government Regime of Korea

(1) Elements of the Presidential System

① Because the President has the status and authority of the Head of the Executive Branch as the Head of State (Article 66 Section 1 and 4 of the Constitution), the supreme authority and final responsibility with regard to execution shall be vested in the President.

② Because the President is elected by direct ballot by the people (Article 67 Section 1 of the Constitution), the representativeness is directly authorized by the people.

③ During the five year term of office (Article 70 of the

Constitution), the President shall not assume the political responsibility toward the National Assembly, except impeachment, and the National Assembly shall not resolve a vote of nonconfidence in the President.

④ The principle of separation of power has been reflected in terms that the President is not authorized to dissolve the National Assembly.

⑤ The President shall prevent the imprudence and arbitrariness of the National Assembly through the right of objection to the bill (Article 53 Section 2 of the Constitution).

(2) Elements of the Parliamentary Cabinet System

① The State Council, which is analogous to a cabinet of the parliamentary cabinet system, was established to deliberate on significant policies belonging to the Executive Branch (Article 88 Section 1 of the Constitution), and the President is the head of the State Council.

② The Prime Minister shall be appointed by the President with the consent of the National Assembly (Article 86 Section 1 of the Constitution).

③ The Prime Minister shall direct the Executive Ministries under the order of the President (Article 86 Section 2 of the Constitution), recommend the appointment and removal of the members of the State Council

(Article 87 Section 1 and 3 of the Constitution).

④ The National Assembly may pass a recommendation for the removal of the Prime Minister or a member of the State Council from office (Article 63 Section 1 of the Constitution).

⑤ The acts of the President under law shall be counter-signed by the Prime Minister and the concerned members of the State Council (Article 82 of the Constitution).

⑥ Bills may be introduced by the Executive (Article 52 of the Constitution).

⑦ The Prime Minister, members of the State Council or government delegates may attend a meeting of the National Assembly or its committees, as the National Assembly or its committees may request to attend any meeting of the National Assembly, and report on the state administration or deliver opinions and answer questions (Article 62 Section 1 and 2 of the Constitution).

3. The Feature of the Government Structure under the Current Korean Constitution

First, the current Korean Constitution abolished the power to dissolve the National Assembly and the power to take special emergency measures of the President, thereby curtailing the President's power to curb the National Assembly.

Second, the independence of the National Assembly has been reinforced in that the current Korean Constitution repealed the provision to limit the annual opening day of the National Assembly and the provision to limit the agenda of the extraordinary session of the National Assembly convened upon the request of the President. Third, the Constitutional Court was established to adjudicate competence disputes between government agencies for the separation of powers. Fourth, the check and balance of powers was reinforced in terms that the National Assembly is granted the authority of national audit, the Constitutional Court is granted the jurisdiction on the concrete review of statutory legislation, and the Court is granted the jurisdiction to review administrative rule-making and administrative action.

[Table 1] The Government Regime of Korea and the Relations between the Executive Branch and the National Assembly under the former and current Constitutions

	Government Regime	Relations between the Executive and the National Assembly
Founding Constitution (1948)	- Presidential System: Indirect election (by the National Assembly) for a term of 4 years. May be re-elected for another term. - Vice President System	- The President has the power to veto and request an extraordinary session of the National Assembly The Executive has the power to propose bill and attend and address the National Assembly
First Revision	- Presidential System: Revised to adopt direct	- The National Assembly has the power to vote non-confidence in the State

		Council - The Prime Minister and members of the State Council have joint responsibility
	election	
Second Revision	- Presidential System: The one-time re-election limit not apply to the first President	- It repealed the Prime Minister system - The members of the State Council are individually liable
Constitution of the Second Republic (1960)	- Parliamentary system - Executive power vested in the State Council - President as a symbolic chief of the state with a term of 5 years. May be re-elected for another term. Indirect election (by the Bicameral Committee Meeting).	- The State Council has the power to dissolve the House of Representatives - The Prime Minister and half of the State Council members are the members of the National Assembly. - The members of the House of Representatives have the power to vote non-confidence in the State Council. The State Council has joint responsibility.
Constitution of the Third Republic (1962)	- Presidential system: Direct election for a term of 4 years	- The President has the power to veto bill and request an extraordinary session of the National Assembly - The Executive has the power to submit bill - The National Assembly has the power to recommend removal of the Prime Minister or a State Council member
Constitution of the Fourth Republic (1972)	- Presidential system: Indirect election (by the National Council for Unification) for a term of 6 years	- The President has the power to nominate members of the National Assembly to be appointed by the National Council for Unification - The President has the power to take emergency measures
Constitution of the Fifth Republic (1980)	- Presidential system: Indirect election (by the Election Committee) for a term of 7 years and no re-election	- The President has the power to dissolve the National Assembly, to submit bill, and to take emergency measures - The National Assembly has the power to request attendance of the Prime Minister, member of the State Council, or government delegate at meetings of the National Assembly. It also has the

		power to decide removal of the Prime Minister or a State Council member.
Constitution of the Sixth Republic (1987-current)	- Presidential system: Direct election for a term of 5 years and no re-election.	- The President has the power to submit and to veto bill - The National Assembly has the power to consent to the appointment of the Prime Minister - The National Assembly has the power to request attendance of the Prime Minister, member of the State Council, or government delegate at meetings of the National Assembly. It also has the power to recommend removal of the Prime Minister or a State Council member.

4. Separation of Powers

The current Constitution designs the government regime under the principle of separation of powers. The legislative power is vested in the National Assembly, the executive power is vested in the President and the Executive Branch, and the judicial power is vested in the Court. Specially, the Constitutional Court, a state agency to protect the Constitution, was established for the check and balance of powers.

(1) The National Assembly

The National Assembly shall exercise the legislative power (Article 40 of the Constitution), deliberate and decide upon the national budget bill (Article 54 of the Constitution), have the right to consent to the conclusion and ratification of treaties (Article 60 Section 1 of the Constitution), and have the right to consent to the declaration of war, the dispatch of armed forces to foreign states, or the stationing of alien forces in the territory of the State (Article 60 Section 2 of the Constitution). Besides, the National Assembly may request the Prime Minister, members of the State Council or government delegates to attend any meeting of the National Assembly and answer questions (Article 62 of the Constitution) and pass a recommendation for the removal of the Prime Minister or a State Council member from office (Article 63 of the Constitution). In addition, the National Assembly may pass motions for the impeachment of the President, the Prime Minister, members of the State Council, heads of Executive Ministries, Justices of the Constitutional Court, judges, members of the National Election Commission, the Chairman and members of the Board of Audit and Inspection, and other public officials designated by statutes (Article 65 of the Constitution).

(2) The President

The President shall have the responsibility and duty to safeguard the independence, territorial integrity and continuity of the State and the Constitution and the duty to pursue sincerely the peaceful unification of the homeland as the Head of State (Article 66 of the Constitution). The President shall represent the State vis-à-vis foreign states (Article 66 of the Constitution), conclude and ratify treaties (Article 73 of the Constitution), be Commander-in-Chief of the Armed Forces (Article 74 of the Constitution), issue emergency orders or take emergency financial or economic actions in time of the State emergency (Article 76 of the Constitution), and proclaim martial law (Article 77 of the Constitution).

In addition, the President may call a national referendum (Article 72 of the Constitution), shall appoint and dismiss public officials (Article 78 of the Constitution) including the Prime Minister and the members of the State Council (Article 86 and 87 of the Constitution), the Chairman and members of the Board of Audit and Inspection (Article 98 of the Constitution), the Chief Justice of the Supreme Court and the Supreme Court Justices (Article 104 of the Constitution), the President of the Constitutional Court and the Constitutional Court Justices (Article 111 Section 2 and 4 of the Constitution), members of the National Election Commission (Article 114 of the Constitution), may grant amnesty, commutation and restoration of rights (Article 79 of the Constitution), shall award decorations and honors (Article 80 of the Constitution), may attend and address the National Assembly (Article 81 of the Constitution), may issue presidential decrees concerning matters delegated by him and necessary to enforce statutes (Article 75 of the Constitution), may introduce a proposal to amend the Constitution (Article 128 of the Constitution), may object to the bill (Article 53 of the Constitution), and may request to convene extraordinary sessions of the National Assembly (Article 47 of the Constitution), as the President has the supreme authority in exercising the national sovereignty.

(3) The Executive

The executive power is vested in the Executive Branch headed by the President. The Executive shall be composed of the President, the Prime Minster and members of the State Council (Article 88 of the Constitution) and the Prime Minister shall assist the President and shall direct the Executive Ministries under the order of the President (Article 86 Section 2 of the Constitution). The members of the State Council shall assist the President in the conduct of State affairs and, as constituents of the State Council, shall deliberate on State affairs (Article 87 Section 2 of the Constitution). The head of each Executive Ministry shall execute administration and may issue ordinances of the Executive Ministry concerning matters that are within his jurisdiction (Article 95 of the Constitution). The Board of Audit and Inspection shall examine the settlement of the revenues and expenditures of the State, the accounts of the State and the job performances of the executive agencies and public officials (Article 97 of the Constitution).

(4) The Court

The Judicial power shall be vested in courts composed of judges (Article 101 of the Constitution). The Supreme Court shall have the power to make a final review of the constitutionality or legality of administrative decrees, regulations or actions, when their constitutionality or legality is at issue in a trial (Article 107 of the Constitution).

(5) The Constitutional Court

The Constitutional Court shall have jurisdiction over the constitutional review of statutory legislation, impeachment, dissolution of a political party, competence disputes, and constitutional complaint (Article 111 Section 1 of the Constitution).

5. Checks and Balances of Powers

(1) The National Assembly v. the Executive Branch

As to the President and the Executive Branch, the National Assembly has the following powers: to consent to the President's appointment of the Prime Minister (Article 86 Section 1 of the Constitution); to recommend removal of the Prime Minister or a State Council member (Article 63 of the Constitution); to decide the national budget (Article 54 of the Constitution); to consent to the conclusion and ratification of important treaties (Article 60 Section 1 of the Constitution); to inspect and investigate the state affairs (Article 61 of the Constitution); to consent to the State's action on foreign affairs (Article 60 Section 2 of the Constitution); to ratify the Presidential order or actions pertaining to national emergency or financial or economic crisis (Article 76 of the Constitution); to request the lifting of martial law (Article 77 Section 5 of the Constitution); to decide upon constitutional amendment proposal submitted by the President (Article 130 Section 1 of the Constitution); to consent to general amnesty granted by the President (Article 79 Section 2 of the Constitution); and to request attendance of the Prime Minister, members of State Council, or government delegates, and their answers at meetings of the National Assembly (Article 62 of the Constitution). These powers are designed to check the President and the Executive branch.

In balancing the powers of the National Assembly, the Executive Branch has the following powers: to request convening of an extraordinary session (Article 47 of the Constitution); to veto a bill passed by the National Assembly (Article 53 of the Constitution); to proclaim martial law (Article 77 of the Constitution); to attend and address the National Assembly (Articles 62 and 81 of the Constitution); to submit important policy matters relating to national security to a national referendum (Article 72 of the Constitution); and to propose constitutional amendment (Article 128 of the Constitution).

Special Counsel's Case on the Suspicion to Myong-bak LEE, Presidential Candidate from Grand National Party Case (2007Hun-Ma1468, January 10, 2008)

Constitutionality review on Article 3 of the Act on Appointment of Special Prosecutors for Investigation of Alleged Crimes, regarding whether the pro-vision violates the principle of separation of powers by allowing the Chief Justice of the Supreme Court to recommend two candidates for appoint-ment of special prosecutors.

－　"The principle of separation of powers under the Constitution does not mean a mechanical separation or strict detachment. Rather, it means the control of state powers through checks and balances among the powers. Therefore, in designing a particular state's organizational structure, the sharing of powers and functions among the executive, legislative, and judicial branches is not against the principle of separation of powers but rather realizes the principle.

The Special Counsel System is an institutional meas-ure to check against the monopoly or arbitrariness of prosecutors in prosecutions. This is to ensure the fairness of law and judicial justice by mandating the special prosecutors, who are independent from the President or any political power, to investigate, prosecute, and maintain the case, when the case involves political corruption or has strong political nature. As such, considering the purpose and function of the Special Counsel System that essentially intends to control the powers, the fact that the National Assembly has the power to decide whether to adopt the system, while the power to appoint special prosecutors is distributed among other constitutional organizations, does not render it violation of the principle of separation of powers."

(2) The Executive Branch v. the Courts and the Constitutional Court

As to the Courts and the Constitutional Court, the President has the following powers: to decide the national budget (Article 54 of the Constitution); to grant amnesty, mitigation of sentence and restoration of rights (Article 79 of the Constitution); to issue emergency order (Article 76 of the Constitution); to declare martial law (Article 77 of the Constitution); to appoint the Chief Justice and Justices of the Supreme Court (Article 104 Sections 1 and 2 of the Constitution); and to nominate three Justices of the Constitutional Court and appoint the President and Justices of the Constitutional Court (Article 111 of the Constitutional Court). These powers of the President are designed to check the Courts and the Constitutional Court.

In balancing the powers of the Executive Branch, the

Courts retain the power to make a final review of the constitutionality or legality of administrative decrees, regulations or actions, when their constitutionality or legality is at issue in a trial (Article 107 of the Constitution). And the Constitutional Court retains the powers: to review the constitutionality of administrative legislation (decrees or regulations) that directly infringes upon the citizens' basic rights (2 KCCR 365, 89Hun-Ma178, October 15, 1990); to decide the constitutionality of treaties signed and ratified by the National Assembly, as well as the Presidential order or actions pertaining to national emergency and financial or economic crisis; and to adjudicate cases concerning impeachment of certain high-ranking public officials and dissolution of political party.

(3) The National Assembly v. the Courts and the Constitutional Court

As to the Courts and the Constitutional Court, the National Assembly has the following powers: to consent to the appointment of the Chief Justice of the Supreme Court and the President of the Constitutional Court (Article 104 Section 1 and Article 111 Section 4 of the Constitution); to consent to the appointment of the Justices of the Supreme Court (Article 104 Section 2 of the Constitution); to select three Justices for the Constitutional Court (Article 111 Section 3 of the Constitution); to legislate laws on operation of the Supreme Court and the Constitutional Court (Articles 102 Section 3 and 113 Section 3 of the Constitution); to review and decide the national budget (Article 54 of the Constitution); to impeach judges and Justices of the Constitutional Court (Article 65 Section 1 of the Constitution); to grant general amnesty (Article 79 Section 2 of the Constitution); and to inspect and investigate the state affairs (Article 61 of the Constitution). These powers of the National Assembly are designed to check the Courts and the Constitutional Court.

In balancing the powers of the National Assembly, the Courts retain the power to request a decision of the Constitution Court over the National Assembly's legislation (Article 107 Section 1 of the Constitution), and the Constitutional Court retains the power to nullify the legislation by its decision of unconstitutionality (Article 111(1) of the Constitution).

(4) The Courts v. the Constitutional Court

The Chief Justice of the Supreme Court has the power to nominate three candidates for Justices of the Constitutional Court (Article 111 Section 3 of the Constitution). On the other hand, the Constitutional Court has no controlling power over the organization of the Courts, and a decision of the Courts cannot be subject to the Constitutional Court's review of constitutionality in principle (Article 68 Section 1 of the Constitutional Court Act). In an exceptional case where the decision of the Courts is subject to the Constitutional Court's review of constitutionality, however, the Constitutional Court may have control over the Courts (9-2 KCCR 842, 96Hun-Ma172 · 173 (consolidated), December 24, 1997). In addition, the Constitutional Court has the power to adjudicate cases concerning impeachment of judges (Article 111 Sections 1 and 3 of the Constitution).

IV. Conclusion

I gave you an overview on the Korean government regime and the checks and balances among the government branches which are designed to realize the separation of powers. Although the way that Korean government is organized shows some elements of the parliamentary system, it basically follows the presidential system. While the past Constitutions allowed strong powers to the President including the power to take special emergency measures, the current Constitution strengthens the Legislative Branch and highlights the importance of procedural justice in exercising the sovereign power. This way, it aims to achieve checks and balances between the Legislative Branch and the Executive Branch.

Nevertheless, some scholars argue that there are tasks remaining for the Republic of Korea. Among other things, they point out the following issues: that the President can be elected by a mere plurality even with valid votes of less than half (plurality system); that the Prime Minister who has no democratic legitimacy can act as the acting President; and that no institutional device is in place to respond to a state of national instability that might arise from conflict between the executive and the legislative branches (divided government).

Introduction to the Constitutional Court of Korea and Its Role in Control of Government Power

Dong-Heub LEE*

---

* Justice, Constitutional Court of Korea.

A. Institutional Foundations of Constitutional Review

I. Current Constitutional Adjudication Model and Historical, Legal Reasons for Its Adoption

(1) Establishment of the Constitutional Court

In the Republic of Korea, the Constitutional Court was established as a key part of the constitutional system with the start of the Sixth Republic in 1988.

While amending the Constitution in 1987, political factions were divided on how to structure the constitutional adjudication system. Eventually, it was agreed to establish an independent Constitutional Court for adjudicating all constitutional matters including constitutionality review of statutes as well as the other so-called political issues.

(2) Forms of constitutional litigation or judicial review systems in the past

(i) the Constitutional Committee of the First Republic (1948-1960)

(ii) the Constitutional Court of the Second Republic (1960-1961)[1]

(iii) the American-type judicial review system of the Third Republic (1961-1972)

(iv) the Constitutional Committee of the Fourth Republic (1972-1981) and the Fifth Republic (1981-1988)

II. Relations between the Constitutional Court and Ordinary Courts

Under the Constitution, the judicial function is divided into two institutions; ordinary courts comprising the Supreme Court and lower level courts and the Constitutional Court.

(1) Interpretation and application of statutes of ordinary courts

In interpreting and applying statutes, ordinary courts must seek, first, to interpret and apply the statute in a manner consistent with the Constitution and, second, in case the constitutionality of the statute is at issue, must suspend their

---

1) The Constitutional Court of the Second Republic, however, was not established in practice due to the military coup d'état in 1961.

proceedings and seek a determination by the Constitutional Court. Once the interpreted content of a statute is declared unconstitutional by the Constitutional Court, it loses its legal validity. Ordinary courts are bound by the Court's decision and barred from applying that content to the instant case.

(2) Exhaustion of all other relief

Constitutional complaints are meant to relieve anyone whose basic rights have suffered in the exercise or non-exercise of governmental power. Therefore, constitutional complaints may be in conflict with administrative litigation that deals with the rights of the individual in relation with the exercise or non-exercise of governmental power. For this matter, the Constitutional Court Act (Article 68, Section 1) forbids filing a constitutional complaint without having exhausted all other relief processes by the laws.

(3) Constitutional complaint against ordinary court's judgments

According to Article 68, Section 1 of the Constitutional Court Act, judgments made by ordinary courts cannot be challenged through constitutional complaints. Thus, the Constitutional Court's power to adjudicate constitutional complaint does not extend to ordinary court judgments in principle.

Yet, when an ordinary court applies a statute that was declared unconstitutional by the Constitutional Court, and violates a person's basic rights as a result, such judgment can become the subject matter of constitutional complaints.

(4) Constitutional complaint against executive decrees, regulations, or administrative action

When the constitutionality or legality of executive decrees, regulations, or administrative actions is at issue in a trial, it is the Supreme Court that has the power of final review (Article 107 Section 2 of the Constitution). However, an ordinary court's ruling that an administrative legislation is unconstitutional has the effect of merely precluding its application in the case at hand only in the form of concrete review, rather than striking down the entire administrative legislation. In contrast, the decision by the Constitutional Court universally invalidates the affected decree or regulation.

In case a decree or regulation directly violates a person's basic rights, whether this can be subjected to constitutional complaint was in question. The Supreme Court maintained that the Constitution gives ordinary courts the entire and exclusive power to review decrees and regulations. By contrast, the Constitutional Court has claimed that under Article 107 Section 2 of the Constitution, the Supreme Court has jurisdiction to adjudicate the constitutionality of rules and regulations, but such adjudication is possible only when the con-stitutionality of these rules and regulations is a condition precedent to the outcome of an actual lawsuit, therefore, constitutional complaints must be permitted against admin-istrative legislations that directly violate a person's basic rights because there is no way to file a lawsuit in ordinary courts to challenge the validity of the administrative legis-lation itself. (2 KCCR 365, 89Hun-Ma178, October 15, 1990).

Moreover, to resolve such uncertainty, some maintain that Article 107 Section 2 of the Constitution should be repealed in its entirety, and the power to make a final review of the con-stitutionality of administrative decrees, regulations or ac-tions, should be conferred exclusively upon the Constitutional Court.[2]

(5) Tension over modified holdings

The Constitutional Court and ordinary courts also went through a fair amount of tension over the modified holdings—"limited unconstitutionality" and "limited constitutionality"(also known as "constitutional in certain context" and "unconstitutional in certain context," they are those of unconstitutionality without any deletion of

---

2) Regarding this issue, there had been a heated debate in the Advisory Commission for Constitutional Revision for the Speaker of the National Assembly. In the draft of the final report of the Advisory Committee, Article 107 Section 2 of the Constitution was abrogated, but in the final report, it was decided that the current system should be maintained.

text in the statute, being 'the qualitative unconstitutionality in part'). The Constitutional Court took the view that these are sub-species of the decision of unconstitutionality, whereas ordinary courts argued that they are merely a form of legal interpretation rather than a binding decision of unconstitutionality.

However, the current Constitutional Court Act does not clearly dictate whether the modified holding binds ordinary courts. Meanwhile, some lawmakers attempt to amend and specify the statute to clearly confer the binding effects to the modified holdings of the Constitutional Court.

B. Status and Composition of the Constitutional Court

I. The Constitutional Court as the Judicial Body

In reviewing the constitutionality of statutes, the only criterion for the Constitutional Court is the Constitution, not political preferences. The Constitutional Court has always maintained that it may not interpret the Constitution expansively so as to impose its own views on matters that were deliberately left open-ended by the Constitution to be determined by the political branches. Therefore the general view is that the Korean Constitutional Court is a judicial body rather than a political one.

II. Professional Qualifications for Members of the Constitutional Court

Nomination and appointment of Justices are limited to individuals qualified as attorney at law. Article 5 of the Constitutional Court Act lays down additional requirements. Justices shall be appointed among eligible persons with 40 years or more of age and who have been in any of the following positions for 15 years or more[3]: (1) Judge, Prosecutor, or Attorney; or (2) Person who has been engaged in legal affairs for a governmental agency or a public enterprise; or (3) Person who has been in a position higher than an assistant professor.

Some proposed to relax the qualifications to include law professors, etc. Such proposal was, however, not reflected in the current legislation.[4]

---

3) The provisions were revised in July 18, 2011 to fortify the qualification for appointees, so that the Chief Justice and Justices of the Supreme Court shall be appointed from among those who are forty five years of age or over. This revision will take effect from January 1, 2013. The provisions that stipulate the qualification of the President and Justices of the Constitutional Court, however, have yet to be revised.

4) With regard to this issue, according to the final report of the Advisory Commission for Constitutional Revision for the Speaker of the National Assembly, not only a person who is qualified as a lawyer, but a person who is a law professor or has experience in managing national affairs becomes eligible to be a Justice of the Constitutional Court.

III. Term of Justices and Possibility of Reappointment

The term of office for Justices of the Constitutional Court is a renewable six years with a retirement age of sixty-five while it is seventy in case of the President.

Different from the similar provisions that stipulate the term of office of Justices of the Supreme Court, which has been revised from 65 years of age to 70 years of age, however, the provisions that stipulate the term of office of Justices of the Constitutional Court have yet to be revised.

In recent debates, many have argued for an extended, but non renewable term of at least nine years. Some also argue that the mandatory retirement age should be abolished, or at least be amended to remove the difference between that of the President and other Justices.

IV. Procedure for Nomination and Appointment of Constitutional Court Members and Guarantee of Their Independence

The Constitutional Court is comprised of nine Justices appointed by the President of the Republic, of whom three shall be elected by the National Assembly, three nominated by the Chief Justice of the Supreme Court and three selected by the President of the Republic. Meanwhile, the President of the Constitutional Court of Korea is appointed by the President of the Republic from among the Justices, with the consent of the

National Assembly.

With respect to this appointment process, some say that the role of experts is not significant. Some have also noted that the nomination of three Justices by the Chief Justice of Supreme Court seems democratically inappropriate and may lead to the underestimation of the Constitutional Court. There are also arguments that all Justices should be selected by the National Assembly, while others say that the presidential appointment of Justices other than the Court's President also requires the consent of the National Assembly.

C. Jurisdiction of the Constitutional Court

I. Constitutional Review of Statutory Legislation in Abstracto?

The Korean Constitutional Court does not have the competence of abstract judicial review. However, there is a discussion about adopting one which is requested by the government or one third of total members of National Assembly.

II. Constitutional Review of Statutory Legislation

(1) Purpose

The Constitutional Court shall have the power to review the constitutionality of statutes upon requests from ordinary courts (Article 111 Section 1 of the Constitution). Adjudication on the constitutionality of statutes is an adjudication system which nullifies the statute that has been found unconstitutional by the Constitutional Court. It is a core component of constitutional adjudication, which secures checks-and-balances mechanism against the legislative branch for the purposes of protecting the Constitution.

(2) Causes for request

The ordinary courts may make a request for an authoritative determination by the Constitutional Court, ex officio or by decision upon a motion by the party, when in a pending case there is a reasonable doubt that the contents of a statute might be unconstitutional. When an ordinary court requests to the Constitutional Court adjudication on the constitutionality of statute, the proceedings of the court shall be suspended while the Constitutional Court makes a decision. In this sense, the Korean Constitution adopts a system of "concrete review of statutes." The subject of adjudication on constitutionality includes formal statutes legislated by the National Assembly, as well as emergency presidential order, treaties and universally accepted international laws.

(3) Decision of constitutionality and its effect

The Constitutional Court may decide that a statute is con-

stitutional or unconstitutional, and that a statute is nonconforming to the Constitution, limitedly unconstitutional or limitedly constitutiona as modified decisions on unconstitutionality.

Any statute or provision thereof decided as unconstitutional shall lose its effect from the day on which the decision
is made: Provided, that the statutes or provisions thereof relating to criminal penalties shall lose their effect retroactively. In cases referred to in the proviso, a retrial may be
allowed with respect to a conviction based on the statutes or
provisions thereof decided unconstitutional (Article 47 Section 2
and 3 of the Constitutional Court Act).

Any decision that statutes are unconstitutional shall bind
the ordinary courts, other state agencies and local governments (Article 47 Section 1 of the Constitutional Court Act).

(4) Cases

① *Motion Picture Rating Case* (13-2 KCCR 134, 2000Hun-Ka9,
August 30, 2001)

The Court ruled that the Korean Media Rating Board's
withholding the rating of a film amounts to censorship prohibited by the Constitution and, therefore violates the
Constitution.

② *Case on the House Head System* (17-1 KCCR 1, 2001Hun-Ka9, etc., February 3, 2005)

The Court held that Article 778 of the Civil Act ("A person who has succeed to the household lineage or has set up a branch household or who has established a new household or has restored a household for any other reason shall become the head of a household.") not only goes against the human dignity as a status of house-head is designated by law regardless of the intention or self determina tion of the people concerned, but also discriminates men and women in achieving the status as a house-head.

Also, regarding the latter part of the main text of Article 781 Section 1 ("a child shall be entered into his or her father's household") and the main text of Article 826 Section 3 ("the wife shall be registered to her husband's household.") of the Civil Act, the Court stated that the provisions violate the human dignity as they one-sidedly form marital relations and relations with children and runs afoul of the Constitution by discriminating men and women without justifiable grounds. However, should the Court render a decision of unconstitutionality and thereby the provisions at issue lose their effects immediately, a legal vacuum would occur. In order to prevent such a problem, the Court pronounced a decision of incompatibility with the Constitution to temporarily enforce the provisions at issues until revised.

③ *Comprehensive Real Estate Tax Case* (20−2(B) KCCR 1, 2006Hun−Ba112, 2007Hun−Ba71 · 88 · 94, 2008Hun−Ba3 · 62, 2008Hun−Ka12 (Consolidated), November 13, 2008)

The Court ruled that the comprehensive real estate tax system itself, including the imposition of comprehensive real estate taxes on the subjected lands, does not violate the Constitution, given the legitimacy in legislative purpose and the characteristics and burden of the comprehensive real es-tate tax system. The Court, however, decided that the provi-sion on the comprehensive real estate tax on house that stip-ulates aggregate taxation of households, imposing large amount of real estate taxation without considering the home-owner's circumstances as to possession of houses, excessively restricts the property right of homeowners beyond the neces-sary degree required to achieve the legislative purpose, thereby violating the rule of least restrictive means and bal-ance between legal interests. Also, the Court held that the provision does not conform to Article 36, Section 1 of the Constitution, which ensures people's marriage and family life and gender equality, because it discriminates those who have family such as married couples or those who compose a household with family members against the individually taxed singles, couples in common law marriage, homeowner who are not household members, and etc.

④ *Nighttime Outdoor Assembly Ban Case* (21-2(B) KCCR 427,
2008Hun-Ka25, September 24, 2009)

The Constitutional Court overturned the decision of constitutionality rendered in 1995 and in an opinion of 5(unconstitutional): 2(nonconforming): 2(constitutional), held that provision of the Assembly and Demonstration Act does not conform
to the Constitution. Article 10 of the Act principally bans
outdoor assembly before sunrise or after sunset[5] with an exception in the proviso that permits such outdoor assembly
when the head of competent police authority grants permission in certain cases. Regarding this, the Constitutional Court
stated that the provision sets time limit for outdoor assembly
but the proviso relieves the severity of the restriction, and
the "permission of the head of competent police authority" should not be regarded as the advance permit. Therefore,
regardless of the proviso, Article 10 of the Act does not violate the prohibition of advance permit by Article 21, Section 2
of the Constitution. But, the Court held that the provision
does not conform to the Constitution as it bans outdoor assembly in a wide range of timeframe, thereby violating the
principle of the prohibition of excessive restriction and failing

---

5) But, according to Article 15 of the Act, Article 10 of the Act is not applicable to assemblies relating to academic purpose, art, sports, religion, ritual, social gathering, entertainment, the four ceremonial occasions of coming of age, wedding, funeral and ancestral rites and national celebration.

to strike balance between legal interests.

⑤ *Death Penalty Case* (22-1(A) KCCR 36, 2008Hun-Ka23, February 25, 2010)

The Constitutional Court, in an opinion of 5 (constitutional):4 (unconstitutional), held constitutional the system of death penalty. First, the Court states that although the current Constitution neither directly recognizes nor prohibits the death penalty, it is required that the death penalty system should be regarded as being implicitly recognized by the Constitution through its interpretation in connection with other constitutional provisions. Also, the Court states that even though a person's life in an ideal sense is deemed to have an absolute value, the Constitution does not textually recognize absolute basic rights and moreover, it also pre-scribes that all of the people's freedom and rights may be re-stricted only when necessary for national security, the main-tenance of law and order or for public welfare under Article 37 Section 2. Therefore, the right to life may be subject to the general statutory reservation in accordance with Article 37 Section 2 of the Constitution in order to protect other lives at least with same value or public interests with same importance. Also, as long as the death penalty is sentenced only for the cruel and heinous crime, the death penalty sys-tem itself violates neither the constitutional principle of proportionality, satisfying all the elements of legitimacy of purpose, appropriateness of means, the least restrictive means and balance between legal interests, nor Article 10 of the Constitution which stipulates human dignity and value.

III. Constitutional Complaint

(1) Purpose

The system of constitutional complaint provides a way for individuals to seek relief in cases where their constitutional rights have been violated by exercise or nonexercise of governmental power (Article 111 Section 1 of the Constitution; Article 68 Section 1 of the Constitutional Court Act).

(2) Types and cause for request

To file a constitutional complaint, complainant's basic rights guaranteed under the Constitution should be directly and presently infringed by the exercise or non-exercise of the governmental power, except the judgment of the ordinary courts: Provided, that if any relief process is provided by other laws, no one may file a constitutional complaint without having exhausted all such processes (Article 68 Section 1 of the Constitutional Court Act).

Since the legislative power of the National Assembly is also a public power, a case where a statute that directly infringes upon the basic rights is legislated, or when the rights are infringed by the neglect of legislature by not enacting law which is mandated to be legislated, is also the subject for a constitutional complaint. So even if there is no concrete dispute being litigated at an ordinary court, an individual can file a constitutional complaint on the ground that a specific statute is infringing upon his constitutional rights. And if an individual's constitutional rights are being violated directly and currently by a statute, even before any specific act take places to implement it, the individual may file a constitutional complaint without having to go through prior relief procedures (2 KCCR 200, 89Hun-Ma220, June 25, 1990).

And even when the Supreme Court dismissed certain exercise of administration power on the ground that it did not fit for judicial review, the Constitutional Court has extended its jurisdiction to permit a constitutional complaint against it, if there was a need for providing relief.

Under the American type judicial review system, the ordinary courts were timid in making any request for a review, so that the review powers of the constitutional adjudicator could rarely be exercised. In order to deal with this problem, Article 68 Section 2 of the Constitutional Court Act provides that, when the ordinary court does not make a request, the parties to the suit may trigger the Constitutional Court's power of concrete review by filing a constitutional complaint against the statute. This procedure is said to have worked effectively, in which nearly 15% of these cases have been upheld at the Constitutional Court.

(3) Time limit for request

A constitutional complaint under Article 68 Section 1 shall be filed within 90 days after the existence of the cause is known, and within one year after the cause occurs: Provided, that a constitutional complaint to be filed after taking prior relief processes provided by other laws, shall be filed within 30 days after the notification of the final decision. If the basic rights are infringed by the occurrence of the cause to which the law is applicable, for the first time after the law is entered into force, a constitutional complaint shall be filed within 90 days after the existence of the cause is known, and within one year after the cause occurs (10−2 KCCR 101, 95Hun−Ba19, July 16, 1998). The adjudication on a constitutional complaint under Article 68 Section 2 shall be filed within 30 days after a request for adjudication on constitutionality of statute is dismissed.

(4) Prior review

When a constitutional complaint is filed, the Panel conducts a prior review. In case of any of the followings, the Panel shall dismiss a constitutional complaint with a decision of unanimity: the constitutional complaint is filed without having exhausted all the relief processes provided by other laws, or is directed against the judgment of the ordinary court (except for cases in which the court applied the laws that the Constitutional Court declared as unconstitutional); a constitutional complaint is filed after expiration of the time limit prescribed in Article 69; a constitutional complaint is filed without a counsel, or the court-appointed counsel; a constitutional complaint is inadmissible and the inadmissibility cannot be corrected.

(5) Content of the adjudication

There are three types of decisions in the final judgment of the Constitutional Court: dismissal, rejection and upholding a case. Dismissal is made when the request was made unlawfully; rejection is made when the request of adjudication does not have a rationale behind the request; and upholding is made when the request has reason.

According to Article 68 Section 1 of the Constitutional Court Act, if a request of adjudication was found to have rationale, the Constitutional Court must specify the exercise or non-exercise of governmental power that infringed basic rights. In this case, if the Constitutional Court finds that the cause of such infringement was from the laws or statutes, the Court may hold the statute unconstitutional. Provided, if the unconstitutionality of a clause makes the whole statute un-enforceable, the Court may announce the whole statute unconstitutional.

A concurrent vote of six or more Justices is required to decide a statute as unconstitutional or to uphold a constitutional complaint.

(6) Effect of decision of unconstitutionality

In case of Article 68 Section 1 of the Constitutional Court Act, the upholding decision shall bind the ordinary courts, other state agencies and local governments. In particular, when a decision of upholding was made against the non-exercise of governmental power, the respondent must take new action in accordance with the decision. Regarding Article 68 Section 2 of the Constitutional Court Act, the upholding decision shall bind the ordinary courts, other state agencies and local government. Any statute or provision thereof decided as unconstitutional shall lose its effect from the day on which the decision is made: Provided, that the statutes or provisions thereof relating to criminal penalties shall lose their effect retroactively.

When the constitutional complaint under Article 68 Section 2 of the Constitutional Court Act has been upheld, the party may claim for a retrial with respect to a final judgment having applied the statutes or provisions thereof decided as unconstitutional, whether criminal, civil or administrative. In addition, because the statutes or provisions relating to criminal litigation lose their effect retroactively, a person convicted based on a statute held as unconstitutional may claim a retrial, even if the case is not related to the constitutional complaint.

(7) Cases

1) Cases filed under Article 68 Section 1 of the Constitutional Court Act

① *Relocation of the Nation's Capital Case* (16-2(B) KCCR 1, 2004Hun-Ma554 · 566 (consolidated), October 21, 2004)

The Constitutional Court held unconstitutional the Special Act on the Construction of a New Administrative Capital, which mandated relocation of the capital and set forth procedure of the relocation, on the grounds that although not explicitly stated in the text of the Constitution, Seoul's status as the nation's capital has been legally effective for more than 600 years as an endearing legal custom and regarded as a part of the most fundamental and self-evident customary constitutional norms since the establishment of the Korean constitutional system. Moreover, the Court stated that the wide consensus among the people that the capital of Korea is Seoul has existed even before the drafting of our written constitution and has gained the status of unwritten constitution, and therefore, in order to repeal certain practices exercised on the basis of such a customary constitutional norm, it is required to follow the procedures required for revising the Constitution. In this regard, the Court held that as the 'Special Act on the Construction of a New Administrative Capital' was passed without going through the process of constitutional revision, which is an attempt to make changes to the Constitution through an ordinary statute, it infringes on the right to vote of the citizens in the constitutional revision.

② *Prohibition of Inmates from Exercising Case* (16-2(B) KCCR 548, 2002Hun-Ma478, December 16, 2004)

The Court held that an outdoor exercise is the minimum basic requirement for the maintenance of physical and mental health of the inmates who are imprisoned. Therefore, the absolute ban of exercise of the inmate subjected to the forfeiture of rights is beyond the necessary minimum degree, thus in violation of the human dignity and values under Article 10 of the Constitution and of the bodily freedom under Article 12 of the Constitution.

③ *Case related to Administrative Omission filed by Japanese Military Comport Women* (23 KCCG 602, 1285, 2006Hun-Ma788, August 30, 2011)

In an opinion of 6 (unconstitutional):3 (dismissal), the Constitutional Court confirmed unconstitutionality of an administrative omission by the respondent (Ministry of Foreign Affairs and Trade) that has not resolved the conflict between Korea and Japan in accordance with the procedures stipulated in Article 3 of the "Agreement on the Settlement of Problems concerning Property and the Right to Claim and on the Economic Cooperation between the Republic of Korea and Japan" (hereinafter, the Agreement), regarding the interpreta tion about whether the complainants' right to request com- pensation against Japan as Japanese Military comport women has lapsed by Article 2 Section 1 of the Agreement. Considering Article 10, Article 2 Section 2 and the Preamble of the Constitution and Article 3 of the Agreement, the re- spondent's duty to proceed to dispute resolution procedures according to Article 3 of the Agreement should be regarded as a duty to act derived from the Constitution, and such a duty is concretely stipulated in the Act. Also, given the seriousness of infringement on the complainants' property right and hu- man dignity and value and the urgent necessity and possi- bility of relief, it is hard to say that the respondent has dis- cretionary power not to execute the duty to act and the re- spondent has been faithfully conducting the aforementioned duty to act, or the duty to execute the dispute resolution procedures. Therefore, the respondent's omission infringes on the complai- nants' fundamental rights in violation of the Constitution.[6]

---

6) In this case, I dissented from the Court Opinion on the following

2) Cases filed under Article 68 Section 2 of the Constitutional Court Act

① *Taxation of Married Couple's Income from Assets Case* (14-2 KCCR 170, 2001Hun-Ba82, August 29, 2002)

The Court held that Article 61 of the Income Tax Act, which required the aggregation of assets incomes for married couples for purposes of calculating the income tax, discriminated against married couples, and therefore is unconstitutional.

② *Case on Prohibition of Transmitting False Communication with Intend to Harm the Public Interest* (22-2(B) KCCR 684, 2008Hun-Ba157, December 28, 2010)

The Constitutional Court, in an opinion of 7 (unconstitutional):2 (constitutional), held unconstitutional Article 47 Section 1 of the Electronic Telecommunication Act (hereinafter, the "Instant Provision") which criminalize those who transmit false commu-

---

grounds: on the basis of Article 10, Article 2 Section 2 and the Preamble of the Constitution and Article 3 of the Agreement, no concrete duty to proceed to dispute resolution procedures according to Article 3 of the Agreement for the complainants is imposed on the State. And, resolving the dispute on interpretation of the Agreement through a diplomatic channel or submitting it to arbitration process is neither a 'matter of duty' nor a 'concrete' duty to act. Also, the interpretation of the Court Opinion exceeds the scope of the Constitution, the statutory provisions and constitutional interpretation of legal principles. Therefore, the constitutional complaint should be dismissed as unjustified.

nication through electronic communication facility with the intent to harm the public interest. The part of "public interest" used in the Instant Provision is unclear and abstract, failing to elaborate a concrete standard to constitute the elements of a crime, and since the public interest is such an abstract concept, whether a certain expression violates the public interest drastically varies depending on individual's value system and ethical standard. Furthermore, in the current pluralistic and value subjective society, the public interest at issue is not monolithic when a certain act becomes an issue. Therefore, the Instant Provision runs afoul of the Constitution, violating the clarity required for guaranteeing the freedom of expression and the rule of clarity under the principle of *nulla poena sine lege.*[7]

---

7) In the dissenting opinion, I wrote that "public interest" in the Instant Provision means 'the interest of all or the majority of citizens who live in Korea and the interest of a state composed of those citizens' and "false communication" is about something of which truthfulness or falsity can be objectively verified, thereby meaning something of false contents and of false pretense, and therefore, the meanings of those words are not ambiguous. Meanwhile, the Instant Provision, intended to prevent disorder of the public order and disturbance of social ethics, is an appropriate means to achieve the legitimate legislative purpose. Also, given the facts that dissemination of false information through electric communication has severe ramification; is difficult to be voluntarily and autonomously corrected by communication users in a swift manner although it is clearly and indisputably false; and it takes high social expense for the lengthy discussion surrounding false information, it is required that, to a certain degree, a stricter restriction should be apply to the palpably false information than to the conventional act of expression. Therefore, I dissented from the majority opinion, finding that the Instant Provision does not violate the Constitution, not infringing on the freedom of express in violation of the rule against ex-

IV. Competence Disputes between State Agencies, between a State Agency and a Local Government or between Local Governments

(1) Purpose

When conflicts arise between state and local governments and agencies about the duties and authorities of each institution, it not only endangers the principle of checks and balances between public powers, but also risks paralyzing an important government function. This may pose a threat to the basic rights of citizens, which calls for a systemic coordinating mechanism.

The power to determine competence disputes between agencies of the central government, central and local governments, and between local governments has been given by the Constitution to the Constitutional Court as part of a function to safeguard the Constitution.

(2) Procedures

The request for adjudication may only be allowed when an action or omission by the defendant infringes or is in obvious danger of infringing upon the plaintiff's competence granted by the Constitution or laws (Article 61 Section 2 of the

---

cessive restriction.

Constitutional Court Act).

Article 62 Section 1 of the Constitutional Court Act allows only the National Assembly, the Executive, the ordinary courts and the National Election Commission to become parties to competence disputes.

But, the Court has recognized the need to expand the scope of parties eligible for filing competence disputes and granted standing to individual members of the National Assembly as well as to its Speaker (9-2 KCCR 154, 96Hun-Ra2, July 16, 1997).

(3) Decision and effect of decisions

The content of the decision concerns the interested parties' existence or scope of the competence of a state agency or local government. In the case as referred to in the previous sentence, the Constitutional Court may nullify an action of the defendant which was the cause of the competence dispute or may confirm the invalidity of the action, and when the Constitutional Court has rendered a decision upholding the request for adjudication against an omission, the respondent shall take a disposition in pursuance of the purport of decision. The decision on competence dispute by the Constitutional Court shall bind all state agencies and local governments. The decision to nullify an action of a state agency or a local government shall not alter the effect which

has already been given to the person whom the action is directed against, in order not to cause confusion.

(4) Cases

① *Competence Dispute between the City of Seoul and the Central
Government* (21-1(B) KCCR 418, 2006Hun-Ra6, May 28, 2009)

The main text of Article 158 of the former Local Autonomy
Act stipulates that "the Minister of Government Administration
and Home Affairs ⋯ may receive a report on the autonomous
affairs of a local government, or inspect its documents, books
or accounts." And the proviso of the same Article stipulates
that "in this case, the inspection shall be made only in respect
of matters which are in violation of Acts and subordinate
statutes." Regarding the proviso of Article 158 of the Act, the
Court held that the inspection power of a central administrative
agency on the autonomous affairs of a local government stipulated in the proviso of Article 158 of the Act should not be considered preemptive, general and comprehensive power but be
considered limited power in its subject matter and scope. The
Court states that the subject matter of inspection notified by
the Minister of Public Administration and Security actually covers almost all the autonomous affairs of Seoul City and
therefore, the notification failed to specifically designate the
matters to be inspected. And, when the Minister of Public
Administration and Security notified the plan for joint in-

spection to the city, it did not identify which specific statutory provision was violated and what kind of local government affairs had been conducted in violation of such provision. As such, the joint inspection conducted by the respondents including the Minister of Public Administration and Security failed to fulfill the requirement stipulated in the proviso of Article 158 of the former Local Autonomy Act, thereby violating the self governing authority of Seoul City endowed by the Constitution and the Local Autonomy Act.

② *Competence Dispute between the Members of the National Assembly and the Chairman of the National Assembly* (21–1(B) KCCR 14, 2009Hun–Ra8 · 9 · 10 (consolidated), October 29, 2009)

Regarding the declaration of passing the Bill of the proposed revisions to the Act on the Freedom of Newspapers, etc. and Guarantee of their Functions (the Newspaper Bill), the Constitutional Court denied the request to confirm nullity of declaring passage of the Newspaper Bill on the ground that although there was procedural illegality in question and discussion during the voting process and such illegality infringed on the National Assembly members' right to deliberate and vote on laws, the declaration of passage itself in this case is not void.

V. Dissolution of A Political Party

The Constitutional Court has jurisdiction over the dissolution of a political party. If the objectives or activities of a political party impinge upon the fundamental democratic order, the Executive, upon a deliberation of the State Council, may request a judgment by the Constitutional Court for the dissolution of that political party.

When a decision ordering dissolution of a political party is pronounced, the political party shall be dissolved.

VI. Election Disputes

The Korean Constitutional Court does not have jurisdiction over the election disputes. In cases of presidential elections and general elections for the National Assembly, the Supreme Court has the jurisdiction over election litigation

However, since national election is a democratic process which grants governmental power to its relevant authority under the Constitution, some suggest that the Constitutional Court having jurisdiction over such disputes is more desirable.

VII. Jurisdiction to Impeach High Public Officials

The Constitution provides that in case the President, heads of Executive Ministries, Justices of the Constitutional Court, judges, and other public officials designated by Act

have violated the Constitution or other Acts in the performance of official duties, the National Assembly may pass motions for their impeachment. And then the Constitutional
Court is authorized to adjudicate the charge brought by the
National Assembly.

Article 53 Section 1 of the Constitutional Court Act provides that when a request for impeachment is upheld, the
Constitutional Court shall pronounce a decision that the ac-
cused person be removed from the public office. To date, one
impeachment case was brought before the Court and the case
concerned the President of Korea.

In the Presidential Impeachment Case,[8] the National
Assembly passed a resolution to impeach then President Roh
Moo-hyun. However, the Constitutional Court rejected the request for impeachment. The case is noted as the landmark
case in which the Constitutional Court has resolved the divi-
sions and tensions in a constitutionally viable manner in a
relatively short period of time.

VIII. Advisory Opinions

The Court is not competent to deliver advisory opinions.

---

8) 16-1 KCCR 609, 2004Hun-Na1, May 14, 2004.

D. Conclusion

After having gone through the inactive and sometimes merely ornamental forms of constitutional adjudication systems such as the Constitutional Committee or the American type judicial review system in the past, the Republic of Korea finally established the Constitutional Court in 1988. And, different from its predecessors, the Constitutional Court has been known for its active and successful performance in adjudicating constitutional matters, as the last resort of upholding the Constitution and protecting fundamental rights of the citizens.

Despite its relatively short history of twenty three years, the Constitutional Court has succeeded in firmly establishing both the constitutional adjudication system in this country and itself as a constitutional institution. The Constitutional Court has become rooted in the minds of the people as the final defender of their basic rights, receiving broad support and positive evaluations from jurists, scholars and the people. For example, in polls by the newspaper, the Constitutional Court is voted every year as the most trusted governmental institution. Also, the Constitutional Court is now expending its scope to the outside of the country, exercising its leadership in establishing the "Association of Asian Constitutional Courts and Equivalent Institutions" which was created through Jakarta Declaration in 2010, and the writer was the Chairperson of the Preparatory Committee of the Association. The Inaugural Congress of the Association of Asian Constitutional Courts and Equivalent Institutions will be held in Seoul, in May 2012.

However, there are also some obstacles that should be hurdled by the Court, such as the issues related to its competence and jurisdiction, including lack of jurisdiction over the election disputes, lack of competence of constitutional review of statutory legislation *in abstracto* and no power to adjudicate the constitutional complaint against ordinary court's judgments, and the issues related to the process of nomination and appointment and term of Justices. In order to solve these problems, the Constitutional Court must examine in depth these issues and make necessary improvements.

Keeping all the citizens' support and faith in mind, the Constitutional Court must disseminate through constitutional adjudication the constitutional values grounded in human dignity and worth to the entire society so that the Constitution becomes the living norm that defines the basic conditions of the people's lives. Only then will the Constitutional Court be able to take root and acquire the people's trust and affection, and bear in abundance the beautiful constitutional fruits of human dignity and worth, liberty, and equality.

⟨table 1⟩

Case Statistics of the constitutional Court of Korea

As of September 30, 2010

Type		Total	Constitutionality of Law[1]	Impeachment	Dissolution of a Political Party	Competence Dispute	Constitutional Complaint — Sub total	§ 68 I	§ 68II
Filed		21,621	772	1		75	20,773	17,425	3,348
Settled		20,823	741	1		70	20,011	16,927	3,084
Decided by Full Bench	Unconstitutional[2]	445 ⟨311⟩[7]	221 ⟨202⟩				224 ⟨108⟩	68 ⟨55⟩	156 ⟨54⟩
	Unconformable to Constitution[3]	141 ⟨106⟩	54 ⟨40⟩				87 ⟨66⟩	31 ⟨33⟩	56 ⟨33⟩
	Unconstitutional, in certain context[4]	59 ⟨43⟩	15 ⟨9⟩				44 ⟨34⟩	17 ⟨13⟩	27 ⟨21⟩
	Constitutional, in certain context[5]	28 ⟨29⟩	7 ⟨14⟩				21 ⟨15⟩		21 ⟨15⟩
	Constitutional	1,569	269				1,300	4	1,296
	Annulled[6]	379				16	363	363	
	Rejected	6,124		1		17	6,106	6,106	
	Dismissed	11,391 ⟨9,856⟩	59			26	11,036 ⟨9,856⟩	9,844 ⟨8,598⟩	1,462 ⟨1,258⟩
	Miscellaneous	6					6	5	1
Withdrawn		681	116			11	554	489	65
Pending		798	31			5	762	498	264

1) This type of "Constitutionality of Law" case refers to the constitutionality of statutes cases brought by ordinary courts, i.e., any court other than the Constitutional Court.

2) "Unconstitutional": Used in Constitutionality of Laws cases.

3) "Unconformable to Constitution": This conclusion means the Court acknowledges a law's unconstitutionality but
merely requests the National Assembly to revise it by a certain period while having the law remain effective
until that time.

4) "Unconstitutional, in certain context": In cases challenging the constitutionality of a law, the Court prohibits
a particular way of interpretation of a law as unconstitutional, while having other interpretations remain
constitutional.

5) "Constitutional, in certain context": This means that a law is constitutional if it is interpreted according to the
designated way. This is the converse of "Unconstitutional, in certain context." Both are regarded as decisions
of "partially unconstitutional."

6) "Annulled": This conclusion is used when the Court accepts a Constitutional Complaint which does not include
a constitutionality of law issue.

7) The numbers in 〈 〉 represent the numbers of statutory provisions subject to the review.

Explanation of Abbreviations & Codes

- KCCR ： Korean Constitutional Court Report
- KCCG ： Korean Constitutional Court Gazette

- Case Codes
- Hun-Ka: constitutionality case referred by ordinary courts according to Article 41 of the Constitutional Court Act
- Hun-Ba: constitutionality case filed by individual complainant(s) in the form of constitutional complaint according to Article 68, Section 2 of the Constitutional Court Act
- Hun-Ma: constitutional complaint case filed by individual complainant(s) according to Article 68 Section 1 of the Constitutional Court Act
- Hun-Na: impeachment case submitted by the National Assembly against certain high-ranking public officials according to Article 48 of the Constitutional Court Act
- Hun-Ra: case involving dispute regarding the competence of governmental agencies filed according to Article 61 of the Constitutional Court Act
- Hun-Sa: various motions (such as motion for appointment of state-appointed counsel, motion for preliminary injunction, motion for recusal, etc.)

* For example, "96Hun-Ka2" means the constitutionality case referred by an ordinary court, the docket number of which is No. 2 in the year 1996.

<Table 2>

Case Statistics of the Constitutional Complaints Based on Subject Matter of Review(§68 I)

1988. 9. 1. – 2011. 12. 31.

Type	Filed	Total	Settled											Withdrawn	Pending
			Decided												
			Sub-total	Unconstitutional	Unconformable to Constitution	Unconstitutional, in certain context	Constitutional, in certain context	Annulled	Constitutional	Rejected	Dismissed	Miscellaneous			
Total	17,425	16,927	16,438	68	31	17		363	4	6,106	9,844	5		489	498
the Legislature — Sub total	2,610	2,469	2,379	56	28	14		4	3	493	1,781			90	141
Statutes	2,490	2,355	2,268	56	28	14		1	3	486	1,680			87	135
Omission	107	101	98					3		5	90			3	6
Decision, Process, etc.	13	13	13							2	11				1
the Executive — Sub total	13,005	12,711	12,343	12		3		359	1	5,585	6,374	5		368	294
Administrative Action, etc.	1,607	1,522	1,469	2				22	1	108	1,335	1		83	55
187	181	170	164					3			161			6	11
Non-prosecution Disposition	10,700	10,504	10,266					331		5,391	4,541	3		238	196
Omission — Administrative Legislation	468	432	400	8				3		73	315	1		32	36
Local Legislation	43	42	38	2						13	22			4	1
the Judiciary — Sub total	1,409	1,385	1,372	1						22	1,349			13	24
Judgment	1,271	1,250	1,249							16	1,233			1	21
Omission	30	30	29							1	28			1	
Judicial Action other than Judgment	80	78	74								74			4	2
Judicial Legislation	28	27	20	1						5	14			7	1
Miscellaneous	41	362	344							4	340			18	39

홍콩 시립대학 법률학원 명사특강 참석기

제 1. 머 리 말

2011년 7월 경 중국의 젊은 판사들이 헌법재판소를 방문하였다. 홍콩 시립대학 법률학원이 중국 본토의 젊은 판사들 중에서 영어시험을 통하여 선발하여 1년간 동 대학에서 연수를 시키고 마지막 1달간 미국 콜럼비아 대학에서 연수를 하고 귀국길에 1주일간 한국에 들러 헌법재판소, 대학 등을 견학하러 왔다는 것이었다. 이에 중국 유학을 마치고 귀국한 조혜수 헌법재판소 연구관이 저자가 지난 해에 중국 인민대학에서 강연했던 내용을 가지고 중국판사들에게 설명을 해주었다. 그런데 중국판사들의 인솔자였던 왕 구이궈오(王貴國) 홍콩 시립대학 법대학장이 저자의 방에 인사를 하러 왔다가 인민대학에서만 강연할 것이 아니라 홍콩 시립대학에도 와서 강연해 줄 수 없겠느냐고 말하며 단순히 인사치레로 말하는 것이 아니라 진지하게 강연을 부탁드린다고 하였다.

그런데 과연 왕 학장이 귀국 후에 정식으로 "명사특강" 초청장을 보내왔다. 홍콩 시립대학의 명사특강은 학생들이 수강하면 정식으로 학점을 주는 과정으로서, 갑자기 할 수는 없고 6개월 정도 기간을 가지고 준비를 해야 한다고 하여 강연 날짜를 2012년 3월 1일로 잡았다. 강연 내용은 그 동안 저자가 다른 강연에서 사용하던 원고에 최신 내용을 더하고 설명이 미진하다고 생각되었던 헌법소원심판에 대한 부분을 보완하여 영어로 준비하였다.

준비했던 강연원고는 [별지 1]로 말미에 첨부하였고 강연의 편의를 위해 강연요지를 파워포인트로 준비하기도 하였다.

제 2. 강연 전날의 환영 만찬

2012년 3월 1일이 강연 날짜로 잡혔기 때문에 하루 전인 2월 29일 처와 함께 홍콩에 도착하였다. 마침 한국 무역보험공사에 근무하던 저자의 장녀가 스페인계 국제상업은행인 산탄데르(Santander) 은행에 스카우트되어 산탄데르 은행 홍콩지점에서 근무하고 있었기 때문에 장녀가 공항에 마중을 나왔고, 홍콩 총영사관에서도 신재현 부총영사와 박성일 영사가 마중을 나와 여러 가지 도움을 주었다.

저녁에는 왕 학장이 홍콩 시립대학으로 저자의 가족을 초청하여

〈홍콩 시립대학 법률학원 학장실에서 왕 구이궈오 학장과 함께〉

대학 구내식당에서 만찬을 베풀어 주었다. 만찬에는 저자의 가족 외에도 마침 홍콩 시립대학에 특별 강의를 하기 위해 와 있던 미국 대학의 교수 두 사람도 동석하였다. 두 분 미국 교수는 왕 학장이 미국 콜럼비아 로스쿨에 유학할 때 만난 동창으로서 졸업 후에도 서로 긴밀한 관계를 가지고 있다고 소개하였다. 만찬 중에는 한국의 헌법재판제도와 로스쿨 유학 시절의 이야기 등 다양한 화제로 와인을 곁들여 즐거운 시간을 보낼 수 있었다.

제 3. 명사 특강(Eminent Lecture)

3월 1일 오후 4시부터 2시간 동안 강연 시간이 잡혔다. 강연회

장에 가기 전에 총영사와 샹글리아 호텔에서 오찬 일정이 있었다. 전
총영사는 국정원 차장의 경력을 가진 외교관이었는데 아주 적극적이
면서 친화력을 가진 분이었다. 왕 학장과도 평소에 친분이 있으며 가
끔 같이 술도 마시는 사이라고 하였다.

　　홍콩 시립대학의 강연장에는 신재현 부총영사와 박 영사도 동행
하였다. 강연을 시작하기 전에는 간단한 다과를 차려 놓고 참석자들
이 명찰을 달고 서로 환담하는 시간을 가질 수 있도록 자리를 마련
해 두었다. 강연장에는 60여 명이 참석하였는데 홍콩 시립대학에
연수 온 중국 대륙의 판사들과 홍콩의 개업변호사들이 대부분이었
고, 서양인들도 몇 사람 보였다. 강연회는 한국의 헌법재판제도의 현
황을 최신 주요 판례를 곁들여 소개하였는데 영어로 진행하였으며,

〈홍콩 시립대학 명사 특강을 하고 있는 저자. 옆에 앉아 있는 사람은
구민강 부학장〉

파워포인트 조작은 동행한 저자의 장녀가 하여 큰 도움이 되었다. 발표를 1 시간가량 한 후에 30분 정도 질문시간을 가졌는데 중국 판사들이 활발하게 질문을 하였고, 대표적인 질문으로는 재판도 대표적인 공권력 행사인데 왜 헌법소원의 대상에서 제외되었느냐, 헌법재판소와 대법원의 법률조항에 대한 해석이 상이할 경우에는 어떻게 해결하느냐 등이었다.

강연을 마친 후에는 한식당에 가서 신 부총영사 등과 같이 식사를 하였는데, 한국의 헌법재판관이 홍콩에 와서 한국의 헌법재판제도에 대하여 명사특강을 한 것은 국가의 명예를 드높인 대단한 일이라고 찬사를 하면서 총영사관 홈페이지에 그 내용을 올려야겠다고 하였다. 과연 저자의 홍콩 시립대 강연 소식이 인터넷에 올라 그 내용을 보고 신각수 일본 대사가 축하 메일을 보내오기도 하였다. 또한 홍콩 시립대학에서도 저자의 명사특강 소식을 대학 홈페이지에 올렸다고 그 내용을 메일로 보내왔다. 홍콩 시립대의 홈페이지에 실렸던 저자의 강연소식은 말미에 [별지 2]로 첨부하였다.

Development and Current Situation of the Constitutional Adjudication in Korea

Dong-Heub LEE*

* Justice, Constitutional Court of Korea.

A. Institutional Foundations of Constitutional Review

I. Current Constitutional Adjudication Model and Historical, Legal Reasons for Its Adoption

(1) Establishment of the Constitutional Court

In the Republic of Korea, the Constitutional Court was established as a key part of the constitutional system with the start of the Sixth Republic in 1988.

While amending the Constitution in 1987, political factions were divided on how to structure the constitutional adjudication system. Eventually, it was agreed to establish an independent Constitutional Court for adjudicating all constitutional matters including constitutionality review of statutes as well as the other so-called political issues.

(2) Forms of constitutional litigation or judicial review systems in the past

(i) the Constitutional Committee of the First Republic (1948–1960)

(ii) the Constitutional Court of the Second Republic (1960–1961)[1]

---

1) The Constitutional Court of the Second Republic, however, was not es-

(iii) the American-type judicial review system of the Third Republic (1961-1972)

(iv) the Constitutional Committee of the Fourth Republic (1972-1981) and the Fifth Republic (1981-1988)

II. Relations between the Constitutional Court and Ordinary Courts

Under the Constitution, the judicial function is divided into two institutions; ordinary courts comprising the Supreme Court and lower level courts and the Constitutional Court.

(1) Interpretation and application of statutes of ordinary courts

In interpreting and applying statutes, ordinary courts must seek, first, to interpret and apply the statute in a manner consistent with the Constitution and, second, in case the constitutionality of the statute is at issue, must suspend their proceedings and seek a determination by the Constitutional Court. Once the interpreted content of a statute is declared unconstitutional by the Constitutional Court, it loses its legal validity. Ordinary courts are bound by the Court's decision and barred from applying that content to the instant case.

(2) Exhaustion of all other relief

Constitutional complaints are meant to relieve anyone

---

tablished in practice due to the military coup d'état in 1961.

whose basic rights have suffered in the exercise or non-exercise of governmental power. Therefore, constitutional complaints may be in conflict with administrative litigation that deals with the rights of the individual in relation with the exercise or non-exercise of governmental power. For this matter, the Constitutional Court Act (Article 68, Section 1) forbids filing a constitutional complaint without having exhausted all other relief processes by the laws.

(3) Constitutional complaint against ordinary court's judgments

According to Article 68, Section 1 of the Constitutional Court Act, judgments made by ordinary courts cannot be challenged through constitutional complaints. Thus, the Constitutional Court's power to adjudicate constitutional complaint does not extend to ordinary court judgments in principle.

Yet, when an ordinary court applies a statute that was declared unconstitutional by the Constitutional Court, and violates a person's basic rights as a result, such judgment can become the subject matter of constitutional complaints.

(4) Constitutional complaint against executive decrees, regulations, or administrative action

When the constitutionality or legality of executive decrees, regulations, or administrative actions is at issue in a trial, it is the Supreme Court that has the power of final review (Article 107 Section 2 of the Constitution). However, an ordinary court's ruling that an administrative legislation is unconstitutional has the effect of merely precluding its application in the case at hand only in the form of concrete review, rather than striking down the entire administrative legislation. In contrast, the decision by the Constitutional Court universally invalidates the affected decree or regulation.

In case a decree or regulation directly violates a person's basic rights, whether this can be subjected to constitutional complaint is in question. The Supreme Court maintained that the Constitution gives ordinary courts the entire and exclusive power to review decrees and regulations. By contrast, the Constitutional Court has claimed that under Article 107 Section 2 of the Constitution, the Supreme Court has jurisdiction to adjudicate the constitutionality of rules and regulations, but such adjudication is possible only when the constitutionality of these rules and regulations is a condition precedent to the outcome of an actual lawsuit, therefore, constitutional complaints must be permitted against administrative legislations that directly violate a person's basic rights because there is no way to file a lawsuit in ordinary courts to challenge the validity of the administrative legislation itself (2 KCCR 365, 89Hun-Ma178, October 15, 1990).

Moreover, to resolve such uncertainty, some maintain that Article 107 Section 2 of the Constitution should be repealed in its entirety, and the power to make a final review of the constitutionality of administrative decrees, regulations or actions, should be conferred exclusively upon the Constitutional Court.[2]

(5) Tension over modified holdings

The Constitutional Court and ordinary courts also went through a fair amount of tension over the modified holdings — "limited unconstitutionality" and "limited constitutionality"(also known as "constitutional in certain context" and "unconstitutional in certain context," they are those of unconstitutionality without any deletion of text in the statute, being 'the qualitative unconstitutionality in part'). The Constitutional Court took the view that these are sub-species of the decision of unconstitutionality, whereas ordinary courts argued that they are merely a form of legal interpretation rather than a binding decision of unconstitutionality.

However, the current Constitutional Court Act does not clearly dictate whether the modified holding binds ordinary courts. Meanwhile, some lawmakers attempt to amend and

---

2) Regarding this issue, there had been a heated debate in the Advisory Commission for Constitutional Revision for the Speaker of the National Assembly. In the draft of the final report of the Advisory Committee, Article 107 Section 2 of the Constitution was abrogated, but in the final report, it was decided that the current system should be maintained.

specify the statute to clearly confer the binding effects to the modified holdings of the Constitutional Court.

B. Status and Composition of the Constitutional Court

I. The Constitutional Court as the Judicial Body

In reviewing the constitutionality of statutes, the only criterion for the Constitutional Court is the Constitution, not political preferences. The Constitutional Court has always maintained that it may not interpret the Constitution expansively so as to impose its own views on matters that were deliberately left open-ended by the Constitution to be determined by the political branches. Therefore the general view is that the Korean Constitutional Court is a judicial body rather than a political one.

II. Professional Qualifications for Members of the Constitutional Court

Nomination and appointment of Justices are limited to individuals qualified as attorney at law. Article 5 of the Constitutional Court Act lays down additional requirements. Justices shall be appointed among eligible persons with 40 years or more of age and who have been in any of the following positions for 15 years or more[3]: (1) Judge, Prosecutor, or Attorney; or (2) Person who has been engaged in legal affairs for a governmental agency or a public enterprise; or (3) Person who has been in a position higher than an assistant professor.

Some proposed to relax the qualifications to include law professors, etc. Such proposal was, however, not reflected in the current legislation.[4]

III. Term of Justices and Possibility of Reappointment

The term of office for Justices of the Constitutional Court is a renewable six years with a retirement age of sixty-five while it is seventy in case of the President.

Different from the similar provisions that stipulate the term of office of Justices of the Supreme Court, which has been revised from 65 years of age to 70 years of age, however, the provisions that stipulate the term of office of

---

3) The provisions were revised in July 18, 2011 to fortify the qualification for appointees, so that the Chief Justice and Justices of the Supreme Court shall be appointed from among those who are forty five years of age or over. This revision will take effect from January 1, 2013. The provisions that stipulate the qualification of the President and Justices of the Constitutional Court, however, have yet to be revised.

4) With regard to this issue, according to the final report of the Advisory Commission for Constitutional Revision for the Speaker of the National Assembly, not only a person who is qualified as a lawyer, but a person who is a law professor or has experience in managing national affairs becomes eligible to be a Justice of the Constitutional Court.

Justices of the Constitutional Court have yet to be revised.

In recent debates, many have argued for an extended, but non renewable term of at least nine years. Some also argue that the mandatory retirement age should be abolished, or at least be amended to remove the difference between that of the President and other Justices.

IV. Procedure for Nomination and Appointment of Constitutional Court Members and Guarantee of Their Independence

The Constitutional Court is comprised of nine Justices appointed by the President of the Republic, of whom three shall be elected by the National Assembly, three nominated by the Chief Justice of the Supreme Court and three selected by the President of the Republic. Meanwhile, the President of the Constitutional Court of Korea is appointed by the President of the Republic from among the Justices, with the consent of the National Assembly.

With respect to this appointment process, some say that the role of experts is not significant. Some have also noted that the nomination of three Justices by the Chief Justice of Supreme Court seems democratically inappropriate and may lead to the underestimation of the Constitutional Court. There are also arguments that all Justices should be selected by the National Assembly, while others say that the presidential appointment of Justices other than the Court's President also requires the consent of the National Assembly.

C. Jurisdiction of the Constitutional Court

Ⅰ. Constitutional Review of Statutory Legislation *in Abstracto*?

The Korean Constitutional Court does not have the competence of abstract judicial review. However, there is a discussion about adopting one which is requested by the government or one third of total members of National Assembly.

Ⅱ. Constitutional Review of Statutory Legislation

(1) Purpose

The Constitutional Court shall have the power to review the constitutionality of statutes upon requests from ordinary courts (Article 111 Section 1 of the Constitution). Adjudication on the constitutionality of statutes is an adjudication system which nullifies the statute that has been found unconstitutional by the Constitutional Court. It is a core component of constitutional adjudication, which secures checks-and-balances mechanism against the legislative branch for the purposes of protecting the Constitution.

(2) Causes for request

The ordinary courts may make a request for an authoritative determination by the Constitutional Court, ex officio
or by decision upon a motion by the party, when in a pending
case there is a reasonable doubt that the contents of a statute
might be unconstitutional. When an ordinary court requests to
the Constitutional Court adjudication on the constitutionality
of statute, the proceedings of the court shall be suspended
while the Constitutional Court makes a decision. In this
sense, the Korean Constitution adopts a system of "concrete
review of statutes." The subject of adjudication on constitutionality includes formal statutes legislated by the National
Assembly, as well as emergency presidential order, treaties
and universally accepted international laws.

(3) Decision of constitutionality and its effect

The Constitutional Court may decide that a statute is constitutional or unconstitutional, and that a statute is nonconforming to the Constitution, limitedly unconstitutional or limitedly constitutional as modified decisions on unconstitutionality.

Any statute or provision thereof decided as unconstitutional shall lose its effect from the day on which the decision is
made: Provided, that the statutes or provisions thereof relating

to criminal penalties shall lose their effect retroactively. In cases referred to in the proviso, a retrial may be allowed with respect to a conviction based on the statutes or provisions thereof decided unconstitutional (Article 47 Section 2 and 3 of the Constitutional Court Act).

Any decision that statutes are unconstitutional shall bind the ordinary courts, other state agencies and local govern-ments (Article 47 Section 1 of the Constitutional Court Act).

III. Constitutional Complaint

(1) Purpose

The system of constitutional complaint provides a way for individuals to seek relief in cases where their constitutional rights have been violated by exercise or nonexercise of gov-ernmental power (Article 111 Section 1 of the Constitution; Article 68 Section 1 of the Constitutional Court Act).

(2) Types and cause for request

To file a constitutional complaint, complainant's basic rights guaranteed under the Constitution should be directly and presently infringed by the exercise or non-exercise of the governmental power, except the judgment of the ordinary courts: Provided, that if any relief process is provided by other laws, no one may file a constitutional complaint without having exhausted all such processes (Article 68 Section 1 of the Constitutional Court Act).

Since the legislative power of the National Assembly is also a public power, a case where a statute that directly infringes upon the basic rights is legislated, or when the rights are infringed by the neglect of legislature by not enacting law which is mandated to be legislated, is also the subject for a constitutional complaint. So even if there is no concrete dispute being litigated at an ordinary court, an individual can file a constitutional complaint on the ground that a specific statute is infringing upon his constitutional rights. And if an individual's constitutional rights are being violated directly and currently by a statute, even before any specific act take places to implement it, the individual may file a constitutional complaint without having to go through prior relief procedures (2 KCCR 200, 89Hun-Ma220, June 25, 1990).

And even when the Supreme Court dismissed certain exercise of administration power on the ground that it did not fit for judicial review, the Constitutional Court has extended its jurisdiction to permit a constitutional complaint against it, if there was a need for providing relief.

Under the American type judicial review system, the ordinary courts were timid in making any request for a review, so that the review powers of the constitutional adjudicator could rarely be exercised. In order to deal with this problem, Article

68 Section 2 of the Constitutional Court Act provides that, when the ordinary court does not make a request, the parties to the suit may trigger the Constitutional Court's power of concrete review by filing a constitutional complaint against the statute. This procedure is said to have worked effectively, in which nearly 15% of these cases have been upheld at the Constitutional Court.

(3) Time limit for request

A constitutional complaint under Article 68 Section 1 shall be filed within 90 days after the existence of the cause is known, and within one year after the cause occurs: Provided, that a constitutional complaint to be filed after taking prior relief processes provided by other laws, shall be filed within 30 days after the notification of the final decision. If the basic rights are infringed by the occurrence of the cause to which the law is applicable, for the first time after the law is entered into force, a constitutional complaint shall be filed within 90 days after the existence of the cause is known, and within one year after the cause occurs (10-2 KCCR 101, 95Hun-Ba19, July 16, 1998). The adjudication on a constitutional complaint under Article 68 Section 2 shall be filed within 30 days after a request for adjudication on constitutionality of statute is dismissed.

(4) Prior review

When a constitutional complaint is filed, the Panel conducts a prior review. In case of any of the followings, the
Panel shall dismiss a constitutional complaint with a decision
of unanimity: the constitutional complaint is filed without
having exhausted all the relief processes provided by other
laws, or is directed against the judgment of the ordinary
court (except for cases in which the court applied the laws that the
Constitutional Court declared as unconstitutional); a constitutional
complaint is filed after expiration of the time limit prescribed
in Article 69; a constitutional complaint is filed without a
counsel, or the court-appointed counsel; a constitutional
complaint is inadmissible and the inadmissibility cannot be
corrected.

(5) Content of the adjudication

There are three types of decisions in the final judgment of
the Constitutional Court: dismissal, rejection and upholding a
case. Dismissal is made when the request was made unlawfully; rejection is made when the request of adjudication does
not have a rationale behind the request; and upholding is
made when the request has reason.

According to Article 68 Section 1 of the Constitutional

Court Act, if a request of adjudication was found to have rationale, the Constitutional Court must specify the exercise or non-exercise of governmental power that infringed basic rights. In this case, if the Constitutional Court finds that the cause of such infringement was from the laws or statutes, the Court may hold the statute unconstitutional. Provided, if the unconstitutionality of a clause makes the whole statute unenforceable, the Court may announce the whole statute unconstitutional.

A concurrent vote of six or more Justices is required to decide a statute as unconstitutional or to uphold a constitutional complaint.

(6) Effect of decision of unconstitutionality

In case of Article 68 Section 1 of the Constitutional Court Act, the upholding decision shall bind the ordinary courts, other state agencies and local governments. In particular, when a decision of upholding was made against the non-exercise of governmental power, the respondent must take new action in accordance with the decision. Regarding Article 68 Section 2 of the Constitutional Court Act, the upholding decision shall bind the ordinary courts, other state agencies and local government. Any statute or provision thereof decided as unconstitutional shall lose its effect from the day on which the decision is made: Provided, that the statutes or provisions thereof relating to criminal penalties shall lose their effect retroactively.

When the constitutional complaint under Article 68 Section 2 of the Constitutional Court Act has been upheld, the party may claim for a retrial with respect to a final judgment having applied the statutes or provisions thereof decided as unconstitutional, whether criminal, civil or administrative. In addition, because the statutes or provisions relating to criminal litigation lose their effect retroactively, a person convicted based on a statute held as unconstitutional may claim a retrial, even if the case is not related to the constitutional complaint.

IV. Competence Disputes between State Agencies, between a State Agency and a Local Government or between Local Governments

(1) Purpose

When conflicts arise between state and local governments and agencies about the duties and authorities of each institution, it not only endangers the principle of checks and balances between public powers, but also risks paralyzing an important government function. This may pose a threat to the basic rights of citizens, which calls for a systemic coordinating mechanism.

The power to determine competence disputes between agencies of the central government, central and local governments, and between local governments has been given by the Constitution to the Constitutional Court as part of a function to safeguard the Constitution.

(2) Procedures

The request for adjudication may only be allowed when an action or omission by the defendant infringes or is in obvious danger of infringing upon the plaintiff's competence granted by the Constitution or laws (Article 61 Section 2 of the Constitutional Court Act).

Article 62 Section 1 of the Constitutional Court Act allows only the National Assembly, the Executive, the ordinary courts and the National Election Commission to become parties to competence disputes.

But, the Court has recognized the need to expand the scope of parties eligible for filing competence disputes and granted standing to individual members of the National Assembly as well as to its Speaker (9-2 KCCR 154, 96Hun-Ra2, July 16, 1997).

(3) Decision and effect of decisions

The content of the decision concerns the interested parties' existence or scope of the competence of a state agency or local government. In the case as referred to in the previous sentence, the Constitutional Court may nullify an action of the defendant which was the cause of the competence dispute or may confirm the invalidity of the action, and when the Constitutional Court has rendered a decision upholding the request for adjudication against an omission, the respondent shall take a disposition in pursuance of the purport of decision. The decision on competence dispute by the Constitutional Court shall bind all state agencies and local governments. The decision to nullify an action of a state agency or a local government shall not alter the effect which has already been given to the person whom the action is directed against, in order not to cause confusion.

Competence Dispute between the City of Seoul and the Central Government (21-1(B) KCCR 418, 2006Hun-Ra6, May 28, 2009)

The main text of Article 158 of the former Local Autonomy Act stipulates that "the Minister of Government Administration and Home Affairs ⋯ may receive a report on the autonomous affairs of a local government, or inspect its documents, books or accounts." And the proviso of the same Article stipulates that "in this case, the inspection shall be made only in respect of matters which are in violation of Acts and subordinate statutes." Regarding the proviso of Article 158 of the Act, the Court held that the inspection power of a central administrative agency on the autonomous affairs of a local government stipulated in the proviso of Article 158 of the Act should not be considered preemptive, general and comprehensive power but be considered limited power in its subject matter and scope. The Court states that the subject matter of inspection notified by the Minister of Public Administration and Security actually covers almost all the autonomous affairs of Seoul City and therefore, the notification failed to specifically designate the matters to be inspected. And, when the Minister of Public Administration and Security notified the plan for joint inspection to the city, it did not identify which specific statutory provision was violated and what kind of local government affairs had been conducted in violation of such provision. As such, the joint inspection conducted by the respondents including the Minister of Public Administration and Security failed to fulfill the requirement stipulated in the proviso of Article 158 of the former Local Autonomy Act, thereby violating the self governing authority of Seoul City endowed by the Constitution and the Local Autonomy Act.

Competence Dispute between the Members of the National Assembly and the Chairman of the National Assembly (21-1(B) KCCR 14, 2009Hun-Ra8, 9, 10 (consolidated), October 29, 2009)

Regarding the declaration of passing the Bill of the proposed revisions to the Act on the Freedom of Newspapers, etc.

and Guarantee of their Functions (the Newspaper Bill), the Constitutional Court denied the request to confirm nullity of declaring passage of the Newspaper Bill on the ground that although there was procedural illegality in question and discussion during the voting process and such illegality infringed on the National Assembly members' right to deliberate and vote on laws, the declaration of passage itself in this case is not void.

V. Dissolution of A Political Party

The Constitutional Court has jurisdiction over the dissolution of a political party. If the objectives or activities of a political party impinge upon the fundamental democratic order, the Executive, upon a deliberation of the State Council, may request a judgment by the Constitutional Court for the dissolution of that political party.

When a decision ordering dissolution of a political party is pronounced, the political party shall be dissolved.

VI. Election Disputes

The Korean Constitutional Court does not have jurisdiction over the election disputes. In cases of presidential elections and general elections for the National Assembly, the Supreme Court has the jurisdiction over election litigation.

However, since national election is a democratic process

which grants governmental power to its relevant authority under the Constitution, some suggest that the Constitutional Court having jurisdiction over such disputes is more desirable.

VII. Jurisdiction to Impeach High Public Officials

The Constitution provides that in case the President, heads of Executive Ministries, Justices of the Constitutional Court, judges, and other public officials designated by Act have violated the Constitution or other Acts in the perform-ance of official duties, the National Assembly may pass mo-tions for their impeachment. And then the Constitutional Court is authorized to adjudicate the charge brought by the National Assembly.

Article 53 Section 1 of the Constitutional Court Act pro-vides that when a request for impeachment is upheld, the Constitutional Court shall pronounce a decision that the ac-cused person be removed from the public office. To date, one impeachment case was brought before the Court and the case concerned the President of Korea.

In the Presidential Impeachment Case,[5] the National Assembly passed a resolution to impeach then President Roh Moo-hyun. However, the Constitutional Court rejected the re-quest for impeachment. The case is noted as the landmark

---

5) 16-1 KCCR 609, 2004Hun-Na1, May 14, 2004.

case in which the Constitutional Court has resolved the divi-
sions and tensions in a constitutionally viable manner in a
relatively short period of time.

VIII. Advisory Opinions

The Court is not competent to deliver advisory opinions.

D. Binding Effect of Constitutional Decisions

I. The Binding Effect on the Legislature

(1) Holding v. Reasoning

That the holding of the Court in the decision of unconstitutionality has the binding effect cannot be questioned.
However, the theories and Constitutional Court's precedents
are not clear as to whether the reasoning of the Court also
has the binding effect, and whether the lawmakers are bound
to follow the decisions of unconstitutionality without any exception is still subject to debate.

This is an issue when the lawmakers enact a statute or a
provision that is identical or substantially similar to the statute or provision once held unconstitutional, that is, when so
called repetitive enactment has occurred.

When considering the decisions of the Constitutional

Court collectively, the basic attitude of the Constitutional Court would be interpreted into two possible ways which would have no particular difference in the way of problem solving: the first interpretation recognizes the binding effect on the National Assembly in a very limited way, admitting the exception when there are reasonable justifications of the repetition of legislation; and another interpretation does not recognize the binding effect on the National Assembly, however, it permits the legislature to enact the repetitive legislation only if there are reasonable justifications of the repetition of legislation, instead of allowing the unrestricted freedom of the repetition of legislation.

(2) Decision of nonconformity to the Constitution as a way of respecting the authority of the legislature

The Constitutional Court may provide a guideline to the legislature in the reasoning when rendering a decision of unconstitutionality, although such guideline would not directly bind legislators. Or, the Constitutional Court, as a way of respecting the authority of the legislature, may render a decision of nonconformity to the Constitution despite some part of the statute is unconstitutional, setting a time limit for the enactment of a new legislation. In that case, if the time for the enactment expires, the existing statute, which has not been amended within the time limit, would automatically lose its effect.

The Constitutional Court has rendered 140 decisions of nonconformity to the Constitution, while declaring 101 statutes as nonconformity to the Constitution, during the 23 years of the history of the Constitutional Court. However, 7 statutes have still remained unamended even after the time has expired (as of October 31, 2011).

II. The Binding Effect on the Ordinary Courts

(1) Effect of statutory provisions ruled as unconstitutional

In principle, the statute or the provision thereof ruled as unconstitutional shall lose its effect from the day on which the decision is made. However, if the statute or provision thereof relates to criminal penalties, it shall lose its effect retroactively. Nonetheless, the Constitutional Court has said that the retroactive effect exceptionally may be applied to the following cases: Firstly, when retroactive effect is necessary to safeguard the effectiveness of concrete judicial review such as; (i) to the case which brought an opportunity to adjudicate on the constitutionality whether by request from ordinary courts or by constitutional complaint, (ii) to the case under which the request for review of the statute is made to the ordinary courts or to the Constitutional Court before the ruling of the unconstitutionality on such statute, or (iii) to the ongoing case though the request for review has not been made, in which the statute or provision in question thereof applies. Secondly, to the case where concrete validity to relieve the party is imminent while legal certainty will not be decreased by applying the retroactive effect. On the other hand, the case where legal certainty would not be decreased and the vested rights formed by the old law would not be infringed, while denial of retroactive effect in such a case would be against the constitutional rights of equality and justice, the retroactive effect may also be applied. In addition, whether the case fits within these categories is the matter to be stated in the holding of the case as the Constitutional Court, having an authority of judicial review, holds the statute as unconstitutional. However, when it is not stated within the holding, whether the above exception should apply to the case, will be decided by ordinary courts in a reasonable way and in a way that fits the purpose, by reviewing history, nature, and purpose of the statute and by balancing all the interests in the case(92Hun-Ka10, May 13, 1993).

(2) Tension over the binding effect of modified holdings

The Constitutional Court has held that the decisions of unconstitutionality of a statute include the decision of holding a statute as limitedly constitutional, limitedly unconstitutional as well as nonconforming to the Constitution, and as such all of these decisions have binding effect in accordance with Article 47, section 1 of the Constitutional Court Act (9-2 KCCR 842, 96Hun-Ma172, 173 (consolidated), December 24, 1997).

Nevertheless, the Supreme Court maintains that the decision of limited constitutionality and unconstitutionality is merely an expression of the Constitutional Court's view on how the statutory provision should be interpreted, and since interpretation and application of statutes are the exclusive province of the ordinary courts, the Constitutional Court's preference on statutory interpretation does not have binding effect on ordinary courts (Sup. Ct. 95Jaeda14, April 27, 2001).

Example: Income Tax Act Case

When the Constitutional Court declared that some provisions of the Income Tax Act were limitedly unconstitutional (7-2 KCCR 616, 94Hun-Ba40, 95Hun-Ba13 (consolidated), November 30, 1995), the Supreme Court stated that such a decision is not binding on ordinary courts since it is merely an expression of the Constitutional Court's view on how the statutory provision in question should be interpreted and refused to follow the decision of the Constitutional Court.

In a constitutional complaint case requesting cancellation of the decision, however, the Constitutional Court held that Article 68 Section 1 of the Constitutional Court Act is unconstitutional to the extent the provision is interpreted to exclude from constitutional review those judgments that enforce law already ruled as unconstitutional by the Court, and cancelled the decision of the Supreme Court (9-2 KCCR 842, 96 Hun-Ma172, 173 (consolidated), December 24, 1997). The tax administrative decided not to enforce the taxation, and thus the decision of the Constitutional Court prevailed.

III. The Binding Effect on the Constitutional Court

The Constitutional Court may change its decision from its prior decisions having same or similar statutes at issue. In this respect, the binding effect of the decision does not reach the Constitutional Court itself. Nonetheless, the Court should respect prior decisions and their reasons if there is no change of circumstances or necessity to rule otherwise.

When the Court changes its previous views on the interpretation of the Constitution or statutes, six votes are also required (Article 23 of the Constitutional Court Act). To date, the Constitutional Court has overruled its cases 20 times.

IV. The Binding Effect on the Executive

The executive has showed a good record in following the decisions of the Constitutional Court.

And no specific issues have not been founded yet regarding binding effect on the executive.

E. Constitutional Review in Practice

I . Cases Concerning Civil Liberties

Extension of Detention Period for Criminal Suspects under the National Security Act Case (4 KCCR 194, 206, 210, 90Hun—Ma82, April 14, 1992)

The Court held that Article 19 of the National Security Act extending detention period up to 50 days in relation to the crimes prescribed in the Act allows unnecessarily long detention, and therefore, clearly violates the personal liberty, the principle of the presumption of innocence and the right to a speedy trial.

Prohibition of Inmates from Exercising Case (16—2(B) KCCR 548, 2002Hun—Ma478, December 16, 2004)

The Court held that an outdoor exercise is the minimum basic requirement for the maintenance of physical and mental health of the inmates who are imprisoned. Therefore, the absolute ban of exercise of the inmate subjected to the forfeiture of rights is beyond the necessary minimum degree, thus in violation of the human dignity and values under Article 10 of the Constitution and of the bodily freedom under Article 12 of the Constitution.

Motion Picture Rating Case (13-2 KCCR 134, 2000Hun-Ka9, August 30, 2001)

The Court ruled that the Korean Media Rating Board's withholding the rating of a film amounts to censorship prohibited by the Constitution and, therefore violates the Constitution.

Prior Censorship of Broadcast Advertisements Case (20-1(B) KCCR 397, 2005Hun-Ma506, June 26, 2008)

The Constitutional Court decided that subjecting broadcasting advertisements to prior review by the Korea Advertising Review Board, to which the Korea Broadcasting Commission has entrusted prior review, is prior censorship prohibited by the Constitution, and therefore violates the Constitution.

Military Secret Leakage Case (4 KCCR 64, 89Hun-Ka104, February 25, 1992)

The Court said that the military secrets should be limited to the necessary minimum in order to maximize the scope of the subject matter open to people's freedom of expression and right to know.

Ban on Assemblies near Foreign Diplomatic Missions Case (15-2(B) KCCR 41, 58-59, 2000Hun-Ba67 etc., October 30, 2003)

The Constitutional Court held that the part of "foreign diplomatic missions" in Article 11, Section 1 of the Assembly and Demonstration Act, which imposed a blanket ban without exception on outdoor assemblies within one hundred meters from the perimeters of foreign diplomatic missions stationed in Korea, violated the principle of the least restrictive means, exceeding the scope of necessary measures required to achieve the legislative purpose.

Nighttime Outdoor Assembly Ban Case (21-2(B) KCCR 427, 2008Hun-Ka25, September 24, 2009)

The Constitutional Court overturned the decision of constitutionality rendered in 1995 and in an opinion of 5(unconstitutional):2(nonconforming):2(constitutional), held that provision of the Assembly and Demonstration Act does not conform to the Constitution. Article 10 of the Act principally bans outdoor assembly before sunrise or after sunset[6] with an exception in the proviso that permits such outdoor assembly when the head of competent police authority grants permis-

---

6) But, according to Article 15 of the Act, Article 10 of the Act is not applicable to assemblies relating to academic purpose, art, sports, religion, ritual, social gathering, entertainment, the four ceremonial occasions of coming of age, wedding, funeral and ancestral rites and national celebration.

sion in certain cases. Regarding this, the Constitutional Court stated that the provision sets time limit for outdoor assembly but the proviso relieves the severity of the restriction, and the "permission of the head of competent police authority" should not be regarded as the advance permit. Therefore, re-gardless of the proviso, Article 10 of the Act does not violate the prohibition of advance permit by Article 21, Section 2 of the Constitution. But, the Court held that the provision does not conform to the Constitution as it bans outdoor assembly in a wide range of timeframe, thereby violating the principle of the prohibition of excessive restriction and failing to strike balance between legal interests.

Joint Penal Provision Case (21-2(A) KCCR 64, 2008Hun-Ka10, July 30, 2009)

The Constitutional Court held unconstitutional the provi-sion of the Juvenile Protection Act which punishes a juristic person when an employee or other service workers of a ju-ristic person commit an offense with respect to the business of such juristic person, without considering whether the ju-ristic person is jointly or contributorily liable for the offense committed by the employee or service workers. Regarding this, the Constitutional Court stated that although it is nec-essary to keep a tight rein on the prevalent wrongful activ-ities of juristic persons in this modern society by imposing

direct punishment on them, once the legislature opts to criminally punish a certain wrongful act, such punishment should
be imposed to the extent that it does not violate the constitutional principle of the rule of liability derived from the rule of
law and the principle of nulla poena sine lege.

Partial Pretrial Detention Credit Case (21-1(B) KCCR 784,
2007Hun-Ba25, June 25, 2009)

The Constitutional Court held unconstitutional the provision of Criminal Act that allows a judge's discretion of giving
partial pretrial detention credit, on the ground that the provision infringes on the freedom of body and violates the constitutional principle of the presumption of innocence and due
process. Also, the Court articulated that the "pretrial credit
provision" cannot be a proper measure to achieve the legislative intent of deterring appeals and preventing frivolous appeals, but it obstructs a criminal defendant's right to trial and
an appeal under the pretext of preventing frivolous appeals.

Adultery Case (20-2(A) KCCR 696, 2007Hun-Ka17, etc., October
30, 2008)

In this case, although the majority of five Justices presented
the opinion of unconstitutionality, the Constitutional Court decided that, in an opinion of 5(unconstitutional):4(constitutional),
Article 241 of the Criminal Act, which imposes imprisonment

as the only statutory sentence in the criminal punishment of adultery or fornication with a married person, does not contradict the Constitution since the quorum of six votes required for the holding of unconstitutionality is not met.

The Court stated that the provision at issue restricts adultery and fornication in order to protect marital relationship and preserve social order and acts as an appropriate means to serve the legitimate legislative purpose. Whether the restrictive regulation involving criminal punishment is excessive may be of issue, but this basically falls into the freedom of legislation. Given the Korean legal awareness that adultery harms social order and violates others' rights as well as the strong demand for preemptive prevention of adultery, the legislature's judgment to criminally punish adultery is not arbitrary. Also, the Court stated that the provision at issue cannot be regarded as infringing on the individual right to sexual autonomy and privacy in violation of the rule against excessive restriction, and although it is true that the provision imposes only imprisonment as statutory sentence, this does not necessarily mean that the punishment is overly excessive.

Meanwhile, regarding the dissenting opinion of five Justices, three Justices presented an opinion of unconstitutionality on the ground that the provision restricts the individual right to sexual autonomy and privacy in violation of the rule against excessive restriction and one Justice presented an opinion of incompatibility with the Constitution on the ground that the provision goes beyond the legitimate boundary of state power over criminal punishment under the rule of law. Also, one Justice presented an opinion of unconstitutionality on the ground that the provision violates the principle of proportionality between the criminal responsibility and the punishment.

Engagement Fraud (having sexual relationship/intercourse on false promise of marriage) Case (21-1(B) KCCR 520, 2008Hun-Ba25, 2009Hun-Ba191 (consolidated), November 26, 2009)

The Constitutional Court held unconstitutional a statutory provision that makes illegal for a man to have sexual relations with a woman by making a false marriage offer, by a vote of 6:3, overruling its 2002 ruling where seven justices upheld the constitutionality of the aforementioned provision. The Court said that having sexual relationship is located in the heart of people's privacy against which the state's interference should be as minimum as possible. But, the provision not only infringes on men's right to decide on sexual behavior, privacy and freedom but also denies women's right to make her own decision to have sex under the guise of protecting women. Also, as the subject of protection is limited to women who have no habit of acting obscenely, thus focusing sexual ideology based on patriarchy and moralism on women, it is in violation of equality in gender.

Death Penalty Case (22-1(A) KCCR 36, 2008Hun-Ka23, February 25, 2010)

The Constitutional Court, in an opinion of 5(constitutional):4(unconstitutional), held constitutional the system of death penalty. First, the Court states that although the current Constitution neither directly recognizes nor prohibits the death penalty, it is required that the death penalty system should be regarded as being implicitly recognized by the Constitution through its interpretation in connection with other constitutional provisions. Also, the Court states that even though a person's life in an ideal sense is deemed to have an absolute value, the Constitution does not textually recognize absolute basic rights and moreover, it also pre-scribes that all of the people's freedom and rights may be re-stricted only when necessary for national security, the main-tenance of law and order or for public welfare under Article 37 Section 2. Therefore, the right to life may be subject to the general statutory reservation in accordance with Article 37 Section 2 of the Constitution in order to protect other lives at least with same value or public interests with same importance. Also, as long as the death penalty is sentenced only for the cruel and heinous crime, the death penalty system itself violates neither the constitutional principle of proportionality, satisfying all the elements of legitimacy of purpose, appropriateness of means, the least restrictive means and balance between legal interests, nor Article 10 of the Constitution which stipulates human dignity and value.

Case on Real Name Verification for Election Campaign via Internet (22-1(A) KCCR 347, 2008Hun-Ma324, 2009Hun-Ba31 (Consolidated), February 25, 2010)

The Constitutional Court, in an opinion of 7(constitutional):2(unconstitutional), held constitutional Article 82-6 Section 1, Section 6 and Section 7 of the former Public Officers Election Act which stipulate that every internet press agency shall, if it allows anyone to post information expressing his support for or opposition to candidates or political parties on the bulletin board and chatting page of its web page, take technical measure to have his real name identified and shall delete such postings without the sign of "real name verification."

Case on Prohibition of Transmitting False Communication with Intend to Harm the Public Interest (22-2(B) KCCR 684, 2008Hun-Ba157, December 28, 2010)

The Constitutional Court, in an opinion of 7(unconstitutional):2(constitutional), held unconstitutional Article 47 Section 1 of the Electronic Telecommunication Act (hereinafter, the

"Instant Provision") which criminalize those who transmit false communication through electronic communication facility with the intent to harm the public interest. The part of "public interest" used in the Instant Provision is unclear and abstract, failing to elaborate a concrete standard to constitute the elements of a crime, and since the public interest is such an abstract concept, whether a certain expression violates the public interest drastically varies depending on individual's value system and ethical standard. Furthermore, in the current pluralistic and value subjective society, the public interest at issue is not monolithic when a certain act becomes an issue. Therefore, the Instant Provision runs afoul of the Constitution, violating the clarity required for guaranteeing the freedom of expression and the rule of clarity under the principle of nulla poena sine lege.[7]

---

7) In the dissenting opinion, I wrote that "public interest" in the Instant Provision means 'the interest of all or the majority of citizens who live in Korea and the interest of a state composed of those citizens' and "false communication" is about something of which truthfulness or falsity can be objectively verified, thereby meaning something of false contents and of false pretense, and therefore, the meanings of those words are not ambiguous. Meanwhile, the Instant Provision, intended to prevent disorder of the public order and disturbance of social ethics, is an appropriate means to achieve the legitimate legislative purpose. Also, given the facts that dissemination of false information through electric communication has severe ramification; is difficult to be voluntarily and autonomously corrected by communication users in a swift manner although it is clearly and indisputably false; and it takes high social expense for the lengthy discussion surrounding false information, it is required that, to a certain degree, a stricter restriction should be apply to the palpably false

Blockading Seoul Plaza Case (177 KCCG 974, 2009Hun-Ma406, June 30, 2011)

In an opinion of 7(unconstitutional):2(constitutional), the Constitutional Court decided that blockade of Seoul Plaza by encircling it with police buses according to the command of Commissioner General of the National Police Agency, thereby restricting the access to Seoul Plaza of complainants, is unconstitutional as it infringes general freedom of action. Despite a conceded possibility that illegal and violent assemblies or demonstrations may take place, a preventing measure should be taken to the minimal extent necessary to prevent riot, depending on the specific and individual circumstances. The restriction of any assembly and passage of ordinary citizens at Seoul Plaza would not be a necessary and minimal measure under the circumstances. Even if the necessity is recognized, the less restrictive means would be available as by establishing some passageways or permitting transit when the possibility of assembly is low or traffic is congested. Because the complete control over passage of citizens exceeds the minimal necessity, it violates the principle against excessive restriction as it infringes the basic rights.[8]

---

information than to the conventional act of expression. Therefore, I dissented from the majority opinion, finding that the Instant Provision does not violate the Constitution, not infringing on the freedom of express in violation of the rule against excessive restriction.

8) Assuming Article 3 of the Police Act and Article 2 of the Act on the

Case on Conscientious Objectors (23 KCCG 602, 1205, 2008Hun-Ka 22, August 30, 2011)

In an opinion of 7(constitutional):2(limited constitutionality), the Court rendered a decision of denial regarding the request for a constitutional review of Article 88 Section 1 of the Military Service Act (hereinafter, the Instant Provision), which stipulates punishment against those who have received a notice of enlistment in the active service or a notice of call (including a notice of enlistment through recruitment) and fail to enlist in the army or to comply with the call without any justifiable reason. The Court stated that although the Instant Provision limits the freedom of conscience of the conscientious objectors, legitimacy of the legislative purpose and appropriateness of means are recognized as the Instant Provision aims to protect national security and maintain equality in compulsory military service. Also, the Instant Provision does not violate the principle of least restrictive means although it provides for a criminal punishment without introducing the alternative military service system, as long as

---

Performance of Duties by Police Officers may be the legal ground, I am of the opinion that the restriction of passage does not violate the principle against excessive restriction as following reasons: the passage restriction is not excessive because it was temporary and the place, Seoul Plaza, was limited; the alternative methods suggested by the Court Opinion would not be practical under the dangers at that time; and the public interests to protect life, body, and property of Citizens from the illegal and riot demonstrations exceed the private interests of temporary passage.

it is hard to clearly conclude that allowing alternative service to be approved does not interfere with achievement of such public interests. The Instant Provision also strikes balance between legal interests. Therefore, the Instant Provision does not infringe on the freedom of conscience.

II. Cases Concerning Social Rights in Pursuit of Social Justice and Property Right

Right to Receive Social Protection

The legislature enjoys broad legislative-formative power in making laws regarding the fundamental social rights such as the right to receive social protection. The legislature can make a legislative decision within reasonable standard combining all necessary socio-economic considerations. The legislative decision is not in violation of the Constitution unless such a decision is absurdly arbitrary or falls far short of providing the minimum necessary protection for the fundamental social rights (13-2 KCCR 422, 433, 2000Hun-Ma342, September 27, 2001).

Taxation of Married Couple's Income from Assets Case (14-2 KCCR 170, 2001Hun-Ba82, August 29, 2002)

The Court held that Article 61 of the Income Tax Act, which required the aggregation of assets incomes for married couples for purposes of calculating the income tax, discriminated against married couples, and therefore is unconstitutional.

Comprehensive Real Estate Tax Case (20-2(B) KCCR 1, 2006Hun-Ba112, 2007Hun-Ba71 · 88 · 94, 2008Hun-Ba3 · 62, 2008 Hun-Ka12 (Consolidated), November 13, 2008)

The Court ruled that the comprehensive real estate tax system itself, including the imposition of comprehensive real estate taxes on the subjected lands, does not violate the Constitution, given the legitimacy in legislative purpose and the characteristics and burden of the comprehensive real estate tax system. The Court, however, decided that the provision on the comprehensive real estate tax on house that stipulates aggregate taxation of households, imposing large amount of real estate taxation without considering the homeowner's circumstances as to possession of houses, excessively restricts the property right of homeowners beyond the necessary degree required to achieve the legislative purpose, thereby violating the rule of least restrictive means and balance between legal interests. Also, the Court held that the provision does not conform to Article 36, Section 1 of the Constitution, which ensures people's marriage and family life and gender equality, because it discriminates those who have family such as married couples or those who compose a household with family members against the individually taxed singles, couples in common law marriage, homeowner who are not household members, and etc.

Reversion of Pro-Japanese Collaborators' Property to the Nation Coffers Case (174 KCCG 548, 2008Hn-Ba141, March 30, 2011)

By a 5(constitutional):2(limitedly unconstitutional in part)[9]: 2 (partially unconstitutional) vote, the Constitutional Court ruled that the later part of Article 2 Item 2 of the Act on Reversion of Pro-Japanese Collaborators' Property to the Nation Coffers presuming the property acquired by pro-Japanese collaborators from Russo-Japanese War(1904–1905) to the National Liberation Day(August 15, 1945) was rewards for pro-Japanese activities and the main text of Article 3 Section 1 of the above Act stipulating the pro-Japanese collaborators' property should be reverted to the Nation Coffers at the time of acquiring do not violate the

---

9) Because the modern property ownership of Korea has been developed with preparing the cadastral map (or land registration map) by Japan in 1912, a land that had been acquired regardless of pro-Japanese activities before cadastral survey (or land survey) would be presumed to be the land acquired during the above period. As a result, such land is presumed as the property of pro-Japanese collaborators according to the presumption provision. In order to reverse such presumption, a party should prove that the land had been actually acquired before 1904. However, there had been no public notification method with general effects with regard to the land ownership before drafting a cadastral map, and it is difficult to prove factual backgrounds more than a hundred years ago, implying the property which is not related to pro-Japanese activities may be reverted under the presumption provision. Therefore, I am of the opinion that it is unconstitutional to include "acquisition according to the cadastral survey" to the "acquisition" of the presumption provision.

Constitution. While the legislature has a broad discretion in allocating the burden of proof and the Nation would have difficulty in proving pro-Japanese collaborators' property which had been acquired long ago, a person who acquired the property would presumably know the acquisition statement, thereby the presumption provision with regard to pro-Japanese collaborators' property not infringing the right to trial or due process, beyond the legislative discretion. Even if the above provision is truly retroactive, it should be allowed when the retroactive provision is exceptionally justified. Considering of the nature of betrayals of the people implied by pro-Japanese collaborators' property and the contents of the Preamble of the Constitution, the retroactive reversion of pro-Japanese collaborators' property would be reasonably foreseeable. Besides, the property subject to the reversion is limited to four categories whose cases are significant and whose scopes are clear; and a party who is subject to the reversion of the pro-Japanese collaborators' property can defend against the reversion by proving the property had not been the reward for pro-Japanese activities. Therefore, the provision of reversion of pro-Japanese collaborators' property to the Nation Coffers does not violate Article 13 Section 2 of the Constitution and nor infringe the right to property.

III. Cases Concerning Other Fundamental Rights

Relocation of the Nation's Capital Case (16-2(B)) KCCR 1, 2004 Hun-Ma554, 566 (consolidated), October 21, 2004)

The Constitutional Court held unconstitutional the Special Act on the Construction of a New Administrative Capital, which mandated relocation of the capital and set forth procedure of the relocation, on the grounds that although not explicitly stated in the text of the Constitution, Seoul's status as the nation's capital has been legally effective for more than 600 years as an endearing legal custom and regarded as a part of the most fundamental and self-evident customary constitutional norms since the establishment of the Korean constitutional system. Moreover, the Court stated that the wide consensus among the people that the capital of Korea is Seoul has existed even before the drafting of our written constitution and has gained the status of unwritten constitution, and therefore, in order to repeal certain practices exercised on the basis of such a customary constitutional norm, it is required to follow the procedures required for revising the Constitution. In this regard, the Court held that as the 'Special Act on the Construction of a New Administrative Capital' was passed without going through the process of constitutional revision, which is an attempt to make changes to the Constitution through an ordinary statute, it infringes on the right to vote of the citizens in the constitutional revision.

Case on Prohibition of Appeal against Decision of Criminal Compensation (22-2(B) KCCR 180, 2008Hun-Ma514, October 28, 2010)

The Constitutional Court unanimously held that Article19 Section 1, which stipulates a single trial system for criminal compensation by prohibiting any appeal against the decision of criminal compensation, is unconstitutional. The provision of this case is not compatible with the nature of the judicial system that pursues the appropriateness and justice of trial since it overemphasizes legal stability, and therefore, infringes the right to criminal compensation and right to trial, in violation of the Constitution.

Case related to Administrative Omission filed by Japanese Military Comport Women (23 KCCG 602, 1285, 2006Hun-Ma788, August 30, 2011)

In an opinion of 6 (unconstitutional):3 (dismissal), the Constitutional Court confirmed unconstitutionality of an administrative omission by the respondent (Ministry of Foreign Affairs and Trade) that has not resolved the conflict between Korea and Japan in accordance with the procedures stipulated in Article 3 of the "Agreement on the Settlement of Problems concerning

Property and the Right to Claim and on the Economic Cooperation between the Republic of Korea and Japan" (hereinafter, the Agreement), regarding the interpretation about whether the complainants' right to request compensation against Japan as Japanese Military comport women has lapsed by Article 2 Section 1 of the Agreement. Considering Article 10, Article 2 Section 2 and the Preamble of the Constitution and Article 3 of the Agreement, the respondent's duty to proceed to dispute resolution procedures according to Article 3 of the Agreement should be regarded as a duty to act derived from the Constitution, and such a duty is concretely stipulated in the Act. Also, given the seriousness of infringement on the complainants' property right and human dignity and value and the urgent necessity and possibility of relief, it is hard to say that the respondent has discretionary power not to execute the duty to act and the respondent has been faithfully conducting the aforementioned duty to act, or the duty to execute the dispute resolution procedures. Therefore, the respondent's omission infringes on the complainants' fundamental rights in violation of the Constitution.[10]

---

10) In this case, I dissented from the Court Opinion on the following grounds: on the basis of Article 10, Article 2 Section 2 and the Preamble of the Constitution and Article 3 of the Agreement, no concrete duty to proceed to dispute resolution procedures according to Article 3 of the Agreement for the complainants is imposed on the State. And, resolving the dispute on interpretation of the Agreement through a diplomatic channel or submitting it to arbitration process is

IV. Cases Concerning Principle of Equality for Protecting Women or Particularly Vulnerable Minorities

Same-Surname-Same-Origin Marriage Ban Case (9-2 KCCR 1, 17-18, 95Hun-Ka6, etc., July 16, 1997)

The Court held that Article 809 of the Civil Act, which prohibits marriage between two persons who have the same family names and come from the same ancestral line, not only loses its social acceptance or rationality as a marriage ban, but also is in direct conflict with the constitutional ideas and provisions regarding "human dignity and worth and the right to pursue happiness" and the constitutional provisions regarding establishment and maintenance of marriage and family life on the basis of "individual dignity and gender equality." In addition, since the scope of prohibition is limited to the same surnames, in other words, those with the same patrilineal blood ties, it is gender discrimination without any rational ground, thereby violating the constitutional principle of equality.

---

neither a ˙matter of duty˙ nor a ˙concrete˙ duty to act. Also, the interpretation of the Court Opinion exceeds the scope of the Constitution, the statutory provisions and constitutional interpretation of legal principles. Therefore, the constitutional complaint should be dismissed as unjustified.

Nationality Act Case (12-2 KCCR 167, 97Hun-Ka12, August 31, 2000)

The former Korean Nationality Law adopted the patrilineal lineage system that coincided a child's nationality at birth to its father's nationality and discriminatingly granted the mother's nationality only supplementary importance. Such discrimination between the child of a Korean father and a foreigner mother and that between a Korean mother and a foreigner father disadvantage the children of Korean mothers and the mothers themselves, and thus the Court held that the law violates the principle of male-female equality under Article 11 Section 1 of the Constitution.

Case on the House Head System (17-1 KCCR 1, 2001Hun-Ka9, etc., February 3, 2005)

The Court held that Article 778 of the Civil Act ("A person who has succeed to the household lineage or has set up a branch household or who has established a new household or has restored a household for any other reason shall become the head of a household.") not only goes against the human dignity as a status of house-head is designated by law regardless of the intention or self determination of the people concerned, but also discriminates men and women in achieving the status as a house-head.

Also, regarding the latter part of the main text of Article

781 Section 1 ("a child shall be entered into his or her father's household") and the main text of Article 826 Section 3 ("the wife shall be registered to her husband's household.") of the Civil Act, the Court stated that the provisions violate the human dignity as they one-sidedly form marital relations and relations with children and runs afoul of the Constitution by discriminating men and women without justifiable grounds. However, should the Court render a decision of unconstitutionality and thereby the provisions at issue lose their effects immediately, a legal vacuum would occur. In order to prevent such a problem, the Court pronounced a decision of incompatibility with the Constitution to temporarily enforce the provisions at issues until revised.

Visually Handicapped Massagist Case (20-2(A) KCCR 1089, 2006Hun-Ma1098, 1116, 1117 (Consolidated), October 30, 2008)

The Court states that the challenged provision which authorizes the massagist license only to visually impaired people aims to enable rewarding lives and realization of the right to humane living conditions for the visually impaired, and satisfies the legitimacy of the legislative purpose. Therefore, the Court held that the provision is neither against the right of equal treatment nor the freedom of occupational choice, and is within the constitutionally permitted level of restriction of basic rights under Article 37 Section 2.

Restriction on Authority to Prosecute Offenders of Traffic Accidents Causing Serious Injury Case (21-1(A) KCCR 156, 2005Hun-Ma764, 2008Hun-Ma118 (consolidated), February 26, 2009)

The Constitutional Court decided that Article 4 Section 1 of the Act on Special Cases Concerning the Settlement of Traffic Accidents which prevents the prosecution of a driver who causes a traffic accident leading to serious injury by negligence in the conduct of business or gross negligence violates the victim's right to be heard at trial stipulated in the Constitution.

Also, regarding the discrimination between severely injured victims of traffic accident which does not fall under the proviso of Article 3 Section 2 and those who are seriously injured from the traffic accidents that fall under the proviso, or the victims who died from any traffic accidents, the Court held that such discrimination does not have reasonable ground because it prevents victims from exercising the right to be heard at trial due to the coincidence that the victims happened to be injured by accidents not falling under the proviso. Also the Court held that the discrimination between the victims who died from any traffic accident and the severely injured victims who are in a vegetative state or suffer incurable injury caused by accidents not falling under the proviso is also without proper ground because the illegality of the result of the serious injury cannot be less than the accident causing death. Therefore, the part of Article 4 Section 1 that prevents the prosecution of a driver who causes a traffic accident leading to serious injury by negligence in the conduct of business or gross negligence runs afoul of the Constitution, in violation of the equality right.

Case on Imposition of the Duty to Serve in the Military only on Men (22-2(B) KCCR 446, 2006Hun-Ma328, November 25, 2010)

The Constitutional Court, in an opinion of 6(denial):2(unconstitutional):1(dismissal), denied a constitutional complaint on Article 8 Section 1 of the Military Service Law(hereinafter the "Instant Provision") which stipulates that every man who is a national of the Republic of Korea shall be enlisted into the first militia service when he attains eighteen years of age.

Given the facts that men as a group are better equipped with physical condition suitable to combats than women as a group; that it is practically impossible to come up with objective comparison among individuals about suitability for combat based on physical capacity of every single person; and that even for a woman who has superior physical capacity, some of woman's physical peculiarities such as menstruation, pregnancy, or delivery could be burden to be used as military manpower, the Instant Provision's stipulation by which only men can be subject to mandatory military service cannot be considered as distinctively arbitrary treatment, and therefore does not violate the right to equality.

F. Conclusion

After having gone through the inactive and sometimes merely ornamental forms of constitutional adjudication systems such as the Constitutional Committee or the American type judicial review system in the past, the Republic of Korea finally established the Constitutional Court in 1988. And, different from its predecessors, the Constitutional Court has been known for its active and successful performance in adjudicating constitutional matters, as the last resort of upholding the Constitution and protecting fundamental rights of the citizens.

Despite its relatively short history of twenty three years, the Constitutional Court has succeeded in firmly establishing both the constitutional adjudication system in this country and itself as a constitutional institution. The Constitutional Court has become rooted in the minds of the people as the final defender of their basic rights, receiving broad support and positive evaluations from jurists, scholars and the people. For example, in polls by the newspaper, the Constitutional Court is voted every year as the most trusted governmental institution. Also, the Constitutional Court is now expending its scope to the outside of the country, exercising its leadership in establishing the "Association of Asian Constitutional Courts and Equivalent Institutions" which was created through Jakarta Declaration in 2010, and the writer was the Chairperson of the Preparatory Committee of the Association. The Inaugural Congress of the Association of Asian Constitutional Courts and Equivalent Institutions will be held in Seoul, in May 2012.

However, there are also some obstacles that should be hurdled by the Court, such as the issues related to its competence and jurisdiction, including lack of jurisdiction over the election disputes, lack of competence of constitutional review of statutory legislation in abstracto and no power to adjudicate the constitutional complaint against ordinary court's judgments, and the issues related to the process of nomination and appointment and term of Justices. In order to solve these problems, the Constitutional Court must examine in depth these issues and make necessary improvements.

Keeping all the citizens' support and faith in mind, the Constitutional Court must disseminate through constitutional adjudication the constitutional values grounded in human dignity and worth to the entire society so that the Constitution becomes the living norm that defines the basic conditions of the people's lives. Only then will the Constitutional Court be able to take root and acquire the people's trust and affection, and bear in abundance the beautiful constitutional fruits of human dignity and worth, liberty, and equality.

⟨Table 1⟩
Case Statistics of the Constitutional Court of Korea

As of December 31, 2011

Type	Total	Constitutionality of Law[1]	Impeachment	Dissolution of a Political Party	Competence Dispute	Constitutional Complaint		
						Sub total	§ 68 I	§ 68 II
Filed	21,621	772	1		75	20,773	17,425	3,348
Settled	20,823	741	1		70	20,011	16,927	3,084
Decided by Full Bench — Unconstitutional[2]	445 ⟨311⟩[7]	221 ⟨202⟩				224 ⟨108⟩	68 ⟨55⟩	156 ⟨54⟩
Unconformable to Constitution[3]	141 ⟨106⟩	54 ⟨40⟩				87 ⟨66⟩	31 ⟨33⟩	56 ⟨33⟩
Unconstitutional, in certain context[4]	59 ⟨43⟩	15 ⟨9⟩				44 ⟨34⟩	17 ⟨13⟩	27 ⟨21⟩
Constitutional, in certain context[5]	28 ⟨29⟩	7 ⟨14⟩				21 ⟨15⟩		21 ⟨15⟩
Constitutional	1,569	269				1,300	4	1,296
Annulled[6]	379				16	363	363	
Rejected	6,124		1		17	6,106	6,106	
Dismissed	11,391 ⟨9,856⟩	59			26	11,036 ⟨9,856⟩	9,844 ⟨8,598⟩	1,462 ⟨1,258⟩
Miscellaneous	6					6	5	1
Withdrawn	681	116			11	554	489	65
Pending	798	31			5	762	498	264

1) This type of "Constitutionality of Law" case refers to the constitutionality of statutes cases brought by ordinary courts, i.e., any court other than the Constitutional Court.

2) "Unconstitutional": Used in Constitutionality of Laws cases.

3) "Unconformable to Constitution": This conclusion means the Court acknowledges a law's unconstitutionality but merely requests the National Assembly to revise it by a certain period while having the law remain effective until that time.

4) "Unconstitutional, in certain context": In cases challenging the constitutionality of a law, the Court prohibits a particular way of interpretation of a law as unconstitutional, while having other interpretations remain constitutional.

5) "Constitutional, in certain context": This means that a law is constitutional if it is interpreted according to the designated way. This is the converse of "Unconstitutional, in certain context." Both are regarded as decisions of "partially unconstitutional."

6) "Annulled": This conclusion is used when the Court accepts a Constitutional Complaint which does not include a constitutionality of law issue.

7) The numbers in $\langle \ \rangle$ represent the numbers of statutory provisions subject to the review.

Explanation of Abbreviations & Codes

- KCCR : Korean Constitutional Court Report
- KCCG : Korean Constitutional Court Gazette

- Case Codes
- Hun-Ka: constitutionality case referred by ordinary courts according to Article 41 of the Constitutional Court Act
- Hun-Ba: constitutionality case filed by individual complainant(s) in the form of constitutional complaint according to Article 68, Section 2 of the Constitutional Court Act
- Hun-Ma: constitutional complaint case filed by individual complainant(s) according to Article 68 Section 1 of the Constitutional Court Act
- Hun-Na: impeachment case submitted by the National Assembly against certain high-ranking public officials according to Article 48 of the Constitutional Court Act
- Hun-Ra: case involving dispute regarding the competence of governmental agencies filed according to Article 61 of the Constitutional Court Act
- Hun-Sa: various motions (such as motion for appointment of state-appointed counsel, motion for preliminary injunction, motion for recusal, etc.)

* For example, "96Hun-Ka2" means the constitutionality case referred by an ordinary court, the docket number of which is No. 2 in the year 1996.

⟨Table 2⟩
Case Statistics of the Constitutional Complaints Based on Subject Matter of Review(§68 I)

1988. 9. 1. – 2011. 12. 31.

	Type	Filed	Total	Settled											Pending
				Decided										Withdrawn	
				Sub-total	Unconstitutional	Unconformable to Constitution	Unconstitutional, in certain context	Constitutional, in certain context	Annulled	Constitutional	Rejected	Dismissed	Miscellaneous	Withdrawn	
	Total	17,425	16,927	16,438	68	31	17		363	4	6,106	9,844	5	489	498
the Legislature	Sub total	2,610	2,469	2,379	56	28	14		4	3	493	1,781		90	141
	Statutes	2,490	2,355	2,268	56	28	14		1	3	486	1,680		87	135
	Omission	107	101	98							5	90		3	6
	Decision, Process, etc.	13	13	13					3		2	11			1
the Executive	Sub total	13,005	12,711	12,343	10	3	3		359	1	5,588	6,374	5	368	294
	Administrative Action, etc.	1,607	1,522	1,469	2				22	1	108	1,335	1	83	55
	Omission	187	181	170					6		3	161		11	6
	Non-prosecution Disposition	10,700	10,504	10,266					331		5,391	4,541	3	238	196
	Administrative Legislation	468	432	400	8	3	3				73	315	1	32	36
	Local Legislation	43	42	38							13	22		4	1
the Judicature	Sub total	1,409	1,385	1,372	2						21	1,349		13	24
	Judgment	1,271	1,250	1,249	1						16	1,233		1	21
	Omission	30	30	29								28		1	
	Judicial Action other than Judgment	80	78	74								74		4	2
	Judicial Legislation	28	27	20	1						5	14		7	1
	Miscellaneous	41	362	344							4	340		18	39

[별지 2]

Justice from Korea Constitutional Court Speaks at Eminent Speaker Lecture Series

CityU Law School is privileged to invite Mr. Lee Dong Heub, Justice of Korea Constitutional Court, to give a public lecture entitled Development and Current Situation of the Constitutional Adjudication in Korea. Along with him, two honorable guests, Mr. Shin Chae-hyun, Vice Consul General and Mr. Park Sung-il, Consul, Consulate General of The Republic of Korea in Hong Kong, attended the lecture.

The lecture unfolded a complete picture of the history, current situation and prospects of the Korea Constitutional Court. After having gone through the inactive and sometimes merely ornamental forms of constitutional adjudication systems, the Republic of Korea finally established the Constitutional Court in 1988. And, different from its predecessors, the Constitutional Court has been known for its active and successful performance in adjudicating constitutional matters, as the last resort of upholding the Constitution and protecting fundamental rights of the citizens. Despite its relatively short history of twenty three

〈Mr. Lee Dong Heub〉

years, the Constitutional Court has succeeded in firmly establishing both the constitutional adjudication system in this country and itself as a constitutional institution. The Constitutional Court has become rooted in the minds of the people as the final defender of their basic rights, receiving broad support and positive evaluations from jurists, scholars and the people.

For better understanding of the Korean Constitutional Court, in this lecture, institutional foundations of constitutional review in Korea and status, composition and jurisdiction of the Korean Constitutional Court were briefly reviewed. Also, important cases in practice classified by the types of fundamental rights including civil, social and property rights and others were presented. The lecture also introduced the arguments over the necessary improvement to overcome some obstacles that the Korean Constitutional Court is facing, including issues related to its competence and jurisdiction and the process of nomination, appointment and term of office of Justices.

Mr. Lee Dong Heub has started to serve as Justice of Constitutional Court of Korea since 2006. Before that, he was assigned to various levels of courts in Korea. He was the Chief Presiding Judge of Suwon High Court from 2000 to 2001 and Chief Presiding Judge of Seoul High Court in 2005. He was also the Chairperson of Preparatory Committee for Association of Asian Constitutional Court.

In his remarks before the lecture, Mr Lee said that he is honored to make a speech in front of the lawyers and students in

Hong Kong. He hopes that the speech would help Hong Kong practitioners to obtain a better understanding of the responsibilities and functions of Korea Constitutional Court and deepen the exchanges between China and Korea.

The lecture has attracted over 60 attendees, among whom, 28 are the Chinese judges studying in the LLM stream at CityU Law School. The Chinese judges took strong interest in the lecture and had comprehensive discussions with Justice Lee after his lecture. Mr Gu Minkang, Associate Dean of CityU Law School described the lecture as insightful and inspiring.

제 11 장

폴란드 헌법재판소, 루마니아 헌법재판소 및 터어키 이스탄불 지방법원 방문기

제 1. 들어가는 말

재판관 임기 중 마지막 해외출장 일정을 잡아야했다. 여러 가지 방안을 궁리하다가 임한택 대사가 근무하고 있는 루마니아 헌법재판소와 동구권에서는 평판이 높은 폴란드 헌법재판소를 방문하고, 귀국길에 터어키 헌법재판소를 방문하는 것으로 일정을 잡았다. 그런데 터어키 헌재는 그 쪽에서 방문을 요청하였음에도 불구하고 우리 헌재

252 제11장 폴란드 헌법재판소, 루마니아 헌법재판소 및 터어키 이스탄불 지방법원 방문기

소장의 방문일정이 가까이 잡혀 있다는 이유로 앙카라에 있는 헌재는 방문하지는 못하고 이스탄불 지방법원을 방문하는 것으로 일정을 변경하였다.

폴란드 헌재를 방문하는 데는 오스트레일리아 시드니 대학의 헌법 교수인 Sadorsky 교수가 많은 도움을 주었다. Sadorsky 교수가 한국의 헌법재판에 관하여 알아보기 위해 저자의 사무실을 방문했을 때 저자가 루마니아 등 동구권 국가를 방문할 예정이라고 했더니 마침 폴란드 헌재소장이 자신의 친구라고 하면서 자신이 직접 소장에게 메일을 보내겠다고 했다. Sadorsky 교수도 폴란드 출신이고, 폴란드 헌재소장도 교수출신이어서 친구 사이라는 것이었다. 그래서 출발 전에 미리 폴란드 헌재소장에게 메일도 보내고, 한국의 헌법재판제도를 소개한 저자의 영문 논문을 메일로 보내 면담 시 충실한 토의가 가능하도록 준비하였다. 이번 해외출장에는 고일광 연구관이 수행하였다.

루마니아 헌재 방문에는 지난 번 제네바 UN 인권위원회 방문 시 도움을 주었던 임한택 대사가 루마니아 헌재 측과 긴밀히 연락하여 면담일정을 잘 잡아 주었고, 터어키 방문에는 터어키 헌재 측과 이스탄불 총영사관에서 우리 사무처와 연락하여 일정을 짜임새 있게 잡아 주었다.

제 2. 폴란드 헌법재판소 방문

2012년 4월 10일 오후 2시경 백영선 주폴란드대사 등과 같이 폴란드 헌재에 도착하였다. 안제이 제프란스키 헌재소장은 키가 190센티미터도 넘어 보이는 거구였는데 소장실과 붙어 있는 회의실에서 서로 인사를 나누자마자 폴란드와 한국의 헌법재판제도에 관하여 심

도있는 대화를 나누었다.

아래 내용은 제프란스키 폴란드 헌재소장과의 대화내용들과 폴란드 헌법재판제도를 고일광 연구관이 정리한 것이다.

1. 폴란드 헌법재판소

가. 연　　혁

○ 1982. 3. 26. 헌법 개정으로 헌법재판소 규정 신설
○ 1985. 4. 29. 헌법재판소법 제정으로 헌법재판소 출범
○ 사법부에 포함되지만, 대법원과는 독립된 최고 사법기관

나. 조직 및 구성

○ 헌법재판소장(President), 부소장(Vice-President) 포함한 15인의 재판관(Judge)으로 구성
○ 재판관은 모두 국회(하원, Sejm)에서 재적 과반수 출석과 출석 과반수의 찬성으로 선출
○ 헌법재판소장과 부소장은 재판관 전체회의(General Assembly of the Judges)에서 추천한 후보자 중에서 대통령이 임명
○ 재판관 임기는 9년 단임(중임 불가)
○ 법학교수가 재판관으로 임용되는 비율이 2/3 상당에 이름

2. 폴란드 헌법재판제도

가. 규범통제권한

○ 사전적 규범통제는, ① 대통령만이, ② 법률과 국제조약에 대하여, 위헌여부심판을 청구할 수 있음

○ 사후적 규범통제는, ① 국제조약·법률 및 법규명령의 헌법
  위반 여부, ② 법률·법규명령의 국제조약 위반 여부, ③ 법
  규명령의 법률 위반 여부(법규명령의 위법성은 헌법 위반에 이른
  다고 봄), 3가지 심판청구로 나뉨[1]
○ 추상적 규범통제는, ① 대통령, 국무총리, 상원의장, 하원의
  장 등의 헌법기관이 청구할 수 있는 경우, ② 사법위원회, 지
  방정부, 국립노동조합 등이 해당기관의 활동범위와 관련 있
  는 규범에 대해 청구할 수 있는 경우, 2가지 심판청구로 나뉨
○ 구체적 규범통제는, 구체적인 사건에서 재판에 적용되는 규
  범에 대하여 법원이 위헌심판제청 하는 형태로 이루어짐

나. 헌법소원심판

○ 법원이나 행정부의 결정에 의하여 헌법상 자유나 권리가 침
  해된 자가 헌법소원심판을 청구할 수 있음
○ 적법요건
  ⅰ) 위 결정은 최종적인 것이어야 하고, 필요한 구제수단을
    모두 거쳤어야 함
  ⅱ) 헌법상 자유나 권리가 침해된 경우이므로 청구원인은 헌
    법위반 여부이어야 함
  ⅲ) 최종 결정이 송달된 날로부터 3개월 내에 청구해야 함
  ⅳ) 변호사나 법률조력자에 의한 소송대리
  ⅴ) 자연인(국민 또는 외국인)뿐만 아니라 법인도 청구인 자격
    있음

---

1) 일반법원도 법규명령에 대해서는 헌법재판소에 위헌심판제청하거나 스스로 심
  리하여 헌법, 국제조약, 법률에 위반되면 법규명령을 적용하지 않을 수 있음.

○ 사전심사(적법요건 심사)는 재판관 1인에 의하여 이루어짐
○ 문제되는 결정 등의 효력을 연기시키거나 중지시키는 가처분 신청도 가능
○ 헌법재판소의 위헌결정은 모든 사람에 대해 효력이 있음

다. 권한쟁의심판

○ 국가기관간의 특정 사안에 대한 권한의 존부나 범위를 확인
○ 국가기관 상호간 권한쟁의만 가능하고, 국가기관과 지방기관 간의 권한쟁의는 불가능

라. 정당의 목적 또는 활동의 위헌여부심판

○ 정당의 목적이나 활동이 위헌임을 헌법재판소가 확인하면 해당 정당은 정당명부에서 삭제되고 해산됨

마. 대통령 궐위여부 확인심판

○ 대통령이 자신의 업무를 수행할 수 없음을 하원의장에게 통지할 수 없는 경우, 헌법재판소는 대통령에 의한 직무수행에 장애사유가 있는지 여부를 판단함

바. 심리 및 결정

○ 결정 정족수(다수결원칙)
　ⅰ) 전원재판부(9인 이상 출석) 결정사항 ― 권한쟁의심판, 대통령 궐위여부 확인, 정당의 목적·활동의 위헌여부심판, 법률 및 국제조약의 사전적 규범통제, 특별히 복잡하거나 예

산법률에 확보되지 않은 재정적 지출과 관련이 있는 사후
적 규범통제

ii) 5인재판부 결정사항 — 법률 및 국제조약의 헌법 위반 여부
또는 법률의 국제조약 위반 여부(추상적, 구체적 규범통제)

iii) 3인재판부 결정사항 — 기타 법규명령의 헌법, 국제조약,
법률 위반 여부(추상적, 구체적 규범통제)

iv) 헌법소원심판의 경우, 문제가 되는 규범의 순위에 따라 5
인재판부 또는 3인재판부가 담당하며, 특별히 복잡한 사
안에 대하여는 전원재판부가 담당함

○ 원칙적으로 위헌으로 선언된 규범은 위헌결정을 한 날 효력을
잃지만, 법률의 경우 18개월, 다른 규범은 12개월 이내의 날
짜로, 해당 규범이 효력을 상실하는 날짜를 지정할 수 있음

○ 한정위헌결정, 한정합헌결정 등의 형식도 가능

3. 폴란드 헌법재판소장과의 대담[2]

가. 대담일시 및 장소

○ 일 시 : 4. 10.(화) 14:30 ~ 15:30
○ 장 소 : 폴란드 헌법재판소 2층 재판관회의실
○ 배석자 : 안제이 제프란스키(폴란드 헌법재판소장)
        이동흡 재판관
        백영선 주폴란드대사
        고일광 헌법연구관
        김식 서기관(한-폴 통역)

---

2) 대담내용 중 일부는 "2. 폴란드 헌법재판제도"에 흡수시켰음.

나. 대담내용(○ : 이동흡 재판관, □ : 제프란스키 헌법재판소장)

○ 이번 폴란드 방문을 계기로 양국의 헌법재판제도에서 동일점
과 차이점에 관해서 생각해 보게 되었습니다. 재판관의 임기
문제, 특히 사전적 규범통제제도를 두고 있는 것이 특이하다
고 생각됩니다.

□ 체코(10년 중임)를 제외한 유럽의 나머지 나라들은 대부분 단
임으로 규정하고 있습니다. 폴란드는 9년 단임으로 되어 있
는데, 단임으로 규정한 이유는 헌법재판의 정치적 중립성을
좀더 담보하기 위한 노력으로 평가되고 있습니다.

예전에 인권법 학자 시절(2002년경) 태국에 간 적이 있는데,
태국의 헌재관계자가 그들의 목표가 대만, 한국의 헌법재판
수준으로 올라가는 것이라고 말한 적이 있습니다. 그걸 보
면, 연임을 허용하고 있는 한국의 제도 역시 훌륭한 것으로
평가할 수 있겠습니다. 특히 폴란드의 경우 단순과반수가 위
헌을 결정하기 때문에 좀 신중하지 못한 인상을 주기도 하는
데, 한국처럼 2/3라는 가중치를 주는 것도 의미있다고 보입
니다. 일장일단이 있다고 생각합니다.

○ 폴란드 헌법재판소의 영문 이름이 좀 특이합니다. 대부분은
'Constitutional Court'라고 하고 있습니다만⋯⋯.

□ 법원에 대하여 헌재가 독립적 지위에 있다는 점을 밝히기 위해
서 이름도 'Court'와 다르다는 의미에서 'Constitutional
Tribunal'이라고 지었습니다.

○ EU재판소와 폴란드 헌법재판소의 위상관계는 어떻습니까?

□ 법원의 경우 EU재판소와 폴란드 헌재 양쪽에 위헌여부 제청

이 가능하므로 EU재판소와 폴란드 헌재의 위치가 애매해지는 경우가 생기는데, 기본적으로 어느 일방이 우위에 있지 않는 상호협력관계에 있다고 보시면 됩니다. 최근 체코 헌재의 결정에 EU재판소가 이의를 제기한 적이 있으나, 체코 헌재는 이를 받아들이지 않아 논란이 되었는데, 다른 나라의 경우도 마찬가지 상황이 발생할 수 있습니다. 하지만 EU협정에 대한 해석은 EU재판소가 전권을 가집니다.

일응 1974년 독일 헌재판결(소위, Solangen[3] 판결)이 그 기준이 되고 있습니다. EU재판소는 EU협정에 대해서만 전권을 가지고, 각국의 고유권한을 침범하지 않는 범위 내에서 판결을 내린다면 존중되어야 한다. 즉, 각국의 독립성을 침해하면 인정하지 않을 수도 있다는 의미입니다.

○ 우리나라에서도 재판관의 임기 6년이 짧다는 논의는 있습니다. 만약 헌법이 개정된다면 폴란드와 같이 갈지도 모르겠습니다. 그리고 위헌정족수가 2/3로서 과반수보다 신중한 결론을 유도하고 있지만, 현재 한국 헌재 재판관들은 매우 적극적인 입장이어서 위헌 사례가 많은 편입니다.

○ 우리나라에서도 추상적 규범통제를 도입하자는 의견이 많습니다. 폴란드는 사전적 규범통제까지 하고 있는데, 이러한 사전적 규범통제와 사후적 규범통제의 비율은 어느 정도 됩니까?

□ 사전적 규범통제는 대통령과 일정 수 이상의 의원들이 제기할 수 있는데, 대통령이 의회다수당과 같은 편이면(코모로프스키 현 대통령, 2011년 2건) 건수가 적은 편이고, 의회다수당과 다른 편이면(레흐 카진스키 전 대통령, 2009년 10건) 건수가

---

3) "만일 ~ 하다면"의 뜻임.

많은 편입니다.

추상적 규범통제의 단점은, 상하원 의원 일정수가 서명하여 청구가 가능하기 때문에, 실제 위헌여부보다는 소수당에 의한 정치적인 악용의 가능성이 많다는 점입니다. 선거철이 되면 실제 운영상 어려움이 가중됩니다. 선거운동의 일환으로 사용하는 경우가 많기 때문입니다. 여당 역시 선거예산을 무리하게 증액 시도하는 사례가 많이 있어 헌재가 정치적으로 곤란해지는 경우가 많습니다.

○ 재판소원제도가 어떻게 실제 운용되고 있는지 궁금합니다. 그리고 우리는 3인의 소재판부를 구성해서 헌법소원의 적법요건을 판단하고 있습니다만, 폴란드에서는 1인의 재판관이 헌법소원의 적법요건에 대해서 판단하는 것으로 알고 있습니다.

□ 한국의 경우와 같이 폴란드에서도 재판에 대한 헌법소원은 배제되어 있습니다. 그리고 적법요건 심사는, 그 자체로 이유 없음이 명백한 경우, 기간을 도과한 청구 등을 조기에 정리하자는 의도에서 1인의 재판관이 하게 된 것입니다.

○ 민사, 형사를 막론하고 법률이 위헌으로 실효되는 날짜를 지정해 주는 제도가 있던데요. 우리의 경우 형사법률은 소급하여 무효가 되고, 이미 확정된 판결에 대해서는 일제히 재심이 가능하게 됩니다. 예를 들어 간통죄의 경우 재심문제가 상당히 어려운 문제로 작용하고 있습니다.

□ 1년에 62건 중 18건 정도가 추상적 규범통제입니다. 추상적 규범통제로 법률이 위헌으로 되면 새로운 법률을 제정하는 데 의회의 의견, EU의회 관계법률까지 자문을 거쳐야 하는 경우도 있으므로 18개월 이내에서(보통은 6월, 1년) 위헌실효

일을 주는 경우가 많습니다. 위헌규정을 그때까지 존속시켜
야 하니 긴장과 불만이 조성될 수도 있으나, 그럴 수밖에 없
는 정책적 이유가 있으니 좋은 면도 있습니다.

○ 우리와 달리 3인재판부와 5인재판부를 구성할 수 있는 것이
독특한 제도라고 생각합니다.

□ 3인재판부와 5인재판부의 관할과 기능은 책자에 소개되어 있
는 바와 같습니다. 작년에는 12건만 전원재판부에 의해 처리
되었고, 변론한 60~80건의 대부분은 5인재판부 사건이었습
니다.

다. 법정견학 및 사진촬영

대담이 끝난 뒤에는 제플란스키 소장이 직접 안내하여 법정을
둘러보고 여러 가지 대화를 나누었다. 특이한 것은 법정의 외벽이 유
리로 되어 있어 바깥에서 법정 내부를 볼 수 있게 되어 있는 것이었
다. 헌법재판의 투명성을 강조한 것으로서 독일의 헌법재판소와 같
은 이념을 나타낸 것으로 이해되었다.

법정의 재판관 테이블에 랩탑이나 컴퓨터 모니터를 설치하는 시
설이 되어 있긴 하나 현재 재판관들 중 3인은 컴맹이고 여자 재판관
도 4명 있다고 하였다. 현재 재판관 중에는 최연소로 38세에 재판관
이 된 분이 있고, 72세(의회추천의 경우 정년 70세를 넘겨서 봉직 가능)
로 재판관에 봉직하고 있는 분도 있다고 하며 헌재 재판관 구성은 다
양할수록 좋다고 생각한다고 하였다.

〈폴란드 헌법재판소 대법정에서 제프란스키 소장의 설명을 듣고 있는 장면. 앞에 서 있는 사람은 백영선 주 폴란드 대사〉

〈폴란드 헌법재판소 대법정 부속 평의실에서 제프란스키 소장과 함께. 벽이 투명한 유리로 되어 있는 것이 특이하다〉

〈폴란드 헌재소장실에서 제프란스키 소장과 함께〉

제 3. 루마니아 헌법재판소 방문

임한택 대사가 열심히 교섭을 하여 처음에는 루마니아 헌재소장과의 면담이 잡혀 있었으나 부활절 행사 때문에 소장은 다른 일정이 생겨 만나지 못하고 대신 재판관과 면담을 가졌다. 루마니아 헌재청사는 독재자 차우체스쿠가 북한의 인민궁전을 흉내내어 지었다는 소위 지상 최대의 건축물이라는 인민궁전의 일부를 사용하고 있었다. 면담장소도 큰 회의실에 거창하게 차려 놓았고, 루마니아 재판관은 영어를 한마디도 못하여 루마니아 헌재직원이 루마니아어와 영어 통역을 하고 저자는 영어로 피터 라자로위 재판관은 루마니아어로 대화를 진행하였다.

아래 내용은 루마니아 재판관과의 면담 내용과 루마니아의 헌법 제도를 고일광 연구관이 정리한 것이다.

1. 루마니아 헌법재판소

가. 연   혁

○ 1991. 12. 8. 신헌법 제 5 장 제140조~제145조에서 헌법재판 소 설치근거 마련

○ 1992. 헌법재판소법 제정, 1992. 6. 6. 헌법재판소 구성

나. 조직 및 구성

○ 헌법재판소장 포함한 9인의 재판관으로 구성

○ 재판관은 하원, 상원, 대통령이 각 3명씩 지명하되, 매 3년 마다 각 지명기관이 재판관 1명씩, 재판관 3명을 교체

○ 헌법재판소장은 재판관들 사이에 비밀투표를 통하여 3년 임기로 선출, 재선 가능

○ 재판관 임기는 9년 단임(중임 불가, 임기 중 해임 불가)

○ 법학 전공자로서 고도의 법률적 식견을 보유하고 18년 이상 법률에 관한 실무적 내지 학문적 활동을 하였던 자 중에서 임명

○ 직무수행 중 한 행위에 대하여 면책특권이 인정되고, 의회 운 영위원회 또는 대통령의 승인 없이는 기소되지 않으며, 헌법 재판관의 범죄는 대법원이 직접 관할

2. 루마니아 헌법재판제도

가. 사전적 규범통제

○ 대통령, 상원 또는 하원의장, 대법원, 50명 이상의 하원의원, 25명 이상의 상원의원의 요청에 따라 공포 전에 법률의 합헌 여부를 심사할 수 있음

○ 위헌으로 결정된 법률이더라도, 재심의에 회부되거나 따로 제안(주로 정부에 의해)된 후 상하 양원의 각 2/3 이상의 찬성으로 원안이 재통과되면, 위헌결정은 무시되고 원안이 법률로 공포됨

나. 사후적 규범통제

○ ① 당사자의 신청 또는 직권에 따라 '법원의 제청에 의하여', ② '법률 및 명령'에 대하여, 위헌성을 심사함

○ 다만, 사전적 규범통제에서 위헌으로 결정되었으나 의회에서 재통과시켜 공포한 법률과 헌법재판소의 결정으로 이미 위헌으로 결정된 법률 등은 제청할 수 없음

○ 양원 의장과 정부에 의견진술의 기회를 부여하고, 공개청문회를 거침

○ 위헌성이 전체에 미칠 경우에는 위헌범위를 확장하는 것이 가능하고, 위헌으로 결정되면 원칙적으로 장래효를 가지고, 법률 또는 명령에 대한 헌재의 위헌결정은 최종적ㆍ강제적임

다. 헌법개정안에 대한 규범통제

○ 헌법개정안의 발안은 ① 내각의 제안에 의한 대통령, ② 상하

원 각 1/3 이상, ③ 선거권을 가진 50만 이상의 국민(과반 이상의 도[4]에 거주하여야 하며, 각 도 혹은 부쿠레슈티 광역시 내에서 각 2만 이상의 서명이 있어야 함)에 의하여 행해질 수 있음(헌법 제146조 제1항, 제2항)

○ 직권으로 헌법개정발의안에 대한 합헌성을 판단함

라. 의회규칙에 대한 규범통제

○ 상원 또는 하원의장, 의회교섭단체, 50인 이상의 하원의원 또는 25인 이상의 상원의원의 요청에 의하여 의회규칙의 합헌성 여부를 판단함

마. 정당해산심판

○ 신청인은 법률 등에 대한 사전위헌심사의 신청인과 동일
○ 위헌으로 선언된 정당은 정당등록명부에서 삭제됨

바. 대통령선거관련재판 등

○ 대통령 선거에 관한 절차적 정당성에 관한 이의신청이 있을 경우 이를 확인하고 선거결과를 인준하는 결정
○ 선거무효시 재선거 날짜를 지정함

사. 대통령 탄핵소추안에 대한 의견제출

○ 상하 양원 재적의원 3분의 1 이상의 발의로 대통령탄핵소추 절차가 개시되면, 양원 합동회의에서 혐의사실 관련증거 사

---

4) 현재 루마니아는 41개 주와 1개의 자치시(부쿠레슈티)로 구성되어 있음.

본이 헌법재판소로 제출됨

○ 재판관전체회의에서 과반수의 결정으로[5] 의견서를 채택하여 의회에 제출함

아. 대통령 권한대행상황 존재확인

○ 대통령 유고상황 존재확인절차는 상하원의 각 의장 또는 임시대통령의 신청으로 개시

○ 양원 합동회의의장이 합동결의로 대통령 권한정지를 제안하면 이에 대한 자문적 의견을 헌법재판소가 제출함[6]

3. 루마니아 헌법재판관과의 대담

가. 대담일시 및 장소

○ 일   시 : 4. 12.(목) 16:00~17:30
○ 장   소 : 루마니아 헌법재판소 5층 재판관회의실
○ 배석자 : 피터 라자로위(루마니아 헌법재판관)
　　　　　 이동흡 재판관
　　　　　 고일광 헌법연구관
　　　　　 강민구 서기관
　　　　　 루마니아 통역관(루-영 통역)

나. 대담내용(○ : 이동흡 재판관, □ : 피터 라자로위 헌법재판관)

□ 우선 우리 헌법재판소장께서 한국의 헌법재판관 영접을 할

---

5) 재판관전체회의는 재적 2/3 이상의 출석, 과반수의 찬성으로 결정함.
6) 상하원 공동회의에서 상하의원 과반수 찬성에 의하여 권한정지될 수 있고, 이 경우 30일 이내에 대통령 해임을 위한 국민투표를 실시한다(헌법 제95조).

예정이셨는데, 이번 주가 Easter Break(부활절 연휴)기간이
라 제가 대신 재판관님을 영접하게 된 점 죄송하게 생각합니
다. 아무쪼록 오늘 이 자리를 통해서 양국 간에 교류와 협력
이 더욱 증진되기를 바랍니다.

○ 폴란드의 경우도 마찬가지입니다만, 루마니아 헌법재판관의
경우도 임기가 9년 단임으로 되어 있군요. 한국의 헌법재판
관은 임기가 6년이고, 연임은 가능하도록 되어 있으나 실제
연임된 사례는 거의 없어, 제 경우 이번 9월 퇴임을 앞두고
있습니다. 재판관 선정기준에 관해서도 좀 알고 싶습니다.

□ 9년의 임기로서, 임기 연장이나 재임은 불가하지만, 예외적
으로 질병이나 사망의 경우 재판관이 보궐임명 되는 경우는
있습니다. 이 때 잔여임기가 3년 이하이면 9년 임기로 재임
명되는 경우가 있는데, 제가 바로 그런 경우에 해당합니다.
보궐임명 되어 1년 10개월을 근무하였고 2010. 6. 재임명되
어 결국 10년 10개월을 근무하게 되겠죠.

재판관에 임명되기 위해서는 법학 전공자로서 고도의 법률적
식견을 보유하고 18년 이상 법률에 관한 실무적 내지 학문적
활동을 하여야 합니다. 이전에는 15년의 경력을 요구했었는
데, 법률이 개정되어 18년으로 상향되었습니다.

○ 헌법개정안의 위헌성을 심사할 수 있는 권한을 가지고 있던
데, 좀 자세히 설명해 주시죠.

□ 헌법상 헌법개정안에 담을 수 없는 사항들이 규정되어 있습니
다. 루마니아의 국체, 공화정체, 독립과 단일불가분, 공식언
어, 사법부의 독립, 복수정당제도와 관련된 사항 및 현재 보
장되어 있는 국민의 기본권에 관한 사항은 헌법개정안에 담을

수 없습니다(헌법 제148조). 특히 국민이 발의한 헌법개정안의 경우 직권으로 심사할 필요가 더욱 큽니다. 루마니아에 거주 하는 소수민족의 경우도 헌법의 지배를 받기 때문에 하나의 독립된 국가로 통합할 필요성이 있습니다. 하지만 이들 소수 인종의 언어, 교육, 문화, 생활방식은 존중해 줍니다.

○ 법률에 대한 위헌결정이 장래효를 가진다고 알고 있는데, 그 렇다면 형벌규정 역시 장래효를 가지게 되는 겁니까? 한국에 서는 형벌규정의 경우 위헌결정은 소급효를 가집니다.

□ 2010년 전에는 당해 사건에서만 소급효를 가졌습니다(당해 사 건의 재판은 정지되었음). 2010년 법이 개정되어 재심이 보장 되었는데, 민사법(civil law)의 경우는 소급효도 없고 재심도 허용되지 않습니다.

○ 헌법소원제도를 도입하는 것이 헌법재판의 활성화를 위해 좋 다고 생각합니다만⋯⋯.

□ 법률에 대하여 위헌심판이 청구될 때 당사자를 위하여 전문 변호인(advocate of the people)이 선임되는데 이 제도가 비슷 하지 않을까 싶습니다. 그 이외에는 시민이 직접 헌법재판소 에 헌법소원 기타 심판을 제기하는 형태는 없습니다. 직접 국민이 헌법소원을 하게 되면 관점에 따라 위헌, 합헌 결론 이 달라지는 경우가 생기지 않겠는지 의문이 드네요.

○ 한국에는 추상적 규범통제 논의가 있습니다만⋯⋯.

□ 작년까지 그와 같은 사건들이 10,000건 이상 쇄도했었는데, 위헌심판을 제기하면 당해 사건이 정지되도록 운영하니까 심 판사건수가 1/4로 줄어들었습니다.

○ 재판관들 사이에 전문영역이 존재합니까? 일정한 분야에 관한

사건을 전담하여 처리하는 전문재판관제도(expert Justice)같
은 것이 존재하는지요?

□ 사실상 존재할 뿐 법적으로는 없습니다. 저도 상법, 경제법,
노동법 전문가라 그와 관련된 사건을 많이 처리하기는 하지만,
분야의 차별 없이 사건을 맡는 것이 원칙입니다. 자기 전문분
야라도 나머지 재판관이 반대한다면 당연히 다수결(재판관 정
원 2/3 출석과 과반수의 찬성으로 결정)에 따를 것입니다.

○ 재판보조인력현황은 어떠합니까? 연구관제도는 있는지, 판사
나 검사로서 파견근무하는 경우는 있는지, 임기는 얼마인지
궁금합니다.

□ 보조연구관(assistant magistrate)이 22~23명 있는데, 모두 6
년 법조경력이 요구됩니다. 재판관의 전문성에 따라 임명되는
경우가 많습니다. 판사나 검사가 전직하는 경우도 있습니다.

○ 올해 업무량은 어떤 수준입니까?

□ 작년 4,000건이 접수되었고, 올해도 4월까지 1,600건이 접
수되었습니다만, 하반기에는 좀 한산해지는 편입니다.

〈루마니아 국회의사당건물(헌법재판소도 같은 건물에 소재)〉

〈재판관 회의실에서 라자로위 재판관과의 면담 장면〉

〈라자로위 재판관이 안내하는 루마니아 헌재 법정〉

제 4. 터어키 이스탄불 지방법원 방문

　　터어키 헌재에서는 저자가 앙카라에 있는 터어키 헌법재판소를 방문하지 못함에도 불구하고 사무처에서 많은 신경을 써 주었다. 우선 터어키 헌재 사무처에서 연락하여 이스탄불 조세법원에 근무하는 Tank 판사가 승합차까지 렌트하여 와서 관광 안내도 해주었을 뿐더러 이스탄불 지방법원을 방문할 때도 수행하여 통역까지 맡아 주었다. 이스탄불 총영사관에서는 배준호 영사가 나와 이스탄불 지방법원 방문에 수행하는 등 많은 도움을 주었다. 이스탄불 지방법원은 유럽 최대 규모를 자랑하는 법원으로서 2년 전에 신청사를 완공하였다는데 과연 그 규모가 세계 최대라 할만 했다.

이스탄불 지방법원의 장은 판사가 아니라 검사장이 맡고 있는 것이 특이하였고. 투란 촐라카드 법원장은 저자와의 대담 중에 한국 헌법재판소에 관하여 많은 질문들을 하였다. 법원장과의 면담 후에는 법정에 가서 방금 재판을 마친 판사들과 대화도 나누고 터어키 판사 법복을 입고 기념촬영을 하기도 하였다.

이하에서 터어키 헌법재판제도와 이스탄불 지방법원 법원장과의 면담 내용을 고일광 연구관이 정리하였다.

1. 터어키 헌법재판소

가. 조직 및 구성

○ 1961. 헌법 개정으로 헌법재판소 설립, 1982. 헌법 개정으로 헌법재판소 권한 일부 수정, 2010. 9. 12. 헌법 개정으로 헌법재판관의 수 및 선출절차 변경, 헌법소원제도 도입

○ 2010. 헌법 개정을 통해 헌법재판관이 11명에서 17명으로 증원되었고, 기존의 예비재판관 제도를 폐지하였음

○ 구헌법은 대통령이 재판관 11명과 4명의 예비재판관 모두를 임명하였는데, 신헌법은 의회가 3인을 임명하도록 보완하였음

○ 대통령이 임명하는 사람은, 각급법원 등에서 7인, 고등교육위원회가 추천하는 법학 · 경제학 · 정치학 교수 중 3인, 고위행정관료 · 변호사 · 판사 · 검사 · 5년 이상 경력 헌법연구관 중 4인을 임명하도록 함

○ 40세 이상에서 45세 이상으로, 법조경력(고위공무원경력) 등 15년 이상을 20년 이상으로 각 자격요건을 강화, 교수는 정교수 또는 부교수일 것을 명시

○ 소장 1인, 부소장 1인이던 것을 부소장 2인으로 늘림, 임기는
   모두 4년으로 재판관들의 절대다수 득표로 선출되고 재임 가능
○ 헌법재판관 임기는 12년 단임, 정년 65세

나. 헌법재판소의 권한

○ 추상적 규범통제
   - 법률, 법률의 효력을 갖는 명령, 국회의사규칙의 형식 및
     내용에 대한 위헌여부심판
   - 법률의 형식상 하자에 대한 위헌여부심판은 법안의결정족
     수의 충족여부에 대한 심판으로 한정
   - 헌법 개정의 형식상 하자에 대한 위헌여부심판(내용에 대한
     심사는 불가능하고 필요한 제안·표결·논의절차의 위헌여부만을
     심판)
   - 국제조약은 규범통제의 대상에서 제외됨
○ 구체적 규범통제
   - 법원은 재판의 전제가 되는 법률 및 법률의 효력을 갖는 명
     령이 위헌이라고 판단되거나 당사자의 위헌 주장이 상당하
     다고 판단하는 경우 위헌법령심판을 제청함
○ 헌법소원심판
   - 공권력으로 인하여 유럽인권협약 및 부속의정서에 명시된
     헌법상의 기본권을 침해받은 자가 직접 제기하며, 입법·
     행정규제 절차 및 헌법에 따라 헌법재판소의 사법심사에서
     제외되는 절차는 헌법소원의 대상이 아님
   - 재판관 17명으로 두 재판부(부소장이 재판장, 4명의 재판관으
     로 구성)를 설치하여 헌법소원을 담당하게 함

- 보충성 요건 명시

○ 정당해산심판 및 정당재정에 대한 감사

○ 헌법이나 국회의사규칙에 반하는 국회의원의 면책특권 박탈 및 제명결정에 관한 심판

2. 이스탄불 지방법원장과의 대담

가. 대담일시 및 장소

○ 일   시 : 4. 16.(월) 14:00~16:00

○ 장   소 : 이스탄불 지방법원장실

○ 배석자 : 투란 촐라카드(이스탄불 지방법원장)

  이동흡 재판관

  고일광 헌법연구관

  배준호 영사

  Tank 판사(터-영 통역)

나. 대담내용(○ : 이 동흡 재판관, □ : 투란 촐라카드 법원장)

○ 지방법원 청사의 규모가 대단하고 인상적입니다.

□ 예, 전체 18층 건물에, 승강기만 80대로 규모가 큰 편입니다. 승강기 중 48대는 에스컬레이터인데 한국기업인 현대가 건설한 것입니다. 국제회의를 비롯하여 사법기관간 회의도 주최할 수 있는 사법센터(judicial complex)라고 보시면 됩니다. 이 건물을 짓기 전에는 분야별로 법원이 산재해 있어서 불편했었는데 이 건물이 지어진 후로 좀 편해졌습니다.

○ 이 법원 신청사에 방문한 것을 영광으로 생각합니다. 저 역

시 헌법재판관으로 임명되기 전에는 서울 인근의 수원·경기 지역을 관할하는 수원지방법원에서 법원장으로 근무한 적이 있습니다. 이 청사에 근무하는 판사들 현황은 어떻습니까?

☐ 판사만 350명, 검사가 250명, 일반공무원 2,000명 이상에다가 law clerk도 함께 근무하고 있습니다. 민사법원(지적재산권부, 통상부 등 특별부 존재), 형사법원(중범 코트와 경범 코트), 소년법원이 함께 있습니다. 이스탄불 시내에 여러 개의 지원도 존재합니다. Tank 판사가 근무하고 있는 조세법원도 그 중 하나입니다.

○ 한국과 터어키의 교류관계는 특별합니다. 특히 이번 5월에 아시아헌법재판소연합이 서울에서 발족하게 되었는데 터어키 헌법재판소장께서 방문하실 예정으로 있습니다.

☐ 그렇습니다. 한국과 터어키는 한국전쟁으로 특별해진 관계이죠. 도로 중에도 코레아 거리가 있습니다. 형제나라로 터어키 국민들은 생각하고 있습니다.

한국 헌법재판소는 주로 어떤 종류의 사건을 처리하십니까?

○ 주로 법원의 제청에 의한 위헌법률심사와 헌법소원심판입니다. 터어키 역시 헌법소원제도를 2년 전에 도입하였는데, 한국에서는 공권력행사(그 중에는 법률도 포함됩니다)를 대상으로 하는 헌법소원이 활성화되어 있습니다.

☐ 재판관 구성이나 임기는 어떠합니까?

○ 대통령이 3인, 국회가 3인, 대법원장이 3인을 지명합니다. 모두 변호사 자격이 있는 자들이어야 하며, 임기는 6년으로 연임이 가능합니다. 하지만 연임가능성은 희박하고, 역사상 2명만 연임된 적이 있습니다. 저 역시 올해 9월에 임기가 끝

날 예정입니다. 터어키는 헌법재판관의 임기가 12년 단임으로 알고 있는데, 우리나라에서도 현재 임기관련 개정논의가 있습니다.

□ 임기가 끝나면 보통 뭘 하시게 되나요?

○ 보통 변호사로 법률실무에 종사하거나 로스쿨 교수로 가기도 합니다.

□ 국회에서 재판관을 선출하는 선출기준은 무엇입니까?

○ 옛날에는 주로 변호사들 중에 선출했으나, 현재는 판사들 경력을 존중해서 판사들 중에 선출하는 경향이 있습니다. 제 경우도 임명 당시는 야당이었으나 현재는 여당인 정당에 의해 선출된 케이스입니다.

□ 터어키의 경우는 판사시험을 치른 후 2년의 견습기간을 마치면 후에 판사나 검사로 임명되게 됩니다. 판검사위원회(The High Council of Judges and Public Prosecutors)가 있어서 거기에서 검찰총장, 부총장 등을 임명합니다. 판검사위원회는 대통령이 임명하는 22명의 상임위원과 12명의 후보위원으로 구성되는데, 법원·검찰청의 설치 및 폐지, 판·검사의 인사를 담당하는 최고의 독립기구입니다.

〈이스탄불 법원장실에서 촐라카드 법원장과 함께〉

〈이스탄불 지방법원 형사법정에서 터어키 판사의 법복을 입고〉

2012 타이완 사법 민주화 국제회의 참석기

제 1. 머 리 말

2012년 7월 하순경 타이완 사법연수소에서 E-mail이 왔다. 11월 중순경에 개최 예정인 "국민참여재판제도의 비교"를 주제로 한 국제회의에 초청하고 싶다는 내용이었다. 한국은 2008년 1월 1일부터 국민참여재판을 시범실시하고 있고, 일본은 2009년 5월 21일부터 형사재판에 있어 재판원 재판제도를 시행하고 있다. 그런데 타이완에서도 그 동안 오랜 기간 국민참여재판의 도입에 관하여 논의를 하고 있었는데 드디어 2012년 6월 '人民觀審施行條例'를 완성하여 立法院에서 심의 중이라는 것이다. 일본에서는 와세다대학 로스쿨의 형사소송법 교수를 초청하고, 한국에서는 저자를 초청하여 국민참여재판에 관한 한국의 경험을 전해달라는 요청이었다. 국민참여재판제도는 저자가 헌법재판소 재판관으로 취임한 이후에 도입된 제도로서 내가 실무경험을 가진 것도 아니어서 발표를 잘할 수 있을까 망설여지기도 하였으나 그러한 사정을 다 알고서도 특별히 저자를 타이완 사법연수소에서 초청한 것이므로 초청에 응하기로 하였다. 국민참여재판제도는 저자가 수원지방법원장으로 재직 시 실무위원으로 참여하였던 사법개혁추진위원회의 개혁사항 중 중요부문이기도 하였으므로 그러한 선진적인 사법제도를 외국에 소개한다는 점에서도 의의깊은 일이라고 생각되었다.

　　우선 대법원 행정처의 국민참여재판 담당자인 여미숙 부장판사에게 연락하여 사정을 이야기하고 협조를 구하였다. 다행히 여 부장은 관련 논문, 파워포인트 자료, 쟁점정리 사항 등 많은 자료들을 보내주어 주제 발표문을 작성하는 데 큰 도움이 되었다. 발표자료를 작성하는 데는 박준민 헌법재판소 연구관, 소은영 헌법재판소 연구원 등이 큰 도움을 주었고, 영문으로 번역하는 데는 예승연 헌법재판소 연구원, 조수혜 헌법재판소 연구원, 김지혜 헌법재판소 연구원 등이 수고를 하였다. 한편 서울중앙지방법원에서 국민참여재판 실무 경험이 많은 설범식 부장판사와 염기창 부장판사를 직접 만나기도 하고 전화를 통하여 여러 가지 실무적인 문제에 관하여 물어보기도 하였다. 특히 8월 중순에는 서울중앙지방법원에 가서 염기창 부장판사가 진행하는 국민참여재판 케이스를 실제로 하루 종일 방청하면서 배심원 선발과정, 공판중심주의가 강화된 구두변론, 증인신문 등을 직접 목격하였다. 법정 방청 시에는 논문 작성을 도왔던 박준민 헌법재판소 연구관도 동행하였다.

발표자료는 9월 중순에 완성하여 E-mail로 보냈다. 영문 발표자료 및 그에 대한 한글 번역본을 [별지 1], [별지 2]로 첨부하기로 한다. 회의 날이 가까워 오자 저자의 발표원고를 중국어로 번역하여 보내며 내용이 충실하게 번역이 잘 되었는지를 검토해 달라고 하였다. 역시 영어로 된 문장을 중국어로 번역하다 보니 뜻이 명확히 전달되지 않아 오역이 된 부분도 있었고, 또한 중국과 한국의 법률용어 사용의 차이로 인하여 이상한 단어로 불만족스럽게 번역된 부분도 다수 보였다. 그래서 담당 검찰관인 Fran 검사와 여러 차례 메일을 주고 받아 11월 초순경에야 중국어 원고를 확정할 수 있었다. 중국어 발표자료도 대외적으로 의미 있는 자료라고 생각되어 [별지 3]으로 첨부하기로 한다.

제 2. 환영 리셉션

2012년 11월 12일 오후 6시 반경 환영 리셉션이 하워드 플라자 호텔에서 열렸다. 주최 측인 타이완 사법연수소의 林輝煌 소장을 비롯한 간부들과 법무부차관 陳守煌 등 법무부의 간부들뿐만 아니라 타이완 외교부의 외교관과 주 타이베이 한국 대표부의 외교관인 조현규 무관 등 참석자가 30여 명이나 되었다. 먼저 임 소장과 진 차관이 발언대로 나아가 타이완이 국민참여재판제도를 도입함에 있어 외국의 경험이나 전문 지식을 얻기 위하여 개최하는 이번 국제회의의

〈왼쪽부터 蘇 고등법원 부장판사, 저자, 林 사법연수소장, 오오타 교수, 陳 고검장〉

의의를 강조하고, 특히 저자를 화려한 경력을 갖춘 전임 헌법재판소 재판관이라고 소개하고 지난 해에 이어 두 번째로 한국의 발표자로서 온 것을 감사드린다고 하였다. 이어서 저자가 발언대로 나아가 간단히 중국어로 인사를 한 다음 영어로 인사말을 하였다. 저자가 국민참여재판에 대한 전문가는 아니지만 한국의 국민참여재판 경험을 타이완에 전함으로써 한국과 타이완의 사법교류 증진에 일조를 하게 된 것이 영광이라는 취지와 타이완 신문에 한류가 매우 인기 있다는 기사를 보았다고 소개하였다. 일본 대표로 온 오오타 시게루(太田 茂) 교수가 비행기 연착 관계로 조금 늦게 도착한 관계로 환영 리셉션은 9시가 넘어서야 종료되었다.

제 3. 국제회의 본회의 일정

본회의는 2012년 11월 13일 오전 9시경 林輝煌 소장의 개막연설을 시작으로 하여 5시 30분경 타이완 법무부장관인 曾勇夫 部長의 폐막연설이 끝날 때까지 하루 종일 이어졌다.

제1세션 주제는 한국과 일본에서의 국민참여재판제도의 현황과 발전이었다. 법무부 정무차장 吳陳鐶의 사회로 먼저 오오타 교수가 일본의 재판원 제도의 현황과 미래에 대하여 주제발표를 하였다. 그런데 일본에서도 형사재판에 재판원 제도를 도입하는 것이 헌법에 위반되는 것이 아니냐 하는 헌법문제가 제기되었으나 최근에 최고재판소가 합헌이라고 판결함으로써 일단락되었다는 것이다. 한편 2차대전 전 일본 구 헌법에서는 우리나라와 같이 "모든 국민은 자격 있는 법관에 의한 재판을 받을 권리가 있다."라고 규정되어 있어 그 당시 배심재판제도를 도입함에 있어 피고인에게 선택권을 부여하고, 법원이 배심원 평결에 구속되지 않도록 규정하였는데, 일본의 신 헌법에서는 그러한 헌법문제가 생기지 않도록 하기 위하여 당해 조항에서 "법관에 의한"이라는 문구를 삭제하고 "누구나 법원에서 재판을 받을 권리가 있다."라고 규정하였다고 소개하였다.

이어서 저자가 한국의 국민참여재판의 현황과 전망에 대하여 주제발표를 하였는데, 헌법과 법률이 정한 법관에 의한 재판을 받을 권리를 규정한 헌법 제27조의 해석과 관련하여 위헌시비를 벗어나기 위하여 원칙적으로 피고인의 청구에 의하여 참여재판을 실시하는 것으로 하고, 배심원의 평결결과에 판사가 기속되지 않도록 하고 국민

참여재판에 대해서도 상소권을 보장한 것을 설명하였다. 그런데 저
자의 사견임을 전제로 하여 배심원의 평결결과에 기속력을 부여하지
않는 한 피고인에게 국민참여재판 선택권을 부여하지 않더라도 위헌
이라고 보기 어렵지 않느냐는 견해를 밝혔다. 따라서 일정한 중대사
건에 한하여 강제적인 참여재판을 실시하는 것이 바람직하고, 다만
인적 물적 설비가 감당할 수 있는 범위의 사건 수를 잘 예측하여 참
여재판 대상 사건으로 규정해야 할 것이라고 의견을 피력하였다.

　제2세션의 주제는 한국, 일본, 타이완의 제도 차이 비교였다.
임휘황 소장의 사회 아래 먼저 타이완 고등법원 부장판사인 蘇素娥
여사가 人民參與刑事審判制度의 研究라는 제목으로 주제발표를 하였
다. 타이완에서도 법관독립심판 규정(타이완 헌법 제80조)과 법관신분
보장 규정(동 헌법 제81조), 피고 소송권 보장 규정(동 16조), 정당법률
절차 규정(동 8조) 등과의 관계상 위헌시비가 있어 배심원 결정에 기
속력을 부여하지 않았다는 설명이 있었다. 다만 우리와 다른 점은 대
상사건을 주요사건에 한정하여 피고인에게 선택권을 부여하지 않았
고, 배심원의 숫자를 5인으로 한 것, 예외적인 경우 관심원도 법관의
허락을 받아 법관의 평의 장소에 참석할 수 있는 것 등이었다. 이어
서 오오타 교수는 재판원 제도에서 재판원의 숫자를 6인으로 정하게
된 경위, 재판장의 재판원에 대한 설명은 어떻게 하는지, 재판원 제
도 시행 전의 판사, 검사, 변호사에 대한 교육을 어떻게 하였는지,
어떻게 대중의 관심과 지지를 얻어내는지 등에 관하여 설명을 하였
다. 저자는 국민참여재판제도의 개선과제로서 피고인의 신청권을 유
지할 것인지, 배심원 평결에 기속력을 부여할 것인지, 짧은 공판기일
을 개선하는 문제, 국민참여재판에 대하여 상소를 제한할 필요가 있
는지 등에 관하여 설명하였다.

제 3 세션의 주제는 국민참여재판제도 도입이 형사소송절차에 미치는 영향이었다. 타이완 고등검찰청 顔大和 검사장의 사회로 먼저 오오타 교수가 형사소송절차에 대한 영향이라는 주제를 발표하였다. 재판원 재판에서는 판사도 제 1 회 공판기일 전에는 사건 기록이나 증거에 대한 접근이 금지되는지, 증거법칙을 수정할 필요가 있는지, 재판원 재판으로 인하여 항소심 구조 변경의 필요가 있는지 등의 쟁점에 관하여 설명하였다. 뒤이어 저자는 국민참여재판이 형사소송절차에 미치는 영향으로, 공판준비절차를 도입하여 공판준비절차가 일반 형사재판 사건에서는 임의적인 절차임에 반하여 국민참여재판 사건에서는 필수적인 절차로 규정하였고, 형사소송법을 개정하여 공판중심주의를 강화하여 구두변론주의 조항을 신설하였고, 모두절차를 충실화 하였으며, 피고인신문을 증거조사 종료 후에 하는 것으로 변경하였고, 증거서류보다는 법정증언을 중심으로 입증활동이 이루어질 수 있도록 수사기관이 작성한 조서의 증거능력을 인정하기 위한 요건을 개정한 것 등을 소개하였다.

매 세션마다 주제발표가 끝난 뒤에는 Q & A 세션을 두어 방청석으로부터 다양한 질문이 이어졌다. 저자는 주제발표는 영어로 하였으나 질의응답 시간에는 우리말로 답변을 하고 중국어로 통역을 하도록 하였다. 영어로도 답변을 할 수는 있으나 우리말로 하는 것이 내용이 더 충실할 것이라고 생각되었기 때문이다. 마침 통역으로는 지난 해에 저자가 사법원을 방문했을 때 통역을 했던 왕정림 씨가 수고를 해주었다. 왕 씨는 우리나라 화교 출신으로 타이완에 유학을 와 대학을 졸업하고 법원에 일반직으로 취직하였다고 하였다. 다행스러운 것은 그 동안 왕정림 씨가 타이베이 지방법원에서 사법원으로 소속이 바뀌어 국민참여재판 견학을 위해 타이완 사절단이 한국을 방문할 때도

〈왼쪽부터 질문에 답하고 있는 저자, 오오타 교수, 某 법무차관〉

수차 동행하여 통역을 한 경력이 있어 국민참여재판에 관하여 이해도
도 높아 저자의 답변을 충실하게 통역할 수 있는 것이었다. 일본의
오오타 교수는 발표뿐만 아니라 답변도 영어로 하였는데 큰 무리 없
이 자신의 의사를 충실하게 표현하는 것 같았다. 오오타 교수는 교토
고등검찰청 검사장 경력을 가진 분으로서 로스쿨 교수로 진출할 마음
을 먹고 10년 정도 준비를 하였고 검사장 퇴임 후 8개월 정도 준비기
간을 가지고 와세다대학 로스쿨 교수로 취임하였다고 하였다.

　질의 내용 중 주요한 것을 소개해 보면, 국민참여재판 도입에 대
하여 법조계에서 반발이나 거부감이 없었는지, 국민참여재판제도 도입
의 사회적 배경은 무엇이고 그 도입으로 인하여 문제해결에 도움이 되
었는지, 타이완은 항소심의 구조적 특성으로 覆審制를 취하고 있는데
국민참여재판을 도입하기 위해서는 복심제 구조를 續審制나 事後審으

로 변경하여야 하는지, 배심원은 예단을 막기 위하여 제1회 공판기일 전에 사건 기록이나 증거 접근이 금지되어야 하겠지만 판사에 대해서도 사건기록이나 증거에 대한 접근이 금지될 필요가 있느냐 등이었다.

제4. 환송만찬

환송만찬은 타이베이의 자랑인 그랜드 호텔에서 타이완 법무부장관의 주재로 베풀어졌다. 그랜드 호텔은 장개석 총통의 부인이 국가적 행사만을 위해 운영하던 특급호텔인데 근래에는 일반인에게도 개방되어 있다고 소개하였다. 환송만찬에는 법무부장관, 차관, 타이베이 고등검찰청 검사장 및 사법연수소 소장 등 연수소 간부들이 모두 참석하여 주제발표자들을 위하여 성대한 만찬을 베풀어 주었다. 장관까지 직접 나서 환송만찬을 베풀어 주니 타이완에서 이번 국제회의를 얼마나 중시하는가를 짐작할 수 있었다. 曾勇夫 법무장관은 70세 가까운 고령이었으나 건강상태가 아주 양호하게 보였다. 曾 장관은 수영으로 몸을 단련하였는데 강을 헤엄쳐 건너는 정도의 실력을 갖추었다고 옆에 있던 분들이 자랑하였다. 술자리가 무르익었을 때 저자는 張繼의 "楓橋夜泊", 유종원의 "江雪" 등 唐詩 두 首를 암송하여 큰 박수를 받았다.

제5. 마치는 말

우리나라는 5년 동안의 시범실시를 마치고 2013년에는 한국의

〈국제회의를 마치고 발표자 및 주최자들이 기념촬영, 저자의 우측이
曾勇夫 법무장관〉

실정에 맞는 완성된 형태의 국민참여재판 제도를 시행하기 위하여
지난 7월 12일부터 국민사법참여위원회를 구성하여 논의중인 것으로
안다. 우리나라의 국민참여재판 제도 실시의 경험을 전해 주기 위하
여 타이완 국제회의에 참가한 것이지만 덕분에 저자로서는 우리나라
의 국민참여재판에 대한 많은 공부를 할 수 있었고, 더 나아가 일본
의 재판원 재판 제도, 타이완의 관심재판 제도에 관하여 깊이 있는
공부를 하는 기회가 된 것 같다. 국민사법참여위원회에서 완성된 형
태의 국민참여재판 제도를 논의하는 데도 이번 타이완의 국제회의
자료가 도움을 줄 수 있겠다는 생각이 들었다.

[별지 1]

Citizens Participatory Trials in the Republic of Korea

Dong-Heub LEE*

---

* Ex-Justice, Constitutional Court of Korea.

I. Citizens Participatory Trials: Present and Future

1. Background of Introduction of Citizens Participatory Trials

A. The need for the citizens participatory trials system

The legitimacy of citizens' participation in judicial process is supported by the theory that it enhances democratic legitimacy in judicial process, promotes the public confidence in judicial process, reflects the diversity of values and common sense among the general public in trials, and delivers fair and considerate trials. Admittedly, there are oppositions to the citizens' participation in criminal trials, which point out, inter alia, the inefficacy of jury trials, including the excessive cost incurred for a lawsuit, the jury's lack of professional knowledge in law, the difficulty of ensuring fairness in trials due to the Korean culture where personal connections are highly regarded. However, as affirmed by the examples of many developed countries, citizens participation of various types in prosecution and trials can be a way to realize the ideology of democracy and ensure the fairness in exercising the authority in criminal judicial process. Moreover, it can be an alternative or a momentum to resolve the long-lasting problems in the legal profession such as judicial back-scratching alliance, corruptions, and privileges granted to former office. For these reasons, scholars and civil society have urged the government to ensure participation of citizens in judicial process.

B. Theoretical issues

(1) Constitutionality of the citizens' participatory trial system.

Article 27 Section 1 of the Constitution of Korea provides that "[a]ll citizens shall have the right to trial in conformity with the Act by judges qualified under the Constitution and the Act." As to the question whether the 'judges' in the provision is limited to professional judges, constitutional scholars have opined that it may conform with the Constitution if citizens are involved only in decision of facts, while it may be unconstitutional if citizens are involved in decision of laws. According to this approach, a jury system which works only for decision of facts would be constitutional, while a lay assessor system, which deals with decision of both facts and laws (or punishment), may be unconstitutional.

The reference to 'judges' under Article 27 of the Constitution was intended at the time of legislation that it prohibits a trial from being delivered by non-professional judges and guarantees the right of citizens by ensuring trials to be delivered by professional judges. It was not, however,

intended to bar the participation of citizens in judicial process, and it is contended that the Constitution is not violated
when what is asked for by citizens is 'a form of citizens participation in judicial process where professional judges play
the leading role.' In other words, the right to trial under
Article 27 of the Constitution may be understood as 'a right
not to be tried before a court composed of non-professional
judges.'

Because this may not completely defend against all constitutional challenges, however, the Act on Citizens Participation in
Criminal Trials (hereinafter the 'Participatory Act') provides that a
participatory trial is, in principle, initiated at the request of the
defendant and the jury verdict has no binding effect on the
judge's decision (Article 5 Section 2 and Article 46 Section 5 of the
Participatory Act). Moreover, by not having any special provisions
on appeals in the Participation Act, it guarantees the right to
appeal against the lower court decision, whether it is a citizens
participatory trial or an ordinary criminal trial. And because only professional judges are involved in the appeal proceedings,
any possibility of unconstitutionality of citizens' participatory
trials can be avoided.

(2) **Jury system versus lay assessor system**

Jury system means a system where a jury composed of lay
people participates in trial and independently renders verdict

of guilty or not guilty which binds the court. On the other hand, lay assessor system means a system where lay assessors who are lay people participate in trials as a member of the court together with professional judges and exercise the same authority as professional judges in deciding the issues of facts and laws.

The citizens' participatory trials in Korea is a mixed form of the jury system and the lay assessor system. That is, the selected jurors, in principle, render verdict free from any influence by judges (reflecting a component of the jury system), while the jurors must listen to the judge's opinion when they fail to reach a unanimous conclusion and discuss with the judge who presided in the proceedings to determine punishment (reflecting components of the lay assessor system). In addition, there is another element as a modified jury system in that the jury verdict does not have binding effect but only advisory effect on the court.

C. Movement to introduce the participatory trial system

Since 1990s, civil society organizations, as they spearhead monitoring and participation in criminal justice system, have argued for citizens participation in judicial process as a part of judicial reform. The government thereafter has shown interest in the idea, and around December 1999, the Commission on Judicial Reform, which was set up as the presidential advisory entity to lead judicial reform during the Government of People, finally reported that it would study and review ways of citizens' participation, including jury system and lay assessor system for a possible adoption.

On the other hand, the Supreme Court of Korea, as it establishes a comprehensive plan for judicial development, "A Plan for Judicial Development in the 21st century," around February 2000, included in its agenda the citizens participation in judicial process to be studied and reviewed and have conducted research on the subject. Further, on October 28, 2003, the Supreme Court installed the Commission on Judicial Reform within the Court and had it study over plans for judicial reform including the issue of citizens' participation in trials. The Commission on Judicial Reform discussed which system it would introduce between the jury system and the lay assessor system, and concluded that modifications may be necessary to reflect the realities of our society after setting one as the basic model, as it is difficult to decide which system would fit for our society. Accordingly, the Commission on Judicial Reform, on December 30, 2004, proposed that "with an aim to implement the finalized system ensuring citizens' actual participation in judicial process from the year of 2012, the development, implement, and an empirical analysis of the initial form of citizens participatory trials should be made. Then, in 2012, a final model of the citizens' participatory trials system that is suitable for our country will be designed and implemented. At the initial stage of the citizens' participatory trial system, it will not adopt a single model of a jury system or a lay assessor system but rather will use a modified model that embraces elements of both the jury system and the lay assessor system."

The Commission on Judicial Reform prepared the bill on Citizens Participation in Criminal Trials, which stipulated citizens' participation in criminal trials as a jury. The bill passed the State Council and was submitted to the National Assembly on December 6, 2005.

2. Preparation before implementation of the citizens' participatory trial system

A. Amendment of the Criminal Procedure Act

The principle of court-oriented trials, which requires examination of evidence in open proceedings and formulation of conviction on guilty or not guilty and punishment, as well as the principles of oral argument, directness, concentrated trial, and actual examination of evidence, which realize the principle of court-oriented trials, are essential to implement citizens participatory trials. Accordingly, the Criminal Procedure Act was amended to strengthen the elements of the principle of court-oriented trials under the same Act.

B. Enactment of the Act, the Rules and the Established Rules on citizens' participation in criminal trials

The Act on Citizens Participation in Criminal Trials, which comprises 60 provisions, passed the National Assembly on April 30, 2007, promulgated on June 1, 2007 and took in effect as of January 1, 2008.

Accordingly, after its prior announcement of legislation on July 25, 2007, the Supreme Court of Korea in its Supreme Court Justices' Council enacted the Rules on Citizens Participation in Criminal Trials (hereinafter 'Participatory Rules') on October 4, 2007 and the relevant established rules, including the Established Rules on Jury Selection Process, reflecting the Act and Rules on Citizens Participation in Criminal Trials. At the same time, it developed various trial document forms necessary for citizens' participatory trials, as well as practice manual, which serves as the reference to the trial procedure, jury instruction, and jury deliberation process for the courts that conduct citizens participatory trials.

C. Development of jury management system

Article 22 of the Participation Act provides that prospective jurors are selected from a jury pool list generated each year based on the resident registration information on citizens provided by the Ministry of Public Administration and Security. In all procedures concerning the preparation of the jury pool list and the selection and management of prospective jurors, the jury management computer system developed by the Supreme Court of Korea is used.

D. Networking with prosecutors, bar association and academia

The courts, as the organization that prepares the implementation of the citizens participatory trial system, installed on June 18, 2007 the 'Preparatory Committee on Establishment of Judicial Participation Planning Task Force,' and established around February 2008 the Judicial Participation Planning Task Force within the Supreme Court of Korea to implement, research and study the participatory trials at the initial stage.

E. Implementation of mock citizens' participatory trials

(1) Before enacting the Act, the Commission on Judicial Reform conducted four sessions of mock trials in which actual citizens participated as jurors.

- Session 1: August 2005, Seoul Central District Court, homicide
- Session 2: December 2005, Busan District Court, rape resulting in bodily injury
- Session 3: April 2006, Seoul Central District Court, homicide

- Session 4: November 2006, Kwangju District Court, bribe

(2) **After enacting the Act, 18 district courts conducted mock trials in which citizens in their jurisdictions participated as jurors.**

- September 10, 2007. Seoul Central District Court, homicide
- October 29, 2007. 5 district courts (Seoul Southern, Seoul Western, Suwon, Daegu, Ulsan), homicide
- November 12, 2007. 13 courts (Seoul Central, Seoul Eastern, Seoul Northern, Uijeongbu, Incheon, Chuncheon, Daejun, Chungju, Busan, Changwon, Kwangju, Jeonju, Jeju), rape resulting in bodily injury
- November 26, 2007 at Uijeongbu District Court, December 10, 2007 at Seoul District Court, and many other courts

(3) In order to enhance lay people's knowledge in criminal trials and promote the public confidence in judicial process by increasing their understanding in the court system and trials, shadow juries have been established since 2010 as a body separate from the actual juries to observe the entire trial process and discuss the trial results, including guilty or not guilty and punishment, in the same manner as they would in actual jury deliberation.

F. Public education and advertisements

In August 2007, the Supreme Court of Korea developed and distributed a general commentary on the Participatory Act for the use of legal practitioners and the general public.

On October 26, 2007, a 16-page introductory booklet, the Juror Handbook, was published for the use of jurors. The booklet comprises introductory statement, questions and answers, easy-to-understand legal terms, and the questions and answers include 30 items that are frequently asked by people who attend as jurors. The booklets are delivered to prospective jurors along with the notice of selection proceedings and thereby help the prospective jurors have sufficient understanding on the criminal trial procedure before attending the selection proceedings.

For the prospective jurors attending the selection proceedings, the Jury Orientation Video is played to guide the procedure of citizens participatory trials, the roles of jurors, and other matters to take notice. In addition, the advertisement materials on participatory trials on the website of the Supreme Court of Korea, comic-type booklet, and souvenirs have been developed to ensure the information on participatory trials are accessible to the general public.

Besides, recognizing that it is necessary to create conditions in which the participants are not disadvantaged by the participation in trials if it were to facilitate voluntary and active participation of lay people in participatory trials, Article 50 of the Act stipulates provisions on that matter. Moreover, cooperation was requested to the Ministry of Public Administration and Security, the Ministry of Labor and economic organizations.

3. Current Status

A. Substances of citizen participatory trial

(1) Eligible Cases (Revision and Implementation)

At the enactment of the Participatory Act, the following cases were eligible for a participatory trial: cases of intentional act causing death, robbery with rape, robbery or rape with bodily injury or death, or bribery of certain kind, cases of attempt of, abetment, aiding, preparation, or conspiracy to commit offenses falling above, and consolidated cases of those falling above. The scope of eligible cases were expanded to include cases of robbery, special robbery, rape, quasi-rape and habitual theft, with the revision of the Rules of the Supreme Court on July 1, 2009; and the scope of eligible cases has been further expanded to include all cases falling under jurisdiction of collegiate panel under Article 32 Section 1 of the Court Organization Act since July 1, 2012 (Article 5 Section 1 of the Participatory Act).

(2) Authority and Duties of Jurors

Jurors shall have the authority to present opinions on the fact finding, the application of Acts and subordinate statutes and the determination of punishment with respect to the case for which they take part in a participatory trial (Article 12 Section 1 of the Participatory Act). Jurors shall abide by Acts and subordinate statutes and perform his/her duties independently and sincerely (Article 12 Section 2 of the Participatory Act), and shall not divulge confidential information known to him/her in the scope of his/her duties nor shall he/she commit any act of undermining fairness of a trial (Article 12 Section 3 of the Participatory Act).

(3) Number of Jurors and Alternate Jurors

Nine jurors shall participate for an eligible case whose statutory punishment is death penalty or life imprisonment with or without prison labor, while seven jurors shall participate for an eligible case other than those set forth above. However, a court may have five jurors if the defendant or defense counsel admits essential elements of prosecuted facts during the preparatory proceedings (Article 13 Section 1 of the Participatory Act). Notwithstanding above, a court may determine the number of jurors, either seven or nine, by decision, only if it finds that extraordinary circumstances exist in view of the substance of a case and the prosecutor and the defendant or defense counsel consent (Article 13 Section 2 of the Participatory Act).

In addition, a court may have five or less alternate jurors in preparation for a vacancy of the jury (Article 14 Section 1 of the Participatory Act).

(4) Qualifications of Jurors

Jurors shall be selected from among citizens of the Republic of Korea who shall be not less than 20 years of age. A person who is disqualified for public servants shall be disqualified for a juror, and a person who may have excessive influence on jurors or whose occupation makes it difficult to perform jury duty, such as the President of the Republic, a member of the National Assembly, the head of a local government or a member of a local council, a jurist, a public official in a court or public prosecutors' office, a police officer, a correctional officer, a probation officer, a military serviceman, a civilian military employee, or fire officer, shall be excepted. In addition, a victim, a person who is a relative of a defendant or a victim, a legal representative, a witness, a representative of a defendant or a victim, a person who performed duties as a prosecutor or a judicial police officer in connection with the relevant case, or a related person shall be excluded from duties as a juror (Article 16 - 19 of the Participatory Act).

Besides, a court may exempt any of the following persons

from duties as a juror at its discretion or at the request of the person: a person who is not less than seventy years of age, a person who has ever attended selection proceedings as a prospective juror during the past five years, a person whose case prosecuted for an offense punishable by imprisonment without prison labor or any heavier punishment is still pending, a person who is under arrest or confinement pursuant to any Act subordinate statute, a person whose performance of duties is likely to cause harm to a third party or is likely to sustain irrecoverable damage to his/her career, a person who has difficulties in making an appearance before court due to serious illness, injury, or disabilities, or any inappropriate person (Article 20 of the Participatory Act).

(5) Travel Expenses and Allowances

According to Article 15 of the Participatory Act, jurors, alternate jurors, and prospective jurors may be entitled to travel expenses and allowances as prescribed by the Rules of the Supreme Court. The Council of Supreme Court Justices has the authority to determine the amount of travel expenses and allowances within budget: 50,000 Won are paid for prospective jurors who attended selection proceedings; 100,000 Won are paid for jurors and alternate jurors who participated in trials; and travel expenses and accommodations charge are paid in accordance with court public officials.

(6) Selection Proceeding of Jurors

The head of a district court shall prepare a jury pool list from citizens who are not less than twenty years of age and who reside within its jurisdiction each year and a court shall choose a required number of prospective jurors by random selection from the jury pool list and serve summons for proceedings of selection of jurors and prospective jurors.

(7) Procedural Rights and Duties of Jurors

At the trial, the public prosecutor shall sit on the opposite side of the defendant and defense counsel at an equal level and jurors and alternate jurors shall sit at the left side of the space between judges and the public prosecutor, the defendant, and defense counsel. The witness stand shall be located at the right side of the space between judges and the public prosecutor, the defendant, and defense counsel, facing jurors and alternate jurors (Article 39 of the Participatory Act).

Jurors may request the presiding judge to examine a defendant or witness on necessary matters and take notes and use them for deliberation, subject to permission of the presiding judge. However, jurors should not leave the court while the trial is in session or leave the place of deliberation, verdict, or discussion without permission of the presiding judge before deliberation, verdict, or discussion is completed; express or discuss his/her opinion on the relevant case before

deliberation begins; collect information on, or investigate into, the relevant case in addition to the trial proceedings; or
divulge confidential information on deliberation, verdict, or
discussion (Article 41 of the Participatory Act).

(8) Deliberation, Verdict, and Discussion

The jury shall deliberate on whether guilty or not guilty,
without the involvement of judges, and deliver a verdict by
unanimous votes. If the jury fails to reach an unanimous verdict of guilt or non-guilt, the jury shall deliver the verdict of
guilt or non-guilty by majority votes, after hearing opinions
of judges. Judges shall not participate in the verdict, even if
they attend the deliberation and make statements on their
opinions. If a verdict is guilty, the jury shall discuss sentencing with judges and shall express their opinions (Article 46
Section 2, 3, and 4 of the Participatory Act).

(9) Sentencing

No verdict and opinions of the jury shall be binding on
the court, and documents compiled with results of a verdict
and opinions shall be filed in the relevant trial records. The
presiding judge shall notify the defendant of results of the
jury verdict at the time of sentencing, and shall explain, to
the defendant, reasons why the sentence pronounced differs
from the jury's verdict, if such is the case (Article 46 Section 5
and 6, Article 48 Section 4 of the Participatory Act).

A written judgment shall describe the fact that jurors have taken part in the trial and may include the jury's opinions. If a judgment pronounced differs from the jury's verdict, the written judgment shall include reasons therefore (Article 49 Section 1 and 2 of the Participatory Act).

B. Current Status

As of February 29, 2012, 1,551 cases, which is 6.8% of 22,667 eligible cases, have been accepted, and 606 cases have proceeded to participatory trials, except those of being excluded or withdrawn. An eligible case may proceed to a participatory trial only when a defendant desires a participatory trial. During the period of January 1, 2008 through February 29, 2012, 1,551 cases (6.8%) have been accepted for a participatory trial among 22,667 eligible cases. Arranged in order of quantity of case categories, 26.2% are robbery cases, 23.9% are murder cases, 22.1% are sexual offenses, 22.2% are other crimes, and 5.7% are bodily injury resulting in death.

Court-appointed attorneys are appointed in 81.4% of participatory trial cases, which implies high ratio. Since participatory trials were implemented in 2008, the proportion of confession to denial is 3 to 7, and a verdict of the jury and a judgment of judges coincide at a 90% probability, implying the overall consensus. Until February 29, 2012, there have been 4 cases where the jury delivered a verdict of guilt, whereas judges found not guilty, and, in contrast, 50 cases where the jury delivered a verdict of non-guilt, whereas judges found guilty. Among the cases that showed discordance between verdicts and judgments, 2 cases were overturned by the appellate court. The sentencing opinions of the jury, despite they are not binding on the court, accord with sentencing of the court with plus or minus 1 year error at a 90% probability.

4. Survey Result of the Citizens (especially the Jury) on Participatory Trials

According to the survey results regarding the Citizens' evaluation of the judiciary in 2008, when participatory trials implemented, 59.3% of the poll had knowledge of participatory trials and 69.3% of the poll answered participatory trials would improve the credibility of trials. Another survey, conducted 3 years later, revealed that 87.5% of the poll answered participatory trials would improve the credibility of trials and 80% or more of the poll answered participatory trials would achieve the fairness and transparency of trials, the improvement of legal knowledge of the Citizens, and the improvement of the law-abiding spirit of the Citizens.

On the other hand, a juror survey carried out by the Supreme Court from 2008 to 2011 showed 96.5% of the poll satisfied and positively evaluated their juror performances.

88.1% of the poll said they fully or mostly comprehended sub-
stances of trials, 72.9% of the poll said their opinions were
sufficiently expressed, and the instruction of presiding judges
were very (70.2%) or somewhat (28.2%) helpful. On the other
hand, the questioned jurors said the long period of trial
(46.1%), indigestible legal terms (23.6%), difficulties in understanding evidence (10.5%), safety concern such as possible re-
taliation from defendant (9.4%), and reduction in income or
disadvantages at work place (10.4%) were indicated as
difficulties.

II. Improvement Issues of Participatory Trials and Effects of Its Introduction to Criminal Trial Proceedings

1. Improvement Issues

A. Improvement of the Application Rate

(1) Limitations of the Application System

Because the low application rate of participatory trials is
due to the lack of social awareness of participatory trials, the
intents or advantages of participatory trials should be pro-
moted to the Citizens and defendants.

Under the Participatory Act, a defendant shall submit a

written statement, describing whether he/she desires a participatory trial, within seven days from the date on which a duplicate of indictment is served (Article 8 Section 2 of the Participatory Act) and if a defendant fails to submit a written statement, it shall be deemed that the defendant does not desire a participatory trial (Article 8 Section 3 of the Participatory Act).

Despite the short period of application for participatory trials is one of the reasons that the application rate of participatory trials is low, the practice allows a defendant, who failed to submit a written statement within seven days from the date on which a duplicate of indictment is served, to apply for participatory trials by the first trial date and to proceed to participatory trials with the confirmation of the court (2009Mo1032 decided by the Supreme Court on October 23, 2009).

Even if the defendant applies for participatory trials, the data shows the high withdrawal rate from participatory trials: Its possible reason is comprehensive response of attitudes of the court, prosecutor, and attorney toward participatory trials, sentencing, opinions of colleague inmates and others.

(2) Improvements of the Application System

(a) A Suggestion to Abolish the Application System

The current application system is based on a defendant's autonomy in choosing a type of criminal proceedings.

However, participatory trials intend to guarantee 'the right to participate in trials of the Citizens' for the fairness and transparency of the judiciary, not intending the guarantee of the right to choose a proceeding of a defendant. In addition, it was not originally related to the issue of uniformity and equality in the exercise of the criminal jurisdiction. Therefore, a possible suggestion would be to abolish the current application system based on party autonomy, but to adopt a mandatory system where eligible cases shall proceed to participatory trials.

From the perspective of this suggestion, the excessive burden would be resolved by limiting the scope of eligible cases, such as excluding confession cases where a defendant confesses entire or essential part of facts charged.

(b) A Suggestion to Maintain the Application System

A suggestion to maintain the application system is supported by two different views: The first view is to maintain the current application system in order to provide a participatory trial only when a defendant applies; and another view is to amend the current application system where eligible cases would proceed to a participatory trial in principle, but proceed to an ordinary criminal proceeding if a defendant submits a written statement that he/she does not desire a participatory trial.

The second view that suggests providing an ordinary criminal proceeding only if a defendant does not desire a participatory trial is further classified into two different views: the first is the automatic exclusion from a participatory trial if a defendant does not desire a participatory trial; and the second view, which is mostly supported, requires the court's permission to proceed to an ordinary criminal proceeding even if a defendant expresses his/her desire.

This suggestion is justified by following grounds: the respect to autonomy of a defendant is desirable under the principle of sovereignty of the citizens, the protection of basic rights requires the broad recognition of autonomy of a defendant, and a mandatory enforcement of participatory trials would infringe the right to trial by judges, which is one of the fundamental basic rights under the Constitution of Korea.

(c) A Suggestion to limit the Decision of Exclusion

The Participatory Act provides the broad grounds for the decision of exclusion: The general provision for the decision of exclusion, such as "if it is considered inappropriate to proceed to a participatory trial due to any other cause or event" of Article 9 Section 1 Item 4 of the Participatory Act, would be de facto denial of the right of a defendant.

Considering the special circumstances where a participatory trial cannot be tried, the provision could be remained at the Participatory Act. Nonetheless, the scope of the grounds for the decision of exclusion should be limited at minimum and the grounds should be specified.

Accordingly, the Supreme Court revised the Supreme Court Regulation on April 27, 2010, limiting the meaning of the phrase of "if it is considered inappropriate to proceed to a participatory trial due to any other cause or event" into "1. Where additional prosecution is predicted, 2. Where a defendant is suspected to have mental diseases, and 3. Where the right to prompt trial of a defendant would be infringed for excessive delaying if his/her case proceeds to a participatory trial (Supreme Court Regulation on Acceptance and Handling of Participatory Trials)."

B. Short Period of Trial Dates

In most cases, participatory trials are closed within one or two days. The possible reasons are as follows: complex cases involving several issues or witnesses are already excluded by the decision of exclusion; confession cases, forming about 30% of participatory trials, do not require evidence investigation for hours; mandatory preparative proceedings effectively organize issues of laws; and jurors desire to finish their trials within a day even the trial last until the late evening.

Nevertheless, dates for trial may need extension depending on the nature of the individual case. Despite it is desired by jurors and supported by the court and prosecutors, the trial lasting until the late evening would not be desirable. As a matter of fact, the juror survey showed that jurors complained excessively long trials, even lasting until midnight, at most.

C. Advisory effect of the jury verdict

Because the jury verdict has only advisory effect, a judgment different from the verdict may be rendered. In such case, the jurors realize that the effect of their verdict is only advisory, and for a citizen who participated in the trial despite substantial inconvenience, it may be an unpleasant experience to accept the conclusion. Because such an experience can discourage citizens' active participation in participatory trials, it is desirable for the courts to respect the jury verdict whenever possible in administering the citizens participatory trials system.

Although some argue that jury verdict should have binding effect, it can be subject to constitutional challenges because recognizing the binding effect of jury verdict may violate the constitutional fundamental right to trial by judges.

If the binding effect of jury verdict were to be recognized, the present method of verdict would need modification. It is because a decision by a simple majority when a unanimous decision is not reached cannot be acceptable in 'proving the facts beyond the reasonable doubt.' The rule of unanimity should apply in principle, or a majority of at least 80% or more should be required.

D. Relation between Jury's Sentencing Opinion and Sentencing Guidelines

'Sentencing guidelines' mean that after setting basic scope of sentencing for certain crimes and if a specific crime falls into categories of causes for aggravation or mitigation, sentencing for the crime is finally decided within the modified scope of sentencing reflecting the causes.

In practice, it is known that there are some cases in which the sentencing guidelines are provided to jurors. In some cases, judges may pay more attention to the objective application of the sentencing guidelines rather than sentencing opinion presented by jurors.

Regarding this, there are two perspectives: one is that there will be a system in which jurors may even make a decision on sentencing after reviewing the sentencing elements presented in the sentencing guidelines, and the other is that there will be a system in which only judge decides sentencing without juror's participation as it is expected that people's trust in the sentencing will be increased with the adoption of the sentencing guidelines, like done in most states in the

U.S.A.

E. Necessity to Limit Appeal

As the current Participatory Act does not have specific provisions regarding appeal, the appeal proceedings stipulated in the Criminal Procedure Act applies to participatory trial cases like general criminal cases.

Generally, appeal in criminal case in Korea has the characteristics of continued review. According to the Criminal Procedure Act, the appellate court can quash the findings of fact admitted in the trial court, and the appellate court, in principle, shall announce a new judgment when the original judgment is quashed (Article 364 of the Criminal Procedure Act).

In practice, a Supreme Court precedent states that "when jurors unanimously render a non-guilty verdict regarding adoption of evidences such as credibility of witness's statement and admission of the findings of fact after they participate in all the fact-finding proceedings such as witness examination and if such a non-guilty verdict, consistent with the court's conviction, is adopted by the court without changes, the trial court's judgment regarding adoption of evidence and admission of the findings of fact through these proceedings should be more respected as long as any new situation sufficient and convincing enough to change the trial court's judgment does not emerge through new evidence examination at the appellate court."(Supreme

Court Decision 2009Do14065 Decided March 25, 2010)

Meanwhile, there are arguments regarding appeal against judgment at the participatory trial: one is that if there are non-guilty verdict rendered by the jury and following court's judgment consistent with the jury's non-guilty verdict, appeal by public prosecutor should be prohibited on the ground of misunderstanding of facts; and further, the other one is that the characteristics of appealing proceedings as deferential review of the trial court judgment or review on the matter of law should be intensified. This is because, if the findings of fact decided on the basis of the sound common sense of majority of people can easily be reversed by the appellate court, it is worried that there could be the flood of ideas that disparage the value of preparatory trial system, and thereby the system ends up with losing its meaning itself.

But, it is also possible that preventing defendant from appealing against judgment at the participatory trial can be unconstitutional in violation of the right to be tried by judges and the matter of reforming the characteristics of appeal proceedings requires more detailed and synthetic review in relation to levels of court in Korea.

2. Effects of Introduction of Participatory Trial to Criminal Trial Procedure

A. Strengthening Preparatory Proceedings prior to Public Trial

(1) Mandatory Proceedings

As the Criminal Procedure Act (hereinafter, the CPA) was revised on June 1, 2007, with the enactment of the Participatory Act, the preparatory proceedings prior to public trial were adopted (Article 266-5 and below). The preparatory proceedings are mandatory for a citizen's participatory trial, while optional for a general criminal case, in order to promote speedy trial through efficient and focused examination (Main text of Article 36 Section 1 of the Participatory Act). The reason is that in order for the participatory trial to take root as quickly as possible, more focused examination is required for a participatory trial case than an ordinary criminal case to finish a trial promptly, and it is also necessary to prevent jurors who are not legal experts from being exposed to inadmissible evidence through the preparatory proceedings prior to public trial.

The preparatory proceedings prior to public trial are the means to confirm defendant's intention to have a participatory trial, take a leading role in settling the subject matters to be examined through arranging issues, preparing for focused examination proceedings through establishing a plan for proving arguments, fixing trial schedule and advancing jury selection proceedings based on the trial schedule.

(2) Management of Preparatory Proceedings Prior to Public Trial

The court shall designate the date of the preparatory proceedings to arrange arguments and evidence and set the schedule for the trial (Article 37 Section 1 of the Participatory Act), the public prosecutor and the defendant or defense counsel shall collect and arrange evidence in advance and give cooperation otherwise so that the preparatory proceedings can be smoothly progressed (Article 36 Section 4 of the Participatory Act).

The court shall conclude the preparatory proceedings prior to jury selection except when the court puts a case to the preparatory proceedings during trial schedules pursuant to Article 266-15 of the revised CPA (Article 27 of the Participatory Rule). The court shall record the result put in order in connection with issues and evidence of the case in the protocol of the preparatory proceedings (Article 266-10 Section 2 of the revised CPA), and after the conclusion of the preparatory proceedings, the 'effect of concluding date' shall apply (Article 266-13 Section 1 of the revised CPA).

Regarding admission or non-admission of evidence, during the preparatory proceedings, the public prosecutor simply presents a list of evidence without presenting specific eviden tial documents or materials and then requests to call a witness in relation to the evidence with which the defendant does not agree or, if necessary, requests to call a witness to prove facts charged. The defendant also requests a witness favorable to him/her, pointing out the arguments or facts to be proved by the witness. And the court, after hearing arguments of both sides, decides whether to admit the evidence or not.

B. Changes in Public Trial Proceedings

(1) The Revised CPA

The original draft bill of the Participatory Act contained considerable number of provisions stipulating public trial proceedings. But, as the National Assembly simultaneously passed the bill of the revised CPA, the provisions of the Participatory Act overlapped with those of the revised CPA were completely deleted. This means that the public trial proceedings of participatory trial should be same as those of general criminal case but the differences in procedural management in practice between trial with and without jurors seem to be expected.

(A) Strengthening the principle of court oriented trial

Even before the revision of the CPA, Article 254 Section 1 of the CPA has been stipulated that "[t]he institution of public prosecution shall be made by filing a written indictment with a competent court." And Article 118 Section 2 of the Regulations on Criminal Procedure stipulates that "[d]ocuments or any other articles…which may cause the court to create presupposition on the case shall not be attached to and their contents shall not be quoted in an indictment." But, in practice, the public prosecutor has submitted all the records of investigation to the court at the same time of the institution of prosecution, and the court, in some cases, reviews the records of investigation and organizes issues in advance before the first trial schedule.

But with the introduction of the participatory trial, the Regulations on Criminal Procedure has been revised to stipulate that "[w]here the court dismisses or rejects the application for evidence, or withholds the decision on the application for evidences, it shall not receive any evidentiary documents or articles from the person who has applied for evidence." (Article 134 Section 4 of the Regulation on Criminal Procedure)

Actually, without the basis of the principle of court-oriented trial, no participatory trial can be implemented: the proper functioning of the participatory trial is ideally based on the perfect foundation of the principle of court-oriented trial which makes it possible for jurors, who cannot review the records of investigation in person, to accurately understand the issues of a relevant case and reach a proper conclusion by listening and seeing contents of assertion and proof in the court.

Therefore, the revised CPA practically intensifies the elements of principle of court-oriented trial by newly enacting a provision stipulating the principle of oral pleading in order to overcome the shortcomings of protocol-oriented trial in the past and find out accurate facts of the case through active oral pleadings by the parties and relevant persons at the courtroom (Article 275 Section 1 of the CPA), changing the one who shall produce evidential materials or recite or inform the summary of documentary evidence from the presiding judge to the movant and also changing the examination method of evidence so that the movant becomes the one who should recite in principle (Article 292 of the CPA).

(B) Sincere execution of opening proceedings

According to the revised CPA, the execution of opening proceedings becomes more sincere and stricter so that the facts charged, issues of case and plan for proving arguments can clearly be shown at the initial stage of trial proceedings (Article 285, Article 286 and Article 287 of the CPA). The process to recite summary of prosecution (opening statement) by public prosecutor, which used to be optional, become mandatory and in doing so, the public prosecutor shall read all the facts constituting the crime charged, name of the crime and applicable statutory provisions in principle and if necessary, the presiding judge may have the public prosecutor state outlines of the prosecution. Also, the proceedings for defendant's replying statement, the presiding judge's questioning session for organizing issues and the public prosecutor and defendant's statement of plan for proving their arguments are newly added.

In a participatory trial, sincere and sufficient execution of proceedings for organizing issues at the opening proceedings is required, as jurors who are the deciders of facts learn about the case and understand its issues for the first time at the public trial.

(C) Changes in examination of defendant

In the revised CPA, the ways to examine a defendant have been changed (Article 296-2 of the CPA). Before the revision of the CPA, the examination of defendant should be conducted before the initiation of the evidence examination. According to the revised CPA, however, one of the functions of defendant examination that discerns between the parts to be contested and the confessed parts is replaced by defendant's opening statement and defendant's opening statement should be conducted after the completion of the evidence examination in principle in order to use defendant's statement as evidence, challenge defendant's justification and persuade jurors.

(D) Proof on the basis of court testimony

According to the revised CPA, the elements of admissibility of protocol prepared by investigative institution have partially been changed in order to establish authenticity of the protocol based more on court testimony than on evidentiary documents.

Before the revision of the CPA, when a defendant denies the actual authenticity of protocol concerning interrogation of suspect prepared by the public prosecutor at trial, such a protocol cannot be used as evidence because there is no other way to prove authenticity than a 'statement by the original stater.' But the CPA was revised to prove actual authenticity not only by a 'statement made by the defendant at a trial' as stipulated in the former CPA but also by a video-recorded product or any other objective means, and the revised CPA also articulates that besides the proof of authenticity of protocol, a protocol can be admissible as evidence only when it is proved that the statement recorded in the protocol is made in a particularly reliable state, thereby resolving controversy over the interpretation (Article 312 Section 1 and Section 2 of the CPA).

And there was a problem that defendant's right to defense or right to cross examination could be insufficiently guaranteed due to the broad interpretation of "any other cause," among the exceptions to hearsay evidence rule of "stater's death, illness, residence in a foreign country, and any other cause' stipulated in the former CPA. In order to solve the problem, however, the CPA was revised to more strictly stipulate the exceptions as follows: "if a person who is required to make a statement in a preparatory hearing or a trial is unable to make such statement because he/she is dead, ill or resides abroad, his/her whereabouts is unknown or there is any other similar cause." (Article 314 of the CPA)

(2) Special Provisions of the Participatory Act

Regarding seats for participatory trial, jurors sit at the left side of the bench facing it, the public prosecutor sits on the opposite side of defendant and defense counsel and the witness stand is located in front of juror's seats (Article 39 of the Participatory Act).

Ruling on summary trial procedures shall not apply to participatory trial even when the defendant makes a confession on charges at a public trial (Article 43 of the Participatory Act), no jurors or alternate jurors may involve in the court's examination on admissibility of evidence (Article 44 of the Participatory Act).

In a general criminal trial, unless there is any extraordinary reason otherwise, every court shall, upon a motion from a public prosecutor, a defendant or a defense counsel, assign a stenographer to take stenographic notes of a hearing in the court, in whole or in part, or make audio or video records (including those with sound recorded; hereinafter the same shall apply) of a hearing by using an audio or video recording system (Article 56-2 of the revised CPA), but in a participatory trial, stenographic notes and audio recording in trial court become mandatory so that a court shall employ a stenographer to take stenographic notes of the trial or shall record sounds or images by using audio or video recording devices in the absence of any special reasons to the contrary and stenographic notes, audio recording tapes, or video recording tapes shall be preserved separately from trial records, and the public prosecutor, a defendant, or defense counsel may request a copy of stenographic notes, audio recording tapes, or video recording tapes, upon the payment of the cost and expense thereof (Article 40 of the Participatory Act).

The presiding judge shall, upon closing of pleadings and arguments, explain to jurors in the court about essential points of prosecuted facts, applicable provisions of Acts, essential points of pleadings and arguments of the defendant and defense counsel, admissibility of evidence, and other significant matters. In such cases, an explanation about essential points of evidence may be also given, if necessary (Article 46 Section 1 of the Participatory Act). Here, "other significant matters" include principle of presumption of innocence, principle of evidential justice, principle of free evaluation of evidence, the fact that defendant's refusal to produce evidence or to give testimony at the trial cannot be interpreted as presuming the defendant to be guilt, disregard of evidence without admissibility, manner of jury deliberation and verdict, and purpose and manner of the election of representative of jurors (Article 37 Section 1 of the Participatory Rule).

3. Evaluation and Future Tasks

The positive effects of participatory trial include the realization of the ideas of the CPA including the principle of public trial and the improvement of communication in the courtroom through explaining legal terms with plain words to help jurors understand the issues of case and widely using multimedia devices such as PowerPoint and pictures. Further, through citizens' direct participation in trial proceedings, people's suspicion and distrust in the judiciary can be resolved as making sure that the practice of allowing privilege associated with one's former post (judge-turned-attorney) and wealth is not existent, and credibility of the judiciary can be enhanced by realization of the ideals of direct democracy in the judiciary and opportunity to experience judicial system.

Other than the installation of the Judicial Participation Planning Task Force or revision of relevant established rules, the Supreme Court held the Conference of Senior Chief Judges in March 2008, right after the launch of the participatory trial system. The Supreme Court has also been holding Annual Meetings for Presiding Judges of Participatory Trial around March or April every year, and in the first half of every year, providing education on the method of pleading in participatory trial at the Workshop for State-Appointed Defense Counsel held at each High Court, exerting its utmost effort for the settlement of participatory trial system.

But, as reviewed before, there are some future tasks to be carried out in relation to the problems singled out during the execution of participatory trial so far. In order to implement the complete form of participatory trial in 2013, based on the collection of extensive opinions from the public including criticism, the Committee for Citizen's Participation in the Judicial System, which makes a decision on the final form of the participatory trial system through analysis on the progress of implementation of the participatory trial system, was established at July 12, 2012, pursuant to Article 55 of the Participatory Act. This Committee will decide the proper type of participatory trial system suitable for Korea's situation by the end of this year.

한국의 국민참여재판

이　동　흡*

* 대한민국 전 헌법재판소 재판관.

I. 국민참여재판의 현황과 전망

1. 국민참여재판제도의 도입 배경

가. 국민참여재판제도의 도입 이유·필요성

국민의 사법참여는 사법의 민주적 정당성을 강화하고, 사법에 대한 국민의 신뢰 제고와 재판에 있어 일반 국민의 다양한 가치관과 상식을 반영할 수 있으며, 공정하고 신중한 재판이 이루어질 수 있다는 점에서 이론적 정당성을 가지고 있다. 물론 국민이 사법에 직접 참여하는 것에 대해서는 소송비용의 과다소요 등 배심재판의 비효율성, 배심원의 법률적 비전문성이나 인맥 중심의 한국사회에서의 재판 공정성 확보의 어려움 등을 이유로 내세워 국민의 형사재판참여를 반대하는 목소리도 적지 않다. 그러나 선진 각국의 사례에서 확인되는 바와 같이 기소와 재판에 대한 다양한 형태의 국민참여는 민주주의 이념을 실현하는 길이자 형사사법권의 공정성을 확보할 수 있는 방안이 될 수 있고, 고질적인 법조 병폐라고 지적되었던 법조유착과 비리, 전관예우 등의 문제를 치유할 수 있는 하나의 대안이자 계기가 될 수 있다는 이유로 학계 및 시민단체 등을 시작으로 국민의 사법참여를 보장하여야 한다는 주장이 꾸준히 제기되었다.

나. 이론적 논의

(1) 국민참여재판제도의 헌법적합성

대한민국 헌법 제27조 제1항은 "모든 국민은 헌법과 법률이 정한 법관에 의하여 법률에 의한 재판을 받을 권리를 가진다."고 규정하고 있는바, 여기서의 '법관'이 직업법관에 한정되는 것인지 여부에 관하여, 종래 헌법학계에서는 시민이 사실판정에만 관여하는 경우는 합헌이며, 법률판단에까지 관여하는 것은 위헌이라는 의견이 많았다. 이 견해에 따르면 사실판단에만 관여하는 배심제는 합헌인 반면, 사실판단과 법률판단(혹은 양형판단)까지 관여하는 참심제는 위헌이라는 결론이 도출된다.

대한민국 헌법 제27조의 '법관'은 제정 당시에는 직업법관이 아닌 자에 의한 재판을 막기 위한 장치로서 '직업법관'에 의한 재판을 보장함으로써 국민의 권리를 보장하려는 목적으로 제정되었다고 할 수 있다. 그러나 이 조항이 사법절차에 대한 시민참여를 막기 위한 목적으로 제정되었다고는 할 수 없고, 국민이 '직업법관이 주도적인 역할을 하는 가운데, 시민사법참여가 보장되는 형태'를 원하는 경우 이를 허용하는 것이 헌법에 위반된다고는 할 수 없다는 견해가 있다. 즉 헌법 제27조의 재판청구권은 '직업법관이 아닌 자들로 구성된 재판부에 의한 재판을 받지 아니할 권리'로 이해할 수 있다는 것이다.

그러나 위헌의 시비를 완전히 봉쇄하기는 어렵기 때문에 국민의 형사재판 참여에 관한 법률(이하 '참여법'이라 한다)에서는 원칙적으로 피고인의 청구에 의하여 참여재판을 실시하는 것으로 하고, 배심원의 평결결과에 판사가 기속되지 않도록 하였다(참여법 제5조 제2항, 제

46조 제5항). 또한 참여법에 상소에 관한 특별규정을 두지 않음으로
써 국민참여재판이든 통상의 형사재판이든 모두 제1심의 재판에 불
복하여 상소할 권리를 보장하고 있으며, 상소심은 직업법관만에 의한
재판이므로 국민참여재판의 위헌가능성을 배제할 수 있게 되었다.

(2) 배심제 vs. 참심제

배심제란 일반 국민으로 구성된 배심원이 재판에 참여하여 직업
법관으로부터 독립하여 유·무죄의 판단에 해당하는 평결을 내리고,
재판부는 그 평결에 기속되는 제도를 의미한다. 한편, 참심제란 일반
국민인 참심원이 직업법관과 함께 재판부의 일원으로 참여하여 직업
법관과 동등한 권한을 가지고 사실문제 및 법률문제를 판단하는 제
도를 말한다.

한국의 국민참여재판제도는 배심제와 참심제의 요소를 혼합한
형태라고 할 수 있다. 즉, 선정된 배심원은 원칙적으로 법관의 관여
없이 평결한다는 점에서 배심제적 요소를 가지고 있으나, 만장일치
에 이르지 못한 경우 반드시 판사의 의견을 청취하여야 하고, 심리에
관여한 판사와 양형에 관하여 토의하는 것은 참심제적 요소라 할 수
있다. 한편, 배심원의 평결결과는 권고적 효력을 가질 뿐 법원을 기
속하지 않는다는 점에서 수정된 배심제의 요소도 가지고 있다.

다. 참여재판제도의 도입을 위한 움직임

1990년대부터 시민단체가 형사사법제도에 대한 감시 및 참여를
주도하면서 사법개혁의 일환으로 국민의 사법참여를 주장하기 시작
하였다. 이후 정부도 이러한 논의에 관심을 가지면서 '국민의 정부'
당시 사법제도 전반의 개혁을 추진하기 위하여 구성된 대통령 자문

기구인 사법개혁추진위원회는 1999년 12월경 배심제, 참심제 등 국
민의 사법참여방안은 중·장기적으로 긍정적으로 연구·검토할 과제
라고 최종 보고하였다.

　한편, 대법원은 2000년 2월경 21세기에 대비한 종합적 사법발
전계획인 "21세기 사법발전계획"을 수립하면서 국민의 사법참여 방
안에 관한 연구·검토를 주요 계획에 포함시켜 연구를 진행하여 왔
고, 나아가 2003. 10. 28. 그 산하에 사법개혁위원회를 설치하여 국
민의 사법참여를 포함한 사법제도 개혁 방안을 연구하도록 하였다.
사법개혁위원회에서는 배심제와 참심제 중 어느 제도를 도입할 것인
지에 관하여 논의하였으나, 어느 제도가 우리의 현실에 적합한지를
단정하기 어려우므로 향후 지속적인 연구를 통하여 기본 모델을 정
한 후 이를 우리의 현실에 맞게 변용하는 것이 필요하다고 결론지었
다. 이에 따라 사법개혁위원회는 2004. 12. 30. "2012년부터 국민의
사법참여가 실질적으로 보장되는 완성된 제도를 시행하는 것을 목표
로, 우선 제1단계 국민사법참여제도를 고안·실시하여 그 시행성과
를 실증적으로 분석한 후, 우리나라에 적합한 완성된 국민사법참여
제도를 설계하여 2012년에 시행하고, 제1단계 국민사법참여제도의
시행에 있어서는 배심이나 참심과 같은 단일한 형태의 기본모델을
결정하지는 않고, 배심·참심 요소를 혼용한 제도를 모델로 한다."
라고 건의하였다. 그 후 사법제도개혁추진위원회에서는 국민이 배심
원으로서 형사재판에 참여하는 국민참여재판의 도입을 골자로 한 '국
민의 형사재판참여에 관한 법률안'을 마련하였고, 위 법률안은
2005. 11. 29. 국무회의에서 의결되어 2005. 12. 6. 국회에 제출되
었다.

2. 국민참여재판제도 시행 전의 준비

가. 형사소송법 개정

법률에 정해진 절차에 따라 증거를 공개된 법정에서 조사하고 이를 토대로 피고인의 유·무죄 및 양형에 관한 심증 형성을 요구하는 공판중심주의와 그 실현을 위한 구두변론주의·직접주의·집중심리주의·실질적 증거조사는 국민참여재판의 시행에 필수적 요소이므로 형사소송법상 실질적 공판중심주의 요소를 강화하는 형사소송법 개정을 하였다.

나. 국민참여법, 규칙, 예규 제정

2007. 4. 30. 모두 60개 조문으로 구성된 '국민의 형사재판 참여에 관한 법률'이 국회 본회의를 통과하여 2007. 6. 1. 공포되었고, 그 시행일은 2008. 1. 1.로 정해졌다.

이에 따라 대법원은 2007. 7. 25. 규칙안 입법예고 후 다양한 외부 의견을 수렴하여 2007. 10. 4. 대법관 회의에서 국민의 형사재판 참여에 관한 규칙(이하 '참여규칙'이라 한다)을 제정하였고, 국민의 형사재판 참여에 관한 법률 및 규칙을 반영하여 배심원 선정절차 예규 등을 제정하고, 관련 예규를 개정하였다. 동시에 국민참여재판에 필요한 각종 재판서류 양식을 제정하고, 국민참여재판 절차 진행과 재판장 설명(instruction) 및 평의 절차 진행방법에 대하여 국민참여재판을 진행하는 재판부가 참고할 수 있도록 실무 매뉴얼을 발간하였다.

다. 배심원 관리 시스템 개발

참여법 제22조는 행정안전부로부터 송부받은 전산정보를 활용하여 매년 단위로 배심원후보예정자명부를 작성하고 그 명부에서 배심원후보를 선정하도록 하고 있다. 이 명부의 작성 및 배심원후보자의 선정・관리와 관련한 모든 절차는 대법원에서 개발한 배심원 관리 전산시스템에 의하도록 하였다.

라. 검찰, 변호사협회, 학계와의 협조 구축

법원은 국민참여재판제도의 시행을 준비할 기구로서 2007. 6. 18. '사법참여기획단 설립준비위원회'를 설치하고, 2008년 2월경 1단계 참여재판 시행 및 1단계 참여재판 조사・연구를 수행하기 위해 대법원에 사법참여기획단을 설치하였다.

마. 국민참여 모의재판 실시

(1) 법률 제정 이전에 사법개혁추진위원회가 주관하여 실제 국민이 배심원으로 참여하는 모의재판을 4회 실시하였다.

- 1회 : 2005. 8. 서울중앙지방법원, 살인죄
- 2회 : 2005. 12. 부산지방법원, 강간치상죄
- 3회 : 2006. 4. 서울중앙지방법원, 살인죄
- 4회 : 2006. 11. 광주지방법원, 뇌물죄

(2) 법률이 제정된 이후 18개 지방법원 본원에서 관할 구역 주민이 배심원으로 참여하는 모의재판을 실시하였다.

- 2007. 9. 10. 서울중앙지방법원, 살인죄

- 2007. 10. 29. 5개 지방법원(서울남부, 서울서부, 수원, 대구, 울산), 살인죄
- 2007. 11. 12. 13개 법원(서울중앙, 서울동부, 서울북부, 의정부, 인천, 춘천, 대전, 청주, 부산, 창원, 광주, 전주, 제주), 강간치상죄
- 2007. 11. 26. 의정부지방법원, 2007. 12. 10. 서울지방법원 등 여러 법원에서 실시

(3) 2010년부터 일반국민의 형사재판에 대한 이해를 제고하고 법원과 재판에 대한 이해를 높여 사법부에 대한 국민의 신뢰를 제고함과 아울러 참여자들의 법적인 판단능력을 함양하기 위하여 국민참여재판의 정식 배심원과 별도로 그림자 배심원단을 구성하여 재판의 전 과정을 참관한 후 실제 평의와 같은 방법으로 유·무죄 및 양형 등 재판결과에 대한 토론을 하도록 하였다.

바. 교육 및 홍보

대법원은 2007. 8. 참여법률에 대한 해설서를 발간하여 법률실무 종사자 및 일반 국민을 대상으로 참여법률에 대한 개괄적인 해설서를 발간·배포하였다.

2007. 10. 26.에는 배심원을 대상으로 하는 16쪽 분량의 안내서(Juror Handbook)를 발간하였다. 안내서는 인사말, 질문과 답변, 알기 쉬운 법률용어로 구성되어 있는데, 질문과 답변은 배심원으로 참여하게 되는 국민이 궁금해 하는 30개 항목으로 이루어져 있다. 이 안내서는 배심원후보자에게 선정기일 통지서를 발송할 때 함께 송달하도록 함으로써, 배심원후보자들이 형사재판절차에 대하여 충분히 이해하고 선정기일에 출석할 수 있도록 하고 있다.

선정기일에 출석한 배심원후보자에 대해서는 '배심원 오리엔테이션 비디오(Jury Orientation Video)'를 상영하여 국민참여재판절차 및 배심원의 역할과 유의사항에 대하여 안내하고 있다. 또한, 대법원 홈페이지의 참여재판 홍보코너, 만화 형식의 홍보 책자, 기념품을 제작하여 일반 국민이 참여재판에 대하여 쉽게 알 수 있도록 노력하고 있다.

이외에도, 국민참여재판의 원활한 시행을 위하여 일반 국민의 자발적이고 적극적인 참여를 이끌어 내기 위해 재판 참여로 인한 불이익을 당하지 않도록 하는 여건 조성이 필요하다는 인식 하에, 법률 제50조에 관련 내용을 명시하였을 뿐 아니라 법률 시행 전인 2007. 10. 행정안전부, 노동부 및 경제단체에 협조를 요청하였다.

3. 현   황

가. 국민참여재판의 내용

(1) 대상사건(개정 및 시행)

참여법의 제정 당시에는 고의로 사망의 결과를 야기한 범죄 및 강도와 강간의 결합범, 강도 또는 강간으로 치상·치사의 결과가 발생한 경우 및 일정 범위의 수뢰죄, 그리고 해당 범죄의 미수죄·교사죄·방조죄·예비죄·음모죄에 해당하는 사건, 해당 사건의 관련 사건으로서 병합하여 심리하는 사건을 참여재판의 대상사건으로 하였다. 그러나 대법원규칙을 개정하여 2009. 7. 1.부터 강도, 특수강도, 강간, 준강간, 상습절도 등이 추가되었고, 2012. 7. 1. 부터는 법원조직법 제32조 제 1 항에 따른 합의부 관할 사건 전체로 대상을 확대하였다(참여법 제 5 조 제 1 항).

(2) 배심원의 권한과 의무

배심원은 국민참여재판을 하는 사건에 관하여 사실의 인정, 법령의 적용 및 형의 양정에 관한 의견을 제시할 권한이 있다(참여법 제12조 제1항). 배심원은 법령을 준수하고 독립하여 성실히 직무를 수행하여야 하고(참여법 제12조 제2항), 직무상 알게 된 비밀을 누설하거나 재판의 공정을 해하는 행위를 하여서는 아니 된다(참여법 제12조 제3항).

(3) 배심원 및 예비배심원의 수

법정형이 사형·무기징역 또는 무기금고에 해당하는 사건의 경우에는 9인의 배심원이 참여하고, 그 외의 대상사건에 대한 국민참여재판에는 7인의 배심원이 참여한다. 다만, 피고인 또는 변호인이 공판준비절차에서 공소사실의 주요 내용을 인정한 때에는, 법원은 5인의 배심원을 참여하게 할 수 있다(참여법 제13조 제1항). 또한 법원은 사건의 내용에 비추어 특별한 사정이 있다고 인정되고 검사·피고인 또는 변호인의 동의가 있는 경우에 한하여 결정으로 배심원의 수를 7인과 9인 중에서 달리 정할 수 있다(참여법 제13조 제2항).

한편, 배심원의 결원 등에 대비하여 5인 이내의 예비배심원을 둘 수 있다(참여법 제14조 제1항).

(4) 배심원의 자격

배심원은 만 20세 이상의 대한민국 국민 중에서 선정되는데, 공무원의 결격사유가 있는 자는 배심원으로 선정될 수 없고, 대통령, 국회의원, 지방자치단체의 장 및 지방의회 의원, 법조인, 법원·검찰 공무원, 경찰·교정·보호관찰 공무원, 군인·군무원·소방공무원 등 배심원에게 과도한 영향을 줄 수 있거나 배심원으로서의 직무수행에 어려움이 있는 자는 제외된다. 또한 피해자, 피고인 또는 피해자의 친족, 법정대리인, 사건의 증인 및 피해자·피고인의 대리인, 사건을 조사한 경찰·검찰 및 관련자는 제척사유에 해당하여 배심원으로 선정될 수 없다(참여법 제16조~제19조).

그 이외에도, 만 70세 이상의 고령자, 과거 5년 이내에 배심원후보자로서 선정기일에 출석한 사람, 금고 이상의 형의 죄로 기소되어 사건이 종결되지 아니한 사람, 법령에 따라 체포 또는 구금되어 있는 사람, 배심원 직무의 수행으로 제3자에게 위해를 초래하거나 직업상 회복될 수 없는 손해를 입을 우려가 있는 사람, 중병·상해 또는 장애로 인하여 법원에 출석하기 곤란한 사람 등은 법원이 직권 또는 신청에 따라 배심원 직무의 수행을 면제할 수 있다(참여법 제20조).

(5) 여비, 일당

참여법 제15조는 대법원규칙으로 정하는 바에 따라 배심원·예비배심원 및 배심원후보자에게 여비와 일당을 지급하도록 하고 있다. 여비와 일당은 매년 예산의 범위 안에서 대법관 회의로 의결하여 정하는데, 일당은 선정기일에 출석한 배심원 후보자에게는 5만원, 배심원 및 예비배심원으로 선정되어 직무를 수행한 사람에게는 10만원을 지급하고, 여비 및 숙박료는 법원공무원에 준하여 지급하도록 하고 있다.

(6) 선정절차

지방법원장은 매년 관할구역 내에 거주하는 만 20세 이상의 국민 중에서 배심원후보예정자를 무작위로 선정하여 명부를 작성하고, 이 명부에서 필요한 수만큼 배심원후보자를 무작위 추출 방식으로 정하여 선정기일을 통지한다.

(7) 배심원의 절차상 권리와 의무

공판정에서 검사와 피고인 및 변호인은 대등하게 마주 보고 위
치하며, 배심원과 예비배심원은 검사·피고인 및 변호인의 사이 왼
쪽에 위치한다. 증인석은 재판장과 검사·피고인 및 변호인의 사이
오른쪽에 배심원과 예비배심원을 마주 보고 위치한다(참여법 제39조).

배심원은 피고인·증인에 대하여 필요한 사항의 신문을 재판장
에게 요청하고, 재판장의 허가를 얻어 각자 필기를 하여 이를 평의에
사용할 수 있다. 그러나 심리 도중 재판장의 허락 없이 평의, 평결
장소를 이탈할 수 없으며, 평의 시작 전에 견해를 밝히거나 논의하는
것, 재판절차 외에서 당해 사건에 대한 정보를 수집·조사하는 것,
평의·평결 또는 토의에 관한 비밀을 누설하는 것이 금지되어 있다
(참여법 제41조).

(8) 평의·평결·토의

배심원은 판사의 관여 없이 독자적으로 유·무죄에 관하여 평의
하고 전원일치로 평결한다. 전원의 의견이 일치하지 않는 때에는 평
결을 하기 전에 판사의 의견을 들은 후 다수결로 유·무죄의 평결을
한다. 판사는 평의에 참석하여 의견을 진술한 경우에도 평결에 참여
할 수 없다. 배심원의 평결이 유죄인 경우 배심원은 판사와 함께 양
형에 관하여 토의하고 그에 관한 의견을 개진한다(참여법 제46조 제 2
항, 제 3 항, 제 4 항).

(9) 판결선고

배심원의 평결 및 의견은 법원을 기속하지 아니하고, 평결결과
의 의견을 집계한 서면은 소송기록에 편철한다. 재판장은 판결선고

시 피고인에게 배심원의 평결결과를 고지하여야 하며, 배심원의 평
결결과와 다른 판결을 선고하는 때에는 피고인에게 그 이유를 설명
하여야 한다(참여법 제46조 제5항 및 제6항, 제48조 제4항).

그리고 판결서에는 배심원이 재판에 참여하였다는 취지를 기재
하여야 하고, 배심원의 의견을 기재할 수 있으며, 배심원의 평결결과
와 다른 판결을 선고하는 때에는 판결서에 그 이유를 기재하여야 한
다(참여법 제49조 제1항, 제2항).

나. 현   황

2012. 2. 29. 현재 대상사건 22,667건 중 6.8%인 1,551건이 국
민참여재판으로 접수되어 그 중 배제 또는 철회된 사건을 제외하고
606건을 국민참여재판으로 진행하였다. 참여재판은 피고인이 원하
여야 실시되는데 2008. 1. 1.~2012. 2. 29. 사이에 대상사건 22,667
건 중 참여재판은 1,551건(6.8%) 접수되었다. 사건유형별로 보면 살
인이 23.9%로 가장 많고 강도(26.2%), 성범죄(22.1%), 기타(22.2%),
상해치사(5.7%) 순이다.

국민참여재판 사건을 보면 국선변호인 선임 비율이 81.4%로 높
다. 2008년 국민참여재판이 시행된 이래 자백사건과 부인사건의 비
율은 매년 3대 7 정도이고, 배심원의 평결과 판사의 판결이 일치하
는 경우가 90%로서 대체로 일치한다고 할 수 있다. 2012. 2. 29. 기
준으로 배심원이 유죄의 평결을 하였으나 재판부가 무죄의 판결을
한 사건은 4건, 반대로 배심원이 무죄 평결을 하였으나 재판부가 유
죄 판결한 사건은 50건 있었으며, 평결과 판결이 불일치하였던 사건
중 항소심에서 유·무죄의 판단이 바뀐 사례가 2건 있었다. 배심원
의 양형 의견도 법원을 기속하지 않지만 양형의견과 실제 선고형량

의 차이는 ± 1년 이내인 경우가 약 90%를 차지하였다.

4. 국민참여재판제도에 대한 일반 시민(특히 배심원)의 평가

국민참여재판제도가 시행된 2008년에 실시한 일반인 대상 법원 관련 의식조사결과에 의하면, 59.3%가 국민참여재판제도에 대하여 알고 있고 69.3%는 국민참여재판으로 인하여 국민의 재판신뢰도가 개선될 것이라고 응답하였다. 또한 3년간의 시행 후 실시된 설문조사에서는 87.5%의 시민이 참여재판으로 재판결과의 신뢰성이 향상될 수 있다고 보았고, 80% 이상의 시민이 재판의 공정성·투명성 향상, 국민의 법지식 함양, 국민의 준법정신 함양 등의 목적을 달성할 수 있다고 응답하였다.

한편, 대법원이 배심원을 대상으로 2008~2011년에 실시한 설문조사에서는 96.5%의 배심원이 직무 수행에 만족하고 긍정적으로 평가하고 있는 것으로 나타났다. 88.1%의 배심원이 재판 내용을 모두 또는 대부분 이해하였으며, 86.5%의 배심원이 심리에 대부분 집중하였고, 72.9%는 의견을 충분히 밝혔다고 하고 있으며, 재판장의 설명이 매우(70.2%) 또는 어느 정도(28.2%) 유익하다고 응답하였다. 그러나 장시간에 걸친 재판(46.1%), 이해하기 어려운 법률용어(23.6%), 증거 이해의 어려움(10.5%), 보복 등 안전에 대한 우려(9.4%), 수입 감소나 직장에서의 불이익(10.4%)을 어려운 점으로 꼽았다.

II. 국민참여재판의 개선 과제와 그 도입이 형사소송절차 에 미치는 영향

1. 개선 과제

가. 실시율의 제고

(1) 신청주의의 한계

국민참여재판의 신청율이 저조한 것은 참여재판에 대한 사회적 인지도가 낮은 데에도 원인이 있으므로, 시민이나 피고인에게 홍보 를 강화하여 국민참여재판의 제도 취지나 장점 등을 널리 인식시킬 필요가 있다.

참여법에서는 피고인이 공소장 부본을 송달받은 날부터 7일 이 내에 국민참여재판을 원하는지 여부에 관한 의사가 기재된 서면을 제출하도록 하고(참여법 제8조 제2항), 피고인이 그 기간 내에 의사 확인서를 제출하지 아니한 때에는 국민참여재판을 원하지 아니하는 것으로 본다(참여법 제8조 제3항).

이와 같이 참여법상 신청기간이 지나치게 짧게 규정되어 있는 것도 신청율을 떨어뜨리는 원인이 되고 있으나, 실무상으로는 공소 장 부본을 송달받은 날부터 7일 이내에 의사확인서를 제출하지 아니 한 피고인도 제1회 공판기일이 열리기 전까지는 국민참여재판 신청 을 할 수 있고 법원은 그 의사를 확인하여 국민참여재판으로 진행할 수 있도록 하고 있다(대법원 2009. 10. 23.자 2009모1032 결정).

한편 피고인이 국민참여재판을 신청한 경우에도 그 철회율이 높게 나타나는데, 이는 법원이나 검찰, 변호인의 참여재판에 대한 태도, 양형, 동료 재소자들의 의견 등이 종합적으로 반영된 것으로 짐작된다.

(2) 신청주의의 개선 방안

(가) 신청주의를 폐기하여야 한다는 주장

신청주의는 형사재판의 절차방식을 피고인의 처분에 맡기는 것으로 형사재판권 행사의 통일성과 평등성의 관점에서 문제가 있다거나, 국민참여재판제도가 피고인의 절차선택권을 보장하기 위하여 도입된 것이 아니라 사법의 공정성과 투명성을 위하여 '국민이 재판에 참여할 권리'를 보장하기 위한 제도라고 하는 관점에서 피고인의 선택권에 입각한 신청주의 방식을 폐기하고 대상사건에 대한 국민참여재판의 필요적 실시방안으로 전환해야 한다는 주장이 있다.

이러한 견해에서는 피고인이 공소사실의 전부 혹은 주요부분을 자백한 사건은 제외하는 등으로 대상사건 범위를 한정함으로써 과중한 사건 부담을 피할 수 있다고 본다.

(나) 신청주의를 유지하여야 한다는 주장

신청주의를 유지하여야 한다는 입장은, 피고인의 신청이 있는 경우에만 국민참여재판을 실시할 수 있도록 현행 방식을 유지하자는 주장과 국민참여재판의 대상이 되는 사건에 대해서는 원칙적으로 전부 국민참여재판으로 하되, 피고인이 국민참여재판을 희망하지 않는다는 의사를 제출한 경우에는 통상재판을 받도록 하는 방식으로 변경하자는 주장이 있을 수 있다.

피고인이 국민참여재판을 희망하지 않는 경우에만 통상재판을 받도록 하자는 주장은 피고인이 국민참여재판을 희망하지 않는다는 의사를 표시하는 경우에는 자동으로 국민참여재판의 배제효과가 발생하도록 하자는 입장과 그러한 의사를 표시한 경우에도 법원의 판단을 거쳐 통상재판에 회부될 수 있도록 하자는 주장으로 나누어 볼 수 있으나, 대부분 후자의 입장이다.

신청주의를 유지하여야 한다는 주장은, 피고인의 의사를 존중하는 것이 국민주권주의에 비추어 바람직하고 기본권의 보장을 위해서는 피고인의 선택을 폭넓게 인정하여야 하며 국민참여재판의 의무적 실시는 헌법상의 기본권인 법관에 의한 재판을 받을 권리를 침해할 수 있음을 근거로 하고 있다.

(3) 배제결정의 제한

참여법은 배제결정 사유를 폭넓게 규정하고 있고, 특히 제 9 조 제 1 항 제 4 호(2012. 1. 17. 개정 전의 제 3 호)의 "그 밖에 국민참여재판으로 진행하는 것이 적절하지 않다고 인정되는 경우"와 같은 추상적인 배제결정 사유를 인정하는 것은 사실상 피고인의 권리를 보장하지 않는 것과 다를 바 없다.

국민참여재판을 현실적으로 진행할 수 없는 특별한 사정이 있는 경우를 감안하여 예외적으로 이를 존치한다고 하더라도, 배제결정의 사유를 필요최소한도의 범위로 제한하고 그 사유도 구체화해야 할 것이다.

결국 대법원은 2010. 4. 27. 대법원예규의 개정으로 "그 밖에 국민참여재판으로 진행하는 것이 적절하지 않다고 인정되는 경우"를 「1. 추가 기소가 예상되는 경우, 2. 피고인에게 정신이상의 의심이 있는 경우, 3. 그 밖에 국민참여재판으로 진행할 경우 현저한 절차지연 등으로 피고인의 신속한 재판을 받을 권리가 침해될 것으로 우려되는 경우」로 제한하였다(국민참여재판의 접수 및 처리 예규 제 6 조 제 4 항).

나. 단기간의 공판기일

하루 또는 이틀의 공판만으로 국민참여재판이 종결되는 경우가 대부분이다. 이것이 가능한 배경으로는 쟁점이 많거나 증인이 많은 복잡한 사건은 법원의 배제결정으로 이미 배제되었다는 점, 국민참여재판 실시사건의 약 30%를 점하는 자백사건의 경우에는 그다지 장시간의 증거조사를 요하지 않는다는 점, 공판준비절차가 필요적으로 실시되고 있어 이 절차에서 쟁점정리가 잘 이루어지고 있다는 점, 배심원들이 늦은 시각까지 재판을 하더라도 당일 재판을 끝내기를 원한다는 점 등이 거론되고 있다.

그러나 개별사건의 특성에 맞게 심리기일을 더 늘여야 할 필요가 있고, 배심원들의 요청에 근거하고 법원 및 검찰의 열의를 바탕으로 한 것이라 하더라도 밤늦은 시각까지 재판을 진행하는 것이 바람직하다고 할 수는 없다. 실제로 배심원을 대상으로 한 설문조사에서 재판이 지나치게 장시간 지속되고 심지어 심야까지도 계속되는 것에 대하여 가장 많은 응답자들이 불만을 표시하였다.

다. 평결의 권고적 효력

평결결과는 권고적 효력만을 가지고 있으므로 배심원 평결과 다른 판결이 선고될 수 있다. 이러한 경우 배심원은 자신이 내린 평결이 단지 권고적 효력에 그친다는 사실을 실감하게 될 것인데, 상당한 불편을 감수하고 재판에 참여한 국민으로서는 이를 유쾌하게 받아들이기 어려울 것이다. 그러한 경험이 국민참여재판에 적극적으로 참여하는 것을 기대하기 어렵게 하는 요인으로 작용할 수 있기 때문에,

법원은 가급적 배심원 평결의 효력을 존중해 나가는 방향으로 국민참여재판제도를 운영하는 것이 바람직하다.

배심원의 평결에 기속력을 부여하는 방향으로 나아가야 한다는 주장도 있으나, 평결에 기속력을 부여하는 것은 헌법상의 기본권인 법관에 의한 재판을 받을 권리를 침해할 수 있다는 점에서 위헌시비를 불러올 수 있다.

만약 평결에 기속력을 부여하게 된다면 현재의 평결방식에 대한 수정이 수반될 필요가 있다. 만장일치에 이르지 못한 경우 단순다수결로 평결을 내리는 것은 '합리적인 의심을 넘어서는 사실의 증명'의 관점에서 수용될 수 없는 문제점을 가지고 있기 때문이다. 만장일치를 원칙으로 하거나 적어도 80% 이상의 절대적 다수결을 유지할 필요가 있을 것이다.

라. 배심원의 양형의견과 양형기준의 관계

양형기준이란 일정한 범죄의 기본적인 양형 범위를 정한 후 미리 정해 둔 가중·감경사유에 해당하면 그 범위를 수정하여 도출된 최종적인 양형 범위 내에서 형을 양정하는 것을 말한다.

국민참여재판에서 배심원들에게 이러한 양형기준 자체를 제시하는 실무례도 있다고 한다. 판사의 입장에서는 국민참여재판에서 배심원이 개진하는 양형의견보다 양형기준의 객관적 적용에 보다 관심을 기울이는 경우도 있을 것이다.

이와 관련하여 양형기준제에서 제시하는 양형요소들을 배심원들이 심리한 후 형량결정까지 하는 체제로 갈 수 있다는 전망과 양형기준제 도입으로 양형에 관한 국민의 신뢰도 어느 정도 향상될 것이므로 양형기준제가 마련되어 있는 미국의 대다수 주처럼 오히려 배심원의 관여 없는 법관양형제도로 나아갈 수 있다는 전망이 있다.

마. 항소 제한의 필요성

현재 참여법에는 상소에 관하여는 특별규정을 두고 있지 않다. 따라서 제1심이 국민참여재판으로 진행된 사건의 경우에도 항소와 상고 절차는 통상의 형사재판과 마찬가지로 형사소송법의 상소절차가 적용된다.

일반적으로 우리나라 형사재판의 항소심은 속심적 성격이 강한 것으로 이해된다. 형사소송법상 제1심 판결의 사실인정 부분에 대하여 항소심에서 이를 파기할 수 있고, 또한 파기할 경우에는 항소심에서의 자판을 원칙으로 규정하고 있다(형사소송법 제364조).

실무상으로는 "배심원이 증인신문 등 사실심리의 전 과정에 함께 참여한 후 증인이 한 진술의 신빙성 등 증거의 취사와 사실의 인정에 관하여 만장일치의 의견으로 내린 무죄의 평결이 재판부의 심증에 부합하여 그대로 채택된 경우라면, 이러한 절차를 거쳐 이루어진 증거의 취사 및 사실의 인정에 관한 제1심의 판단은 실질적 직접심리주의 및 공판중심주의의 취지와 정신에 비추어 항소심에서의 새로운 증거조사를 통해 그에 명백히 반대되는 충분하고도 납득할 만한 현저한 사정이 나타나지 않는 한 한층 더 존중될 필요가 있다."라고 한다(대법원 2010. 3. 25. 선고 2009도14065 판결).

한편, 국민참여재판에서 배심원의 무죄평결과 그에 따른 재판부의 무죄판결이 있었다면 이에 대해서는 사실오인을 이유로 한 검사의 항소를 금지하자는 주장이 있고, 더 나아가 항소심에 대하여 사후심이나 법률심으로서의 성격을 강화해야 한다는 주장도 있다. 다수 국민의 건전한 상식을 바탕으로 판단된 사실인정이 어렵지 않게 항소심에서 파기된다면, 국민참여재판에 대한 가치를 폄훼하는 인식이 팽배해져 제도 자체의 의미를 퇴색시킬 우려가 있다는 것이다.

그러나 국민참여재판에 대하여 피고인의 항소를 제한하는 것은 헌법상의 기본권인 법관에 의한 재판을 받을 권리를 침해하여 위헌의 가능성이 있고, 항소심의 성격을 개혁하는 문제는 우리나라의 심급제도와의 관련성 속에서 보다 면밀하고 종합적인 검토가 필요하다.

2. 국민참여재판 도입이 형사소송절차에 미치는 영향

가. 공판준비절차의 강화

(1) 필수적 절차

참여법의 제정과 때를 같이하여 형사소송법이 2007. 6. 1. 개정되면서(이하 '개정 형소법'이라 한다) 공판준비절차를 도입하였다(형소법 제266조의5 이하). 공판준비절차는 형사재판의 효율적이고 집중적인 심리를 위한 것으로 일반형사사건에서는 임의적 절차이나 국민참여재판 사건에서는 필수적 절차로 되어 있다(참여법 제36조 제1항 본문).

이는 국민참여재판이 조기에 정착될 수 있도록 하기 위하여 일반 형사재판보다 집중심리에 더욱 충실하여 재판이 신속하게 종결되도록 함과 아울러 공판준비절차를 통하여 법률전문가가 아닌 배심원으로 하여금 증거능력이 없는 증거에 노출되는 것 자체를 막아야 할 필요성이 있기 때문이다.

국민참여재판의 공판준비절차는 피고인의 국민참여재판 희망 여부를 확인하는 수단이 되고, 쟁점정리를 통하여 증명대상을 확정하고 입증계획의 수립과정을 거쳐 집중증거조사를 준비하는 역할을 하며, 본격적인 공판기일을 지정하고 그에 맞추어 배심원 선정절차를 진행할 수 있도록 하는 선도기능을 수행하게 된다.

(2) 공판준비절차의 운영

법원은 공판준비기일을 열어 주장과 증거를 정리하고 심리계획을 수립하여야 하고(참여법 제37조 제 1 항), 검사·피고인 또는 변호인은 증거를 미리 수집·정리하는 등 공판준비절차가 원활하게 진행되도록 협력하여야 한다(참여법 제36조 제 4 항).

법원은 개정 형소법 제266조의15에 따라 공판기일 사이에 공판준비기일을 진행하는 때 이외에는 배심원 선정기일 이전에 국민참여재판의 공판준비절차를 마쳐야 한다(참여규칙 제27조). 법원은 공판준비기일에서 행해진 쟁점 및 증거에 관한 정리결과를 공판준비기일조서에 기재하여야 하고(개정 형소법 제266조의10 제 2 항), 공판준비기일이 종결된 경우에는 실권효의 적용을 받게 된다(개정 형소법 제266조의13 제 1 항).

증거의 채부와 관련하여 검찰측은 공판준비기일에 구체적인 증거서류나 증거물은 제시하지 않은 상태에서 증거목록만을 제시한 다음, 피고인측이 부동의하는 증거에 대하여 증인을 신청하고 그 외에도 필요한 경우 공소사실의 입증을 위하여 증인을 신청하고 있으며, 피고인측도 입증취지를 적시하면서 자신에게 유리한 증인을 신청하고 있다. 이때 양측의 의견을 들어 법원은 그 채부여부를 결정한다.

나. 공판절차의 변화

(1) 개정 형소법의 내용

당초의 참여법안은 상당히 많은 분량의 공판절차에 관한 규정을 포함하고 있었는데 개정 형소법이 함께 국회를 통과하면서 중복되는 조항은 모두 삭제되었다. 이는 국민참여재판의 공판절차도 일반 형사사건의 통상공판절차와 동일하게 진행되어야 함을 의미하나, 배심원이 참여하는 재판과 그렇지 않은 재판의 실무운영은 어느 정도 다를 수밖에 없을 것으로 예상된다.

　(가) 공판중심주의의 강화

　　형소법 개정 이전부터 형사소송법은 제254조 제 1 항에 "공소를 제기함에는 공소장을 관할 법원에 제출하여야 한다."라고 규정하고, 형사소송규칙은 제118조 제 2 항에 "공소장에는 … 사건에 관하여 법원에 예단이 생기게 할 수 있는 서류 기타 물건을 첨부하거나 그 내용을 인용하여서는 아니 된다."라고 규정하고 있었으나, 실제로는 검사가 원칙적으로 공소제기와 동시에 수사기록 일체를 법원에 제출하여 왔고, 재판부로서도 제 1 회 공판기일에 들어가기 전에 수사기록을 살펴보고 쟁점을 사전에 정리해 들어가는 사례가 있었다.

　　그러나 국민참여재판제도가 도입됨과 동시에 형사소송규칙도 개정되어 "법원은 증거신청을 기각·각하하거나, 증거신청에 대한 결정을 보류하는 경우, 증거신청인으로부터 당해 증거서류 또는 증거물을 제출받아서는 아니 된다."라고 규정하기에 이르렀다(형사소송규칙 제134조 제 4 항).

　　사실 공판중심주의가 전제되지 않고는 국민참여재판은 불가능하다. 국민참여재판은 사건기록을 직접 검토할 수 없는 배심원이 법정에서의 주장·입증 내용을 듣고 보는 것만으로 사건의 쟁점을 파악하고 적정한 결론에 도달할 수 있도록 하는 완전한 공판중심주의를 이상으로 삼고 있는 것이다.

　　따라서 개정 형소법에서는 실질적 공판중심주의의 요소를 강화하였다. 즉 종래의 조서재판의 폐해를 극복하고 공판정에서 소송관계인의 활발한 구두변론을 통해 사건의 실체관계를 파악하기 위한 구두변론주의 조항을 신설하고(형소법 제275조의3), 증거물의 제시와 증거서류의 요지 고지의 주체를 재판장에서 증거신청인으로 변경하고, 증거조사의 방법도 변경하여 원칙적으로 증거신청인이 낭독하도록 하였다(형소법 제292조).

(나) 모두절차의 충실화

개정 형소법은 모두절차를 더욱 충실하게 하여 절차진행 초기단계에서 공소사실과 사건의 쟁점, 입증계획이 명확하게 현출될 수 있도록 하였다(형소법 제285조, 제286조, 제287조). 임의적 절차로 되어 있던 기소요지 진술절차를 필수적 절차로 변경함과 동시에 원칙적으로 공소사실, 죄명 및 적용법조 전부를 낭독하게 하고, 필요한 경우 공소요지를 진술할 수 있도록 하였다. 피고인의 답변절차, 재판장의 쟁점정리를 위한 질문과 검사와 피고인측의 입증계획 진술절차 등을 새로 추가하였다.

국민참여재판의 경우 사실판단자인 배심원이 공판절차에서 비로소 처음 대상사건을 접하고 쟁점 등을 이해하게 되므로 모두절차상의 쟁점정리절차를 충실하게 진행할 필요가 있다.

(다) 피고인신문제도의 변경

개정 형소법은 피고인신문제도를 변경하였다(형소법 제296조의2). 개정 전에는 피고인신문은 반드시 증거조사를 개시하기 전에 이루어져야 했다. 개정 형소법은 피고인신문의 기능 중에서 다투는 부분과 자백하는 부분을 구별하는 기능을 피고인 모두진술로 대체하고, 피고인 진술을 증거로 활용하고 피고인의 변소를 탄핵하거나 이를 배심원의 설득에 사용하기 위하여 피고인신문을 원칙적으로 증거조사 종료 후에 실시하도록 하였다.

(라) 법정증언 중심의 입증 유도

개정 형소법은 증거서류보다는 법정증언을 중심으로 입증활동이 이루어질 수 있도록 수사기관이 작성한 조서의 증거능력을 인정하기 위한 요건을 일부 개정하였다.

피고인이 공판정에서 검사 작성의 피의자신문조서의 실질적 진정성립을 부인하는 경우 '원진술자의 진술'이외에 성립의 진정을 인정할 다른 방법이 없으므로 해당 조서를 증거로 사용할 수 없었으나, 개정 형소법은 이 경우 예상되는 실체적 진실발견의 어려움을 방지하기 위하여 실질적 진정성립의 인정 방법을 개정 전의 '피고인의 공판정에서의 진술' 이외에 '영상녹화물 기타 객관적인 방법'에 의해서도 증명될 수 있도록 하되, 조서의 진정성립 외에도 조서에 기재된 진술이 특히 신빙할 수 있는 상태하에서 행하여졌음이 증명되어야 증거능력을 인정할 수 있음을 분명히 하여 해석상의 논란을 해소하였다(형소법 제312조 제1항, 제2항).

그리고 종래 전문법칙의 예외사유로 규정된 "진술자의 사망, 질병, 외국거주, 기타 사유" 중 "기타 사유"를 폭넓게 해석하여 피고인의 방어권이나 반대신문권이 충분히 보장되지 못하였던 문제점이 있었으나, 개정 형소법은 증거능력에 대한 예외사유를 "공판준비 또는 공판기일에 진술을 요하는 자가 사망·질병·외국거주·소재불명 그 밖에 이에 준하는 사유로 인하여 진술할 수 없는 때"로 엄격히 규정하였다(형소법 제314조).

(2) 참여법의 특칙

국민참여재판에서 배심원석은 법대를 향하여 좌측에 위치하고, 검사와 피고인 및 변호인의 좌석은 마주보고 위치하며, 증인의 좌석은 배심원석의 정면에 위치한다(참여법 제39조).

국민참여재판은 피고인의 자백에도 불구하고 간이공판절차에 의한 심판을 할 수 없으며(참여법 제43조), 배심원 또는 예심배심원은 법원의 증거능력에 관한 심리에 관여할 수 없다(참여법 제44조).

그리고 일반형사재판에서는 검사나 피고인 또는 변호인의 신청이 있는 때에 특별한 사정이 없는 한 공판정에서의 심리의 전부 또는 일부를 속기사로 하여금 속기하게 하거나 녹음장치 또는 영상녹화장치를 사용하여 녹음 또는 영상녹화할 수 있으나(개정 형소법 제56조의2 제1항), 국민참여재판의 경우 공판정 심리의 속기·녹음 및 영상녹화를 의무화하여 법원은 검사나 피고인 또는 변호인의 신청 여부와 관계없이 특별한 사정이 없는 한 공판정에서의 심리를 속기사로 하여금 속기하게 하거나 녹음장치 또는 영상녹화장치를 사용하여 녹음 또는 영상녹화하여야 하고, 이에 따른 속기록·녹음테이프 또는 비디오테이프는 공판조서와는 별도로 보관되어야 하며, 검사·피고인 또는 변호인은 비용을 부담하고 속기록·녹음테이프 또는 비디오테이프의 사본을 청구할 수 있도록 하고 있다(참여법 제40조).

재판장은 변론이 종결된 후 법정에서 배심원에게 공소사실의 요지와 적용법조, 피고인과 변호인 주장의 요지, 증거능력, 그 밖에 유의할 사항에 관하여 설명하여야 한다. 이 경우 필요한 때에는 증거의 요지에 관하여 설명할 수 있다(참여법 제46조 제1항). "그 밖에 유의할 사항"이란 무죄추정의 원칙, 증거재판주의, 자유심증주의, 피고인의 증거제출 거부나 법정에서의 진술거부가 피고인의 유죄를 뒷받침하는 것으로 해석될 수 없다는 점, 증거능력이 배제된 증거를 무시하여야 한다는 점, 평의 및 평결의 방법, 배심원 대표를 선출하여야 한다는 취지 및 방법 등이다(참여규칙 제37조 제1항).

3. 평가와 전망

국민참여재판의 긍정적 효과로는 공판중심주의를 비롯한 형사소송법의 정신을 재판에서 구현할 수 있다는 점, 그리고 배심원에게 사건의 내용을 보다 잘 전달하기 위하여 법령용어를 알기 쉽게 설명하고 파워포인트나 사진 등 멀티미디어 수단을 활용함으로써 법정 내의 커뮤니케이션을 원활하게 할 수 있다는 점을 들 수 있다. 나아가 국민이 직접 사법절차에 참여하여 사법 불신의 원인이 되었던 전관예우, 무전유죄 의혹을 해소하고, 사법에 대한 직접민주주의를 실현하고 사법제도 체험함으로써 사법에 대한 신뢰를 높일 수 있다.

앞서 보았던 사법참여기획단의 설치나 관련 예규의 개정 외에도 대법원은 참여재판제도가 시작된 직후인 2008년 3월 수석부장판사 회의를 개최하고, 참여재판장 간담회를 매년 3~4월경 개최하고 있으며, 매년 상반기에 각 고등법원 단위로 국선전담변호인 워크샵에서 국민참여재판에서의 변론기법에 관하여 교육하는 등 제도의 정착을 위하여 많은 노력을 기울여 왔다.

그러나 앞서 보았듯이 시행과정에서 드러난 문제를 바탕으로 앞으로 해결하여야 할 과제도 남아 있다. 여러 비판을 포함한 각계의 의견을 수렴하여 2013년 완성된 형태의 국민참여재판의 실시를 위하여 2012년 7월 12일, 참여법 제55조에 근거하여 국민참여재판의 최

종 형태를 결정하는 국민사법참여위원회가 출범하였다. 이 위원회는
올 연말까지 한국의 실정에 맞는 국민참여재판의 형태를 결정하게
될 것이다.

大韓民國之國民參與審判制

李　東　洽*

Ⅰ. 國民參與審判制：現在與未來

1. 引進國民參與審判制的背景

A. 國民參與審判制之需求

國民參與司法程序有理論上之正當性，為加強司法程序中民主正當性、提高大眾對司法程序之信心、將普羅大眾的多元價值與通念反映於

---

* 前大法官 韓國憲法法院

審判中，並作出公正周全的審判。固然，有反對刑事審判實施國民參與審判制之說，特別指出陪審制的無效率，包括訴訟產生過多費用、陪審團欠缺法律專業知識、韓國文化非常重視人與人之間關係因而難以確保審判公正。然而，經許多已開發國家的例子證明，起訴和審判中不同型式的國民參與，是實現民主意識和確保刑事司法程序公正運作之途徑。再者，還可成為解決法律職業長期積累的問題，如司法包庇循私、貪污、給予前任官僚特權等。基於這些理由，學者和公民社群督促政府保障司法程序中人民之參與。

B. 理論爭議

(1) 國民參與審判制之合憲性

韓國憲法第27條第1項規定「所有人民應有依法律受符合憲法和法律規定之法官審判之權利」，至於法條中的「法官」是否限於職業法官的問題，憲法學者主張若人民僅參與事實之判斷，是合憲的；若人民參與法律之判斷，則可能違憲。

依此見解，僅為事實認定的陪審制是合憲的，而對事實和法律均作判決的參審制，可能是違憲的。

憲法第27條中「法官」之淵源，始於立法當時有意禁止非職業法官之審判，並賦予人民受職業法官審判的權利。但這並非禁止人民參與司法程序，且有論者主張，當人民要求的型式是一種「人民參與以職業法官為主的司法程序」時，並不違憲。換言之，第27條之受審判權可被理解為「不受非職業法官所組成之法院審判的權利」。

由於上述說法無法完全地反駁所有合憲性的質疑，從而，國民參與刑事審判法(以下稱「參與法」)規定，參與審判原則上經被告請求而開始，陪審團之評決不能拘束法官之判決(參與法第5條第2項及第46條第5項)。再者，由於參與法中沒有關於上訴的特別規定，則不論是國民參與審判或普通刑事審判，均保障對下級法院判決上訴的權利。且因為上訴程序僅有職業法官參與，可以避免所有國民參與審判制違憲的疑慮。

(2) 陪審制與參審制

陪審制是指由一般人組成的陪審團參與審判，並獨立地作出有罪或無罪評決，拘束法院。另一方面，參審制係一般人民的參審員與職業法官同為法庭成員之一並就判斷事實與法律爭點，有與職業法官相同的權力。

韓國的國民參與審判評陪審制和參審制的綜合體。也就是說，被選出的陪審員，不受法官之影響作出評決(反映陪審制的成份)；而當陪審員們無法達成一致意見時，必須聽取法官的意見，並與主持審判之審判長討論，以決定刑罰(反映參審制的成份)。另外，此改良式陪審制的另一個元素為陪審團之評決不具拘束力，對法院僅具建議效力。

C. 引進參與審判制的運動

自1990年代起，民間社會組織矛頭指向刑事司法制度之監督和參與，要求人民參與司法程序之改革。政府從那時起對此議題產生興趣，並在約1999年12月，即「人民的政府」時期，為領導司法改革而設立之主要建議機關－司法改革委員會，終於表示將研究並審視國民參與審判之方式，包括陪審制和參審制，作為可能採用的制度。

另一方面，韓國大法院於約2000年2月，為司法發展建立了全盤的計畫，稱為「21世紀司法發展計畫」(A Plan for Judicial Development in the 21st century)，計畫議題包括檢視國民參與司法程序，並對此議題展開研究。接著，在2003年10月28日，大法院下設司法改革委員會，並對

包括國民參與審判制在內的議題進行研究。司法改革委員會就陪審制和
參審制，討論要引進哪種制度，由於決定哪個制度最適合我們的社會非
常困難，最後作出結論認為在建立基礎的制度型式後，必須有些改良以
反應我們社會的真實面貌。因此，司法改革委員會於2004年12月30日提
出「為決定自2012年起實施之人民參與司法程序之最終型式，應分析國民
參與審判制的初始型式之發展、施行，並為實證研究，始能於2012年，設
計完成並施行適合我們國家的國民參與審判制度。在國民參與審判制度
的初始階段，並不會單單採用陪審制或參審制，而會採用含有陪審團和參
審員二者元素的改良式型式」。

　　司法改革委員會草擬國民參與刑事審判的法案，該法案規定人民以陪
審團參與刑事審判。國務院於2005年12月6日通過法案，並送交國會。

2. 施行國民參與審判制前之準備

A. 刑事訴訟法之修法

　　公判中心主義原則，如公開審查證據、有罪或無罪評決和刑罰之制
度要求、言詞辯論原則、直接、集中審理原則、實質審查證據原則等，
對國民參與審判是必要的。因此，刑事訴訟法於修法時強化這些公判中
心主義原則。

B. 制定國民參與刑事審判之法律，規則和準則

　　國民參與刑事審判法(The Act on Citizens Participation in Criminal
Trials)有60條條文，由國會於2007年4月30日通過，2007年6月1日公
布、2008年1月1日生效施行。

　　從而，在2007年7月25日提出立法預告後，韓國大法院於2007年10月4

日在大法官會議上，配合國民參與刑事審判法和規則，制定國民參與刑事審判規則(以下稱參與規則) 和相關準則，包括陪審團選任程序準則。

C. 陪審團管理制度之發展

依參與法第22條之規定，候選陪審員是每年依行政安全部對人民戶籍所作的陪審員庫名單中選出。所有關於準備陪審員庫名單、候選陪審員之選任和管理的程序，均使用韓國大法院研發之陪審團電腦管理系統。

D. 檢察官、律師協會和學院之聯繫網絡

法院身為準備實施國民參與審判制度之組織，於2007年6月18日成立「建制司法參與計劃專責小組之籌備委員會」，並於2008年2月間，在韓國大法院下設司法參與計劃專責小組(Judicial Participation Planning Task Force)，在初始階段執行、研究、與學習參與審判制度。

E. 實施國民參與審判模擬審判

(1) 在法律制定之前，司法改革委員會進行四場模擬審判，由人民實際參與任陪審員。

－ 第一場：2005年8月，中央首爾地方法院，殺人案件

－ 第二場：2005年12月，釜山地方法院，強制性交致傷害案件

－ 第三場：2006年4月，中央首爾地方法院，殺人案件

－ 第四場：2006年12月，光州地方法院，貪污案件

(2) 在法律制定之後，18個地方法院進行四場模擬審判，由該轄區內人民參與擔任陪審員。

－ 2007年9月10日，中央首爾地方法院，殺人案件

- 2007年10月29日，五個地方法院(南首爾、西首爾、水原、大邱、蔚山)，殺人案件
- 2007年12月12日，13個地方法院(中央首爾、東首爾、北首爾、議政府、仁川、春川、大由、忠州、釜山、晶原、光州、全州、濟州)，強制性交致傷害案件
- 2007年11月26日，議政府地方法院
- 2007年12月10日，首爾地方法院和許多其他的法院

(3) 為提昇人民對法院制度和審判之了解，加強一般人民對刑事審判的知識及促進大眾對司法程序的信心，自2010年起即設立與真正陪審員不同之影子陪審員，讓他們以如同在真的陪審團審判之同樣方式，觀察整個審判程序並討論審判結果，包括有罪或無罪及量刑。

F. 民眾教育與宣導

於2007年8月，韓國大法院發展並發布對於參與法之一般性闡述評釋，供法律實務參與者以及一般大眾使用。

於2007年10月6日，出版一本16頁的指導手介紹、問與答、簡冊—陪審員手冊，供陪審員使用。此手冊內容有前言單易懂的法律名詞、及參與為陪審員者常提出的三十項問題與答案。手冊與選任程序通知被一起發送給候選陪審員，藉此使候選陪審員在參加選任程序前，對於刑事訴訟程序有充分的瞭解。

於候選陪審員參加選任程序時，會播放陪審員訓練影片，指導國民參與審判的程序、陪審員的角色、及其他應注意之事項。此外，並有韓國大法院的網站、漫畫形式的手冊、紀念品上之廣告宣傳，以確保一般大眾得接觸到關於參與審判的資訊。

　　再者，認知到若欲促進一般人民自願且主動地參與審判，就必須創造一個參與審判不致對陪審員產生不利的環境，法案第50條即就此事項為規定。另外，並要求行政安全部、勞工部和經濟組織間的合作。

3. 現　　況

A. 國民參與審判內容

(1) 適格之案件(修改與施行)

　　參與法制定時，下述之案件適用參與制審判：故意殺人罪、強盜結合強制性交罪、強盜或強制性交之致傷害或死亡、某些類型之貪污罪；意圖、教唆、幫助、預備、共謀及共同犯上述之罪。隨著2009年7月1日大法院規則之修改，參與制審判適格之案件範圍隨之擴張，包括有強盜案件、特別強盜、強制性交、準強制性交、慣竊。自2012年7月1日起，適格案件之範圍再度擴張為依法院組織法第32條第1 項規定之合議法庭管轄之所有案件(參與法第5條第1項)。

(2) 陪審員的權力與職務

　　陪審員應有權於其所參與之參與制審判，就事實之認定、法律之適用、以及量刑表示意見(參與法第12條第1項)。陪審員應遵守法律和規則，獨立並誠摯地執行職務(參與法第12條第2項)。不得揭露其職務範圍內知悉之秘密，亦不得為任何損害審判公正之行為(參與法第12條第3項)。

(3) 陪審員與備位陪審員名額

　　法定刑為死刑或附勞動或無勞動之無期徒刑的案件，應有9名陪審員參與；前述以外之案件，應有7名陪審員參與。然而，若被告或辯護人於準備程序中就起訴事實重要要素為認罪之案件，法院得不受前述規定之拘束，裁定為5名陪審員(參與法第13條第1項)。但發現案件本身或檢察官與被告或辯護人之間的協議有不尋常之情形，法院得裁定定陪審員名額為7或9名(參與法第13條第2項)。此外，法院得有5名或5名以下的備位陪審員，預備陪審團出缺時遞補(參與法第14條第1項)。

(4) 陪審員之資格

陪審員應自大韓民國年滿20歲以上之公民中選出。不得擔任公職者亦不得擔任陪審員、有過度影響陪審員之虞者、或因其職業難以履行陪審員職務者，例如大韓民國總統、國會議員、地方政府首長或地方議會議員、法官、法院或檢察署內之公務員、警察、矯治官或假釋官、軍人、軍中的職員、消防隊員，應排除為例外。此外，被害人、被告或被害人之親戚、就有關聯之案件為檢察官或司法警察、或有關係者，應被排除而不得任陪審員(參與法第16-19條)。

除此之外，法院得依職權或依下列之人請求，豁免任陪審員之職務：70以上之人、過去五年內曾參與候選陪審員選任程序、曾被起訴求無勞動之有期徒刑以上之刑罰案件或案件仍在進行中、依法令被逮捕或拘禁之人、履行陪審員職務將導致第三人或對其職業產生不可回復損害之虞者、因重病、傷害、或殘障而難以出庭之人(參與法第20條)。

(5) 車馬費與報酬

依參與法第15條，陪審員、備位陪審員、及候選陪審員得依大法院規則領取車馬費和報酬。由大法院法官委員會(Council of Supreme Court Justices) 在預算內決定車馬費之數額：參與選任程序之陪審員和候選陪審員為50,000韓元；參與審判之陪審員和備位陪審員為100,000韓元；車馬費和住宿費依法院職員之標準計算。

(6) 陪審員之選任程序

地方法院院長應以住居在其管轄範圍內20歲以上之公民，準備一份陪審員名冊，且法院應自陪審員名冊中隨機選取，選擇出必要人數的候選陪審員，並發出陪審員和備位陪審員選任程序之傳票。

(7) 陪審員之程序權利與職務

在審判中，檢察官應坐在與被告與辯護人對面平等之位置，而陪審員和備位陪審員應坐在法官與檢察官、被告與辯護人之間空間左邊的位置。證人之位置應位於法官與檢察官、被告與辯護人之間空間右邊的位置，面對陪審員和備位陪審員(參與法第39條)。

陪審員得要求審判長就必要事項詰問被告或證人，經審判長同意得記筆記，且得使用於評議。然而，陪審員在評議、評決、或討論完成之前，於審判休息時無審判長之同意不得離開法院或離開評議、評決、或討論的場所；不得在評議開始前表達或討論其意見；審判程序外，不得蒐集資料、或調查相關案件；不得洩露評議、評決或討論之秘密(參與法第41條)。

(8) 評議、評決及討論

陪審團應於法官不參與之情形下，就有罪或無罪為評議，並以一致表決同意作出評決。若陪審團就有罪或無罪無法達成一致評決，陪審團應在聽取法官之意見後以多數決作出有罪或無罪之評決。法官即使參加評議表達其意見，亦不得參與陪審團評決。若為有罪評決，陪審團應與法官討論量刑並應表達他們的意見(參與法第46條第2、3、4項)。

(9) 量　刑

陪審團之評決與意見不得拘束法院，評決結果和意見所作之文件應列入相關審判紀錄。審判長應於宣判時向被告曉諭陪審團評決之結果，若宣判與陪審團評決不同,並應向被告解釋理由(參與法第46條第5、6 項、第48條第4項)。

　　書面判決應說明陪審團參與審判之事實,並得包含陪審團之意見。若宣示之判決與陪審團評決不同,判決書應記載理由(參與法第49條第1、2項)。

B. 現　況

　　到2011年2月29日為止,有1551件案件,即22667件適格案件的6.8%被收案,扣除排除適用或撤回之案件外,有606件案件進行到參與審判。適格的案件僅於被告希望適用參與制審判時,方得進行參與審判。自2008年1月1日至2012年2月29日止,22667件適格案件中的1551(6.8%)件案件被收案進行參與制審判。依案件類別來分,其中26.2%為強盜案件、23.9%為殺人案件、22.1%為性侵害、22.2%為其他犯罪、而5.7%為傷害致死。

　　法院指定辯護人的比例占參與審判案件的81.4%,屬高比率。由於參與制審判係於2008年施行,自白與不認罪的比率為3:7,而陪審團評決和法官判結果相同的比率約為90%,代表有普遍之共識。直至2012年2月29日,有4件案件陪審團作出有罪的評決,而法官判決無罪,反而有50件案件陪審團作出無罪的評決,而法官判決有罪。在陪審團評決與法官判決不一致的案件中,兩件案件被上訴法院駁回。陪審團的量刑意見,雖然不能拘束法院,但和法院量刑相差在一年以內的案件亦達90%。

4. 民眾(特別是陪審團) 就參與審判之問卷調查結果

　　在參與審判實施之2008年,就民眾對司法評估的問卷調查結果顯

示，59.3%的比例知道參與審判、而69.3%的比例回答參與審判會促進
對審判的信賴。另一個在三年後進行的調查顯示，87.5%的比例回答參
與審判會促進對審判的信賴，而80%以上的比例回答參與審判可以達到
審判的公平與透明、促進人民的法律知識、及增進人民守法之精神。

　　一方面，大法院自2008至2011年進行的陪審員調查顯示，96.5%的比
例對他們任陪審員的表現感到滿意與給予正面評價。88.1%的比例認為他們
完全或幾乎瞭解審判的內容；72.9%認為他們的意見有充足地表達，而審判
長的指揮為「非常有幫助」(70.2%)或「有一些幫助」(28.2%)。另一方面，被問
到困擾陪審員的因素，在於「長時間之審判」(46.1%)、「法律名詞難消化」
(23.6%)、「難以理解證據」(10.5%)、「因被告報復等之安全顧慮」(9.4%)、「收
入減少、職場上不利益」(10.4%)。

II. 參與審判的提升事項及引進刑事審判程序之效果

1. 提升事項

A. 提升聲請率

(1) 聲請制度之限制

　　由於參與審判的低聲請率肇因於社會缺乏對參與審判的認知，因此
應提高人民和被告對參與審判的意願和好處。

　　依參與法之規定，被告應於收受起訴書之日起七日內，提出書面聲
請，說明其欲進行參與審判(參與法第8條第2項)。若被告未提出書面聲
請，應視為被告不欲進行參與審判(參與法第8條第3項)。

　　雖然聲請參與審判的期間短是參與審判聲請率低的原因之一，實務容

許未於收到起訴書七日內提出書面聲請之被告，得於第一次審判期日提出
聲請，經法院認可後進行參與審判(大法院2009年10月23日決定2009Mo1032)。

　　即使被告提出參與審判之聲請，資料顯示出撤回參與審判的高比
例；可能的原因是普遍對於法院、檢察官、律師對於參與審判、量刑、
受刑人和其他意見態度之回應。

(2) 改進聲請制度

(a) 廢止聲請制度之建議

　　目前的聲請制度基礎為被告自主選擇刑事程序。然而，參與審判目
的在於為使司法公平與透明化，係保障人民參與審判的權利，而非在於
保障被告的程序選擇權。而且，聲請制度最初亦非與刑事司法執行的一
致性與平等有關。因此，可能的建議為，廢止基於當事人自主權的聲請
制度，而採用適格案件即應進行參與審判之強制性制度。

　　依此建議的觀點延伸，可以限制適格案件範圍的方式，來解決案件
負擔過重的問題，例如排除被告對起訴事實之全部或必要部分為自白的
認罪案件。

(b) 維持聲請制度之建議

　　支持維持聲請制度之建議，有二個不同的意見：第一個意見為，維
持目前的聲請制度，僅於被告聲請時提供參與審判；另一個意見為，就
參與審判之適格案件原則上進行參與審判，將目前聲請改為若被告提出
書面聲請，表示其不欲進行參與審判，則進行一般刑事程序。

　　第二個意見建議僅於被告不欲進行參與審判時，提供一般刑事程
序；可再進一步分為二個不同意見：第一為若被告不欲進行參與審
判，則自動排除於參與審判之外。第二個受到最多支持的意見為，即使
被告表達其欲進行一般刑事程序之意思，仍須經法院之許可。

此建議之正當理由為：在人民主權原則下尊重被告的自主權，基本權利之保障，也須基於被告自主權之認知，強制地施行參與審判會侵害到韓國憲法所保障的受法官審判之基本權利。

(c) 限制駁回裁定之建議

參與審判制規定了廣泛的理由得裁定排除適用，裁定排除適用的一般規定，如第9條第1項4款「因其他原因或情形，認進行參與審判不適當者」，會事實上否決被告的權利。

考量到參與審判案件不能審判的特殊情況，參與法中可保留此規定，但是，排除裁定之的範圍應限制到最小，且事由應特定。

因此，大法院於2010年4月27日修訂大法院規則，限制「因其他原因或情形，認進行參與審判不適當者」之意涵，為：1. 可預期有另案起訴；2. 被告疑有精神疾病；3. 可預期若進行參與審判將導致被告之速審權因重大程序延宕而有受侵害之虞(大法院參與審判收案和處理規則(Supreme Court Regulation on Acceptance and Handling of Participatory Trials))。

B. 短期審判期間

大部分的案件，參與審判會在一或二天內結束，可能的原因為：有些問題或有證人之複雜案件已被排除；約占參與審判的30%的自白案件，並不需要耗費數小時的證據調查；法定準備程序有效地整理法律爭點；即使審判將持續至深夜，陪審員仍欲在一天內結束審判。

然而，審判的日期可能依個別案件性質而需要延長。雖然陪審員欲如此且受到法院與檢察官之支持，審判持續至深夜仍非所願。事實上，陪審員調查顯示陪審員抱怨審判過久、甚至最晚會持續到午夜。

C. 陪審團評決的建議效力

由於陪審團評決僅具建議之效力，法院可能會作出不同於陪審團評決之判決。

於此案件，陪審員理解其評決僅為建議性質，而對於不顧實際上不便而參與審判的人民來說，要接受此結果可能會是不愉快的經驗。由於如此之經驗可能削減人民主動參與參與審判之動力，法院於國民參與審判制度之運行時，應盡可能尊重陪審團的評決。

雖然有意見議論陪審團評決應具拘束力，但此會成為違憲爭議，因為承認陪審團評決之拘束力可能違反受法官審判之憲法基本權利。

若陪審團評決的拘束力被承認，目前的評決形式將需要修改。因為就「證明事實達到無合理懷疑之程度」而言，當不能達到一致決定時僅以簡單多數決的評決，是不能被接受的。原則上應適用一致決，或要求百分之八十以上的多數決。

D. 陪審團量刑意見和量刑準則之關係

「量刑準則」為制定對某些犯罪的基本量刑範圍後，若有特定犯罪落入加重或減輕事由類別中，該犯罪之刑罰最後會在反應該事項之量刑修正範圍內定之。

實務上有些案件會提供量刑準則給陪審員。有些案件法官可能更著重客觀地適用量刑準則，而非陪審員提出之量刑意見。

就此，有二個面向：一為將會出現一個制度是，陪審員可能在審視量刑準則中所列的量刑要素後就量刑作出決定；另一個將會出現的制度為，如同美國大部分州所採用的，量刑僅由法官決定，陪審員不參與；

由於希望增進人民對量刑之信賴而增加適用量刑準則。

E. 限制上訴之必要

由於現行參與法無上訴之特別規定，參與審判案件與一般刑事案件一樣，均適用刑事訴訟法規定的上訴程序。

一般來說，韓國刑事案件上訴有續審制的特色，依刑事訴訟法，上訴法院得廢棄原審法院認可之事實，上訴法院原則上於廢棄原審判決時，應為新的判決(刑事訴訟法第364條)。

實務上，大法院判決先例表示「陪審員在參與如證人證詞可信度之證據審查、詰問證人，認定事實並為一致無罪評決後，法院對於這些證據未為變更而採用，且法院判決與陪審員之評決一致時，除非有充足且令人信服與判決相反之新情事，於上訴法院再進行新證據之審查外，否則上訴法院關於適用證據、及藉由這些程序認定事實之判決，應更加尊重」(大法院2010年3月25日判決2009Do14065)。

同時，亦有對於參與審判判決上訴之爭議，其一意見表示若陪審團評決無罪，且法院與陪審團評決一致，為無罪判決，應以誤解事實之理由，禁止檢察官上訴；另一意見則表示應強化上訴程序對第一審判決為事後審(deferential review)或法律審之特色。因為，若基於多數人民通念的事實認定輕易地被上訴法院駁回，會產生許多蔑視準備程序制度價值的觀念，從而最後變成失去審判本身的意義。

但是，不許被告對參與審判判決上訴可能會違憲，違反其受法官審判之權利，而韓國各級法院必須更仔細檢討重建上訴程序特色之事項。

2. 刑事訴訟程序引進國民參與審判之影響

A. 強化公開審判前準備程序

(1) 必須的程序

隨著參與法的制定，刑事訴訟法於2007年6月1日修法，採用公開審判前之準備程序(第266條之5以下)。為了以有效且集中的審查促進迅速審判，審判前準備程序就國民參與審判係必要的，而在一般刑事案件則為任意的(參與法第36條第1項主文)。原因在於，為使參與審判儘早生根，參與審判案件必須比一般刑事案件更集中審理，以迅速結束審判。避免使非法律專業的陪審員在公開審判前的準備程序接觸到無證據能力的證據，也是必要的。

公開審判前之準備程序是確認被告欲進行參與審判意思、對整理爭點、藉由建立辯論之計畫來準備集中審理程序、確定審判時程表並根據審判時程表進行陪審團選任程序，扮演了重要的角色。

(2) 公開審判前準備程序之處理

法院應指定準備程序期日以整理爭點和證據，並訂定審判時程表(參與法第37條第1項)。檢察官及被告或辯護人應預先蒐集與整理證據，並提供協助，以使準備程序得以順利進行(參與法第36條第4項)。

當法院依新修正刑事訴訟法第266條之15的審判時程表，就案件進行準備程序時，法院應於陪審團選任前完成準備程序(參與規則第27條)。法院將依案件爭點和證據排列順序之結果記明於準備程序紀錄(刑事訴訟法修法第266條之10第2項)，並於準備程序完成後，應發生準備期日終結之效力(失權效)(修正之刑事訴訟法第266條之13第1項)。

關於準備程序中證據有無證據能力之判斷，檢察官僅提示證據清單，不須提示特定證據文件或資料，然後向法院聲請傳喚關於被告不同意之證據的證人，於必要時，請求傳喚證人證明起訴事實。被告亦聲請對其有利之證人，提出抗辯或待證人證明之事實。至於法院於聽取雙方之主張後，決定是否准許證據。

B. 公開審判程序之改變

(1) 刑事訴訟法修法

參與法原本的草案中含有相當多關於公開審判程序的條文。但是，由於國會同一時間通過刑事訴訟法修法，參與法中與刑事訴訟法新修法規定重複的部分，即全部被刪除。代表參與審判之公開審判程序應與一般刑事案件的一樣，但在實務上有陪審員或無陪審員的審判，在程序處理上不同是可預期的。

(A) 加強公判中心主義原則

刑事訴訟法修法前，刑事訴訟法第254條第1項曾規定：「檢察官起訴應向有管轄法院提出書面起訴」；刑事訴訟規則第118條第2項規定：「有使法院對案件產生預斷之資料或其他文件…不得附於起訴書，起訴書不得引用其內容」。

但是實務上檢察官在起訴的同時，會送交所有的偵查之紀錄給法院，而法院在一些案件中，審查偵查之紀錄並在第一次審判期日前整理爭點。

不過隨著參與審判之採用，刑事訴訟程序細則已修正規定為「就法院駁回或未裁定之證據聲請，法院不得自聲請證據之人處收受任何證據資料或文件」(刑事訴訟程序細則第134條第4項)

事實上，若無公判中心主義之原則基礎，參與審判將無法施行：參與審判的妥善運行，理想上係基於公判中心主義原則的完善基礎，使個人私下不能審查調查紀錄之陪審員，以聽與看在法庭主張與立證的內容，得以正確地理解相關案件的爭點、作出適當的結論。

因此，刑事訴訟法修法藉由新制定條文規定言詞辯論之原則，克服過去審判傾向書面審理的缺點，並透過雙方當事人和法庭上相關人士主動的言詞辯論發現正確的事實，而強化了公判中心主義之原則(刑事訴訟法第275條第1項)。

將提出證據資料或陳述或告知文件資料摘要之人，由審判長改為提出主張者，亦改變審查證據之方法，而使提出主張者成為原則上應提示證據之人(刑事訴訟法第292條)。

(B) 開審程序之誠摯實踐

依新修正之刑事訴訟法，開審程序之實踐變得更認真與嚴格，從而起訴事實、案件爭點、及辯論證明之計畫得以清楚地呈現於審判程序的初始階段(刑事訴訟法第285條、第286條、第287條)。檢察官為開審陳述的程序，曾經是任意的，如今成為必要的，且在為此陳述時，檢察官應朗讀所有構成起訴犯罪之事實、罪名、原則上適用之法律規定，必要時，審判長得令檢察官陳述起訴之要旨。並且新加入被告回應陳述之程序，審判長為整理爭點之詢問時間，及檢察官和被告為陳述抗辯所提之書狀。

在參與審判中，於開審程序誠摯並充分地整理爭點是必要的，因為身為事實認定者的陪審員，是第一次透過該程序認識案件並了解爭點。

(C) 被告詰問之轉變

修正之刑事訴訟法改變了被告詰問的方法(刑事訴訟法第296之2條)。刑事訴訟法修法前，被告之詰問應在證據審查開始前為之。然而，依修正之刑事訴訟法，詰問被告功能之一的區別抗辯和自白，被被告的開審陳述所取代，被告的開審陳述原則上應在證據審查後進行，以使用被告之陳述為證據、挑戰被告的正當理由，並說服陪審員。

(D) 以法庭證詞為基礎之證明

依修正之刑事訴訟法，關於調查機關所作資料之證據能力也有部分修改，以使調查資料之真實性建立於法庭證詞、而非證據文件之基礎上。

刑事訴訟法修法前，若被告否認檢察官為審判所作有關調查嫌疑犯之調查資料的真實性，則不能作為證據，因為此並非「原陳述者所作之陳述」，故無法證明資料之真實性。但刑事訴訟法修法改為除了舊法規定的「被告審判中所為陳述」外，錄影紀錄或其他客觀的工具亦可證明其真實性，刑事訴訟法新修法並訂定，除了資料真實性的證明證據外，資料僅於可證明所載陳述係於具可信性之情況下所為時，具證據能力，此解決了解釋上的爭議(刑事訴訟法第312條第1項與第2項)。

此外，另一個問題為，因舊法就傳聞證據法則之例外規定「陳述者死亡、疾病、住在國外或其他因素」中對「其他因素」的廣泛解釋，使得被告防禦權、或交互詰問權未受到足夠的保障。為解決此問題，刑事訴訟法修法更嚴格地規定例外如下：「若必須於公判準備或公判期日為陳述之人，因死亡、疾病、或住在外國、下落不明或有其他類似之原因」(刑事訴訟法第314條)。

(2) **參與法之特別規定**

關於參與審判之座位，陪審員坐在面對法官的左側，檢察官坐在被告與辯護人的對面，證人席位於陪審員席的前方(參與法第39條)。

即使被告於公開審判時認罪，簡式審判程序之評決仍不得適用參與審判(參與法第43條)。陪審員或備位陪審員不得參與法院判斷證據能力與否之審查(參與法第44條)。

　　於一般刑事審判，除非有特殊的理由，每一法院應依檢察官、被告或辯護人之聲請，指派書記員記錄法庭內聽審之全部或一部，或使用錄音或錄影設備為錄音或錄影(包含聲音錄音；以下亦同，新修正之刑事訴訟法第56條之2)。但是在參與審判，筆記和錄音成為強制必要的，因此法院應僱用書記員為審判記錄，於無記錄或特殊理由時應使用錄音或錄影器材錄下聲音與影像，且錄音帶或錄影帶應與審判紀錄分別保存；檢察官、被告、或辯護人得支付成本費用，請求錄音之筆記、錄音帶、或錄影帶之複本(刑事訴訟法第40條)。

　　審判長應於結辯時，向法院中之陪審員闡明起訴事實之重要爭點、可適用之法律條文、被告與辯護人之聲明與抗辯之重要爭點、證據能力和其他重要事項。

　　必要時得闡明證據之重要爭點(參與法第46條第1項)。此「其他重要事項」包括無罪推定原則、證據審判原則、自由心證原則、不得因被告於審判中拒絕提出證據或作證即推定被告有罪、忽視無證據能力之證據、陪審團評議及評決之方法、選舉陪審團代表之目的與方法(參與法第37條第1項)。

3. 評估與未來課題

　　參與審判的正面效果包含實現刑事訴訟法之理想，如公判中心主義原則、透過用白話語言解釋法律名詞、使用多媒體設備如Powerpoint和圖片幫助陪審員瞭解案件爭點，而促進法庭內之溝通。再者，透過人民直接參與審判程序，可以解決人民對司法的疑心與不信任，確認關於利用過去職位和財富徇私而允許特權的實務不再存在，透過在司法中實現直接民主之理想與體驗司法制度之機會，提升司法的可信度。

　　除了設立建置參審計畫專責小組或修改相關規則外，大法院於國民參與審判制施行後，在2008年3月舉辦資深首席部長判事研討會。大法院已於每年約3月或4月時，舉辦參與審判之審判長年度會議。並在每年的上半年，在高等法院所舉行的國家指定辯護會議工作坊中，教導參與審判中辯論之方法，盡最大的努力以實踐國民參與審判制。

　　但是，如前述所檢討，目前參與審判施行中突顯出的問題，未來仍有一些課題須進行。為了在2013年全面地施行參與審判，2012年7月12日依參與法第55條設立了國民參與司法制度委員會，針對向大眾收集包括批評在內的意見，透過分析參與審判之施行過程，決定國民參與審判制的最終型式。此委員會將於今年底決定適合韓國國情之參與審判類型。

저자 약력

학   력
서울대학교 법과대학 학사
서울대학교 대학원 민사법 석사
죠지타운대학교 대학원 [미국] 법학 석사

경   력
제15회 사법시험 합격
사법연수원 제 5 기 수료
군법무관
부산지방법원 판사
서울고등법원 판사
대법원 재판연구관
대구지방법원 부장판사
헌법재판소 헌법연구부장 파견
사법연수원 교수
대법원 사법제도발전위원회 제 2 분과위 위원
인천지방법원 부천지원 지원장
서울고등법원 부장판사
서울고등법원 수석부장판사
서울가정법원 법원장
수원지방법원 법원장
사법제도개혁추진위원회 실무위원
헌법재판소 재판관
아시아 헌법재판소연합 창립 준비위원회 위원장
제 5 대 헌법재판소 소장 후보자 지명
현   법무법인 우면 대표변호사

주요 저서
- 헌법소송, 사법연수원, 2001
- 주석 행정소송법(공저)
- 주석 민사소송법(공저)
- 세계로 나아가는 한국의 헌법재판, 박영사, 2011
- 헌법소송법, 박영사, 2015

Mr. LEE, DONG-HEUB

Ex Justice of Constitutional Court of Korea

☐ Name : Dong-Heub LEE

☐ Date of Birth : January 27, 1951

☐ Marital Status : Married(Wife, 4 children)

☐ Education :

   ° Received an LL.B. and LL.M. from Judicial Graduate School, Seoul National University

   ° Received an LL.M. from Georgetown University(U.S.A.)

☐ Professional Career

Passed the 15th Judicial Examination

Judge, Busan District Court

Judge, Seoul High Court

Law Clerk, the Supreme Court

Presiding Judge, Daegue District Court

Chief of Constitution Research Officer, Constitutional Court

Professor, Judicial Research & Training Institute

Chief Judge, Bucheon Branch of Incheon District Court

Presiding Judge, Seoul High Court

Chief Presiding Judge, Seoul High Court

Chief Judge, Seoul Family Court

Chief Judge, Suwon District Court

Justice, Constitutional Court

Chairperson of Preparatory Committee for Association of Asian Constitutional Court

Nominated for Candidate to the president of the Constitutional Court of Korea

Representative Partner in Woomyon Lawfirm

세계로 나아가는 한국의 헌법재판 Ⅱ

초판인쇄	2015년 7월 10일
초판발행	2015년 7월 20일
지은이	이동흡
펴낸이	안종만
편 집	김선민 · 이승현
기획/마케팅	조성호
표지디자인	김문정
제 작	우인도 · 고철민
펴낸곳	(주) **박영사**
	서울특별시 종로구 새문안로3길 36, 1601
	등록 1959. 3. 11. 제300-1959-1호(倫)
전 화	02)733-6771
f a x	02)736-4818
e-mail	pys@pybook.co.kr
homepage	www.pybook.co.kr
ISBN	979-11-303-2744-0 93360

* 잘못된 책은 바꿔드립니다. 본서의 무단복제행위를 금합니다.
* 저자와 협의하여 인지첩부를 생략합니다.

정 가   25,000원